GOD SEEKERS

GOD SEEKERS

Twenty Centuries
of Christian Spiritualities

RICHARD H. SCHMIDT

WILLIAM B. EERDMANS PUBLISHING COMPANY
GRAND RAPIDS, MICHIGAN / CAMBRIDGE, U.K.

Published 2008 by

Wm. B. Eerdmans Publishing Co.

2140 Oak Industrial Drive N.E., Grand Rapids, Michigan 49505 /

P.O. Box 163, Cambridge CB3 9PU U.K.

Printed in the United States of America

13 12 11 10 09 08   7 6 5 4 3 2 1

Library of Congress Cataloging-in-Publication Data

Schmidt, Richard H., 1944-

God seekers: twenty centuries of Christian spiritualities / Richard H. Schmidt.

p.   cm.

Includes index.

ISBN 978-0-8028-2840-8 (cloth: alk. paper)

1. Spirituality — History.   I. Title.

BV4501.3.S353   2008

270.092′2 — dc22

2008002950

www.eerdmans.com

Contents

Contents

Contents

Contents

Foreword

Hagiography. It is a commanding word that, with all its circular and draping letters, sits handsomely on the page, just as, when spoken, it usually stops a moment to linger on the tongue. I was half-grown before I ever saw it in print, and an undergraduate before I ever heard it used with ease. Primarily, I suspect this deficiency resulted from the fact that I was raised in a very Presbyterian household by very devout parents. In the 1930s, Protestants of any stripe did *not* have saints. That is to say, if *hagiography* is a substantial and memorable word, what it names is even more so. Meaning "holy writing" literally, it refers to all writing about the holy. Over the centuries, though, it has come to refer almost exclusively to writing about human beings whose lives seem to the rest of us to have been holy and therefore worthy of our study.

It was the "worthy of study" part that Protestants like my parents were leery of, and for good reason. In the early days of Christianity, when hagiography as a genre of Christian literature was almost as new as the faith itself was, the stories were principally about martyrs; the tales those first stories told were written in order that converts and believers might find the courage likewise to suffer and die. However, over the centuries, after Rome's fall and during Europe's Dark Ages, the stories, like the culture around them, became more and more magical. Miracles, some of them too fantastical to be credible at any time, became the principal stuff of hagiographic literature; and the people who performed them were added to the ranks of the church's saints.

ix

It was a short step from hearing miraculous tales to venerating and petitioning the miracle workers. One of the great pushes of the Great Reformation was, as a result, the paring down of the roll call of the saints, assigning that title only to those who were the formative fathers of the church and, long since, safely buried. Even those holy forebears were never to be prayed to, however, and only within specific contexts were they to be emulated. Thus some twenty-five or thirty generations of Christians, growing up within the ethos of Protestantism, were protected from the spiritual danger of human veneration while being, at the same time, robbed of the beauty and sustenance of any elaborated exposure to heroic faith lived in human circumstances. In the end, that has proved to be an unequal and debilitating exchange, and the church's times and ways are changing once again.

Protestantism is no longer young, nor is it so afraid now to look dispassionately at that out of which it came or even, upon occasion, to embrace some of that which once it fought against. New and blended configurations of Christianity rise up among us, as do new ways of being intentional community. The ancient is received into the present from which it should never have been exiled. The traditional liturgies of pre-Reformation times are incorporated into the worship of an emerging and reinvigorated faith; and the celebration of our heroes and heroines is restored to us as a legitimate part of our formation in that faith. Hagiography as literature for all the people of God has gone full circle; and it returns with gifts that are all the sweeter for having been so long withdrawn from so many of us.

Richard Schmidt's *God Seekers: Twenty Centuries of Christian Spiritualities* — like his *Glorious Companions: Five Centuries of Anglican Spirituality,* to which it is a companion volume — is hagiography, hagiography at its redeemed and re-established best. As a collection, it is not without its ironies, of course. One has to smile upon seeing John Calvin included here as a saint newly redefined. Calvin would have been appalled by that association, I suspect, under any definition. But the inclusion of the stories and words of Christians like the great fundamentalist R. A. Torrey and the Pentecostal leader Donald Gee itself affirms the fact that time and distance have brought us perspective upon, and appreciation of, the long way of our coming to this present moment in Christianity's earthly history.

While *God Seekers* may be read with delight or for information or, as probably was Schmidt's intent, for instruction and guidance in one's own formation, it is impossible to engage it for long without being seized as well by the grandeur of the panorama it lays out before us. Here, in living people, in living saints, is the history of the church, the body of Christ as we and our kind have shaped it and are shaping it (for some of Schmidt's seekers are indeed still living).

What is eternal in us is that which studies to be holy, as the early apostles told us. But the holy can all too easily be masked by the falsely holy, by the passing dogma, or by the culturally embedded doctrine. It is time and the fruit borne in time that clarify and then certify the holy. *God Seekers,* like the historic genre of literature from which it comes, presents us with that which is worthy of study, with that which has clarified and been certified. With charm and a kind of studied simplicity, it offers us proofs of what, with prayer and grace, Christians can become. It offers as well a realistic hope that we today can also become living saints within the household of God. And such a thing as that is, beyond all time and question, holy writing indeed.

PHYLLIS TICKLE
The Farm In Lucy
The Fifth Week of Easter 2007

Introduction

WHAT IS SPIRITUALITY?

Spirituality is a relatively new word. Although it derives from a Latin root, it first appeared in seventeenth-century France, where it carried both positive and negative connotations. It referred to a personal relationship with God leading to a holy life, but also to fanatical behaviors suggesting an unbalanced personality. One person's saint was another's kook (a difference in perceptions hardly limited to seventeenth-century France).

In recent decades, *spirituality* has become a buzzword in America. Secular news magazines have run lead articles on it, and television documentaries have been produced about it. Nearly every week another celebrity describes herself as "a spiritual person." Entire aisles in bookstores — and not only religious bookstores — are devoted to it. Everything imaginable (and a few things hard to imagine) are tied to spirituality: I recently came across books on the spirituality of sex, of baseball, of the cinema — even books on the spirituality of knitting and of whole-grain diets. But not everyone has leapt onto the spirituality bandwagon, and the word continues to carry negative connotations for some: it can suggest a self-preoccupation that excludes other people, the denial of physical pleasures, and an unctuous religiosity.

The word begs for definition. Before it was coined, what came to be called spirituality had been called by a variety of other names — Christian perfection, discipleship, faithfulness, devotion, obedience, piety, holiness.

By whatever name, spirituality has traditionally been associated with theology. Theology is disciplined reflection on Christian faith. From earliest Christian times, spirituality has been seen as integral to theology. It was assumed that anyone engaged in theology would have made a personal faith commitment; a theologian's credibility depended on such a commitment. For centuries most theologians were cloistered monks. Since it addressed the most important thing in human life, humanity's relationship to God, theology was known as the "queen of the sciences," and it was the spiritual dimension of theology that justified the title. Theology and spirituality were almost two words for the same thing.

This understanding prevailed in the West until the twelfth century (it prevails even today in the Orthodox East). But with the founding of the European universities, theology departed the cloister and entered the classroom as an academic discipline. Eventually it became formalized and detached from Christian experience, perhaps to make it intellectually respectable. A few years ago, I heard an academic theologian criticize those who allow theology to become "mixed up" with prayer. For most of Christian history, to separate them would have been inconceivable.

Not everyone, even in the West, abandoned the traditional view. P. Pourrat, writing in 1922, defined spirituality as "that part of theology which deals with Christian perfection and the ways that lead to it." Theology was the overarching category for Pourrat, with spirituality a subcategory within it. Pourrat's definition is consistent with the traditional understanding.

But in recent decades, as organized religion has declined in Western Europe and parts of America, spirituality has become increasingly detached not only from theology but from religion in general. Sixty years after Pourrat wrote his definition, Richard O'Brien wrote that spirituality has to do with "our experiencing of God and with the transformation of our consciousness and our lives as outcomes of that experience." Notice that O'Brien included God in his definition but made no mention of religion or theology.

In recent years spirituality has often been defined without reference even to God. In 1972 theologian John Macquarrie defined it as "the capacity of going out of oneself and beyond oneself; or, again, the capacity for transcending oneself." In my book on Anglican spirituality, published in 2002, I defined spirituality as "the search for what is truly important or valuable or beautiful and our relationship to it." And perhaps best known of all is the definition of Alcoholics Anonymous and other twelve-step programs: they call themselves "spiritual" fellowships while avoiding any mention of religion and gingerly referring to God by the pseudonym "Higher Power." I have occasionally heard someone say he is "spiritual but not religious."

This raises several questions. Can we really have spirituality apart from God? Without God, just what is spirituality? What is its focus if not God? If spirituality is "the search for what is truly important or valuable or beautiful and our relationship to it," could someone who relates in that way to his car be said to be "spiritual"? I resist that notion and would now want to include God in any definition of spirituality. But then, who or what is God? How is God known? Who is to say how God is known? God could surely answer those questions, and many would say that God has in fact done so. But we're still left with having to decide who should interpret what God has said and done. Isn't that what religion and theology do? Not that God needs them — if God is self-sufficient, he needs nothing, least of all religion and theology. But we are not self-sufficient and often make a mess of things. We need to be reminded, recalled, reoriented — and hence it would seem we need religion and theology. Yes, religious institutions can be irritating and doctrinal statements dull, but they do point us in some directions and away from others. They point us toward what is important, valuable, and beautiful — that is, toward God. Spirituality is what we see in a person moving toward God.

It seems, then, that religion and theology, just shown the door, have found their way back in through the window. So, which religion and theology should we choose? Will any religion and theology do? Does God draw people to himself in all of them, or must one look for the right religion and theology? Can we perhaps devise a generic, blended spirituality drawing on the insights of all religions? No, we can't. The differences among major faiths — their perceptions of what is important, valuable, and beautiful — are such that they could never be melded into one; their answers to the questions posed in the preceding paragraph diverge too profoundly for merger or compromise. It does matter what religion one professes.

This is not to say that even the "best" religion or theology fully comprehends God. Though God does not operate equally in every faith tradition, I believe that God is present and operative within most of them, and that each has its contribution to make. There is, surely, *some* validity, some shred of insight, in most understandings of what is important, valuable, and beautiful. It is always possible to learn something from those whose experience differs from ours.

Think of the ocean. Someone whose knowledge of the sea is limited to a walk along the beach doesn't know much about the ocean, but what she does know is accurate. Even an experienced sailor might learn something from a casual beach-walker. But if the beach-walker wanted to attain a fuller knowledge, she would do well to talk to the sailor, travel extensively (gain more firsthand experience), and study maps and oceanography (avail herself of the knowledge gained by others before her). Even then, however, her knowledge of the sea would be incomplete, for the sea is too large and complex to be understood fully by the human mind. The same is true of God, only more so.

For a spirituality that moves one toward God and not down some blind alley or dead end, religion and theology are helpful, perhaps even essential. They draw on the wisdom and experience of countless others who have gone before us. They set boundaries and warn us of dangers in the road ahead. Again using the image of the sea, someone wanting to sail across the Pacific would be foolish to buy a boat and set out before learning how to sail, consulting charts, and inquiring of others who have made similar journeys. That's where religion and theology enter in. Spirituality is not identical to them, but it depends upon them. They are, as it were, the casing or structure within which spirituality flourishes. Without it, spirituality can become disoriented, superficial, and an exercise in self-adoration.

CHRISTIAN SPIRITUALITY

The word *spirituality* derives from the Latin *spiritus,* but the concept goes back to the Jewish and Christian scriptures. *Spiritus* was used to translate the Greek *pneuma,* which New Testament authors had earlier used for the Hebrew *ruach.* Prior to their religious usage, both *pneuma* and *ruach* meant "moving air," a reference to gentle breezes, gusty winds, inhaling, exhaling — any air in motion. The biblical words suggest a reality that is dynamic, energetic, powerful, and on the move (just the opposite of sitting quietly and entertaining devout thoughts). Moreover, *ruach* and *pneuma* denote an energy that is *unseen.* As Jesus said, "The *pneuma* blows where it chooses, and you hear the sound of it, but you do not know where it comes from or where it goes. So it is with everyone who is born of the *pneuma*" (John 3:8).

This further suggests that spirituality in the Bible includes mystery. Rudolf Otto, in his 1917 classic *The Idea of the Holy,* calls this the *numinous* and adds to energy and mystery a third quality: fascination. There is much of this in the Bible. In the Judeo-Christian tradition, then (this is true of some other traditions as well), spirituality refers to the search for (and to being sought by) what is all-powerful, beyond understanding, and utterly alluring. This is what I referred to as the search for what is important, valuable, and beautiful. The usual name for this is God.

By a Christian spirituality, I mean any spirituality which sees God in Jesus Christ. I am a Christian, both by birth and by intention. While I believe other spiritualities have something to contribute to our knowledge of God, I believe it is in Jesus Christ that we see most deeply into the heart of God. For this reason, though Judaism, Islam, Buddhism, and other faith traditions have much to contribute, I have limited this book to expressions of Christian spirituality.

The subtitle of this book is meant to suggest that Christian spirituality is not one thing, but many. Just as there are various spiritualities among the religions of the world, so are there various spiritualities among Christians. Each spirituality has a different emphasis, asks different questions, and relates to God through Christ from a different angle. Studies of personality type suggest that different expressions of spirituality appeal to different personalities. One size does not fit all, nor is one size suitable for someone throughout his or her life. People grow and change. It is not a matter of finding the true or right way to relate to God, but of finding the way that is most helpful to you at this time.

Imagine that we are looking at a finely cut diamond on display. Lighting from various places in the room illuminates the diamond. As we walk around the room, the sparkle of the stone changes as the point from which we gaze changes. The diamond does not change, but our perception of it does, and no perception can claim to be the right or the only one. So it is with God. No single point of view can define God, and there is no single "Christian" spirituality. Simon Chan comments that "each spirituality helps to highlight and preserve aspects of the totality of Christian life and belief that would be lost to a single superimposing spirituality." Although Jesus Christ is "the way, the truth, and the life" (John 14:5), he comes to us in many guises. This book explores the various ways that Christians through the centuries have approached God through Jesus Christ (or, as many would say, the ways God has approached them). Though the differences among these spiritualities may appear huge, I see them not as conflicting but as complementing each other.

POLARITIES TO LOOK FOR

One way to look at Christian spiritualities is to consider several polarities on which they can be plotted. Not every spirituality addresses every polarity, but these polarities pop up repeatedly throughout Christian history, and the position someone takes regarding them tells us a great deal about him or her.

Holistic versus Dualistic

The ancient Hebrews saw the material world, including the human body, as God's creation and a manifestation of God's glory. They affirmed human life in this world, including its physical dimension. The Greeks, on the other hand, were suspicious of material things and sought to overcome or rise above them, with the human body in particular needing discipline and constraint. Christianity began as a movement among Jews in Palestine, but soon moved into the Greek and Roman world. As the Hebrew and Greek worldviews came up against each other in the young Christian church, two understandings of spirituality emerged. We see this happening even as early as some of the later books of the New Testament. Irenaeus was an early champion of the Hebrew view, Origen of the Greek view. The two streams have continued into modern times.

Mystical versus Cognitive

The word *mysticism* has become suspect for many people today, suggesting something esoteric, superstitious, and occult. It refers to visions, dreams, and the like — direct, inner experiences of the supernatural, neither mediated nor validated by any doctrine, sacred text, or human influence. Mystics have appeared in virtually every religion, and Christian mysticism seems to date from the earliest Christian times. For roughly a third of the subjects of the chapters that follow, mystical encounters were central to their spirituality, and several others seem to have had such encounters, though they made less of them. While most Christian mystics are orthodox in their beliefs, their souls are energized by their direct experiences of the holy. Others, however, take a more cognitive, rational approach. Their spirituality centers on obedience to Scripture and adherence to Christian teaching, sometimes allowing no place for mystical encounters.

Communal versus Individualistic

For most of Christian history, and certainly during the first few centuries, to be a Christian was to be part of the Christian community and to relate to God and other Christians within that community. This reflected the biblical understanding of the holy people or nation and, later, of the church as the body of Christ. Individual behaviors and beliefs were not overlooked or discounted, but they mattered less than taking one's place in the community. In recent times, however, a more individualistic understanding of Christian spirituality has developed alongside the older view, largely in Protestant circles (though neither Luther nor Calvin nor the early Anglicans could be classed as individualists). One sees the individualistic emphasis today in the focus on the salvation of souls and personal decisions for Christ in Western evangelical circles.

Inward versus Outward

The word *spirituality* suggests to many people an inward focus on the growth of the soul through solitude, prayer, meditation, and acts of self-denial. Certainly this is true of the Carmelites and other enclosed monastic orders, several representatives of which are discussed in the chapters that follow. Though they are engaged with one another and with the world through prayer, and in some cases ecclesiastical responsibilities, God energizes these people mainly during their times of retreat. Others, however, though often prayerful, are energized through their relationships and responsibilities in the world and acts of service such as feeding the hungry, caring for orphans, and working for reconciliation. The tension between the two often produces creative and insightful reflections.

Prophetic versus Institutional

"Thus says the Lord!" the Old Testament prophets often thundered. Prophetic figures throughout history, inspired by mystical experiences, Scripture, or some other disclosure of the divine will, have attracted large followings. Because they challenge institutions and traditions, they usually make enemies as well. Several representatives of this prophetic tradition are discussed in this book. They chafe under what they perceive as insensitive or unfaithful institutional authority. Their goal is to reform the institution and recall it to its roots (though they are also often aware of having been nurtured within the institution and are usually loath to abolish it). Others, while recognizing the failings of the institution, find in the structure and security it affords a setting where they can hear and respond to the voice of the Lord.

SPIRITUALITY AND PEOPLE

One often reads (and I occasionally write) about "Anglican," "Carmelite," "Orthodox," or some other spirituality. These expressions are literary conveniences, mere abstractions — there are no such things. Spirituality is only found in the day-to-day lives of actual people. God lives in the hearts of flesh and-blood human beings, not in mental constructs, inspirational thoughts, and sublime truths. When we speak of "Anglican" spirituality, for example, we are talking about specific people, many thousands of them over a period of centuries, their prayers and poetry, their worship and devotion — everything that is and has been part of their relationship to God through Jesus Christ. Joann Wolski Conn has said that while the definition of spirituality may be generic, there are no generic spiritualities. There are only people experiencing and responding to the love of God. For this reason, as Gordon Wakefield has observed, spirituality "is often best studied in biographies."

This book is therefore not about ideas, thoughts, and truths. It is about people. As I suggested in my list of polarities above, the thirty-two people discussed in these pages are quite diverse. At times during the writing of this book, I marveled at how people so different could all find a place under the Christian tent. What, for example, would R. A. Torrey have had in common with Madeleine L'Engle? Or John Calvin with Donald Gee? Not much, I tell myself — until I realize that I am missing the obvious: God loved them all, they experienced God's love through Jesus Christ, and they responded by giving their lives to him.

One other thing emerges from these biographies: virtually all the people discussed in this book changed as they grew older, and in more than the inevitable ways that come with aging. Some of them ended their lives in a radically different place from where they had begun. They were willing to ask difficult questions and not shy away from hard answers. Their spirituality evolved as they gave of themselves, their time, energy, talent, and in some cases, their very lives. It is hard to imagine many of them doing at an early age what they did after having progressed along this road. Most would have said they were still on that road when they died and that they hoped to continue on it in the next life.

How did I choose the subjects of these chapters? The first question I had to answer was where to begin this study. Surely a book on Christian spiritualities should include a chapter on the spirituality of Jesus, I thought. And one on Paul, John, and perhaps other New Testament authors. And since Christian faith builds upon the faith of the Hebrew people, should one go back before Jesus to the spirituality of the Hebrew scriptures? Tempting and reasonable though that seemed, a book needs some limits. Moreover, biblical studies constitutes a separate field, with its own set of questions and disciplines. Hence I decided to begin this study at the end of the New Testament era.

I wanted as broad a sampling of Christian spiritual masters as possible, embracing divergent viewpoints, practices, denominations, and eras. I had written a similar book on Anglican spirituality, intentionally limited to that strand of the Christian tradition. Here I wanted to cast my net more widely, to include both spiritualities already familiar to me and ones new to me. I sought at least one representative from every major branch of the Christian family tree.

My original list, composed largely of authors whose writings had meant something to me over the years, contained many more men than women. The lives of women and men are equally instructive, but through most of Christian history, women were not encouraged to write about their spiritual lives (or about anything else, for that matter). But to have written a book of this sort and included only two or three women would have given a skewed picture of the varieties of Christian spirituality. I therefore looked for additional women and, when presented with a choice between a woman and a man of comparable stature, I chose the woman. That explains why this book includes Julian of Norwich rather than Walter Hilton or Richard Rolle, Teresa of Ávila rather than John of the Cross, Maria Skobtsova rather than Dietrich Bonhoeffer or Anthony Bloom, and Madeleine L'Engle rather than Frederick Buechner. In no case did I choose a woman solely because she was a woman — all those included in this book, men and women alike, were chosen because of the lives they lived and the literary legacy they left behind. I came to see each as a fellow seeker, chosen and precious, part of the household in which God dwells. As I began reading their biographies and what they had written, I felt as if I was coming to know them personally, and I found myself conversing with them in my head, praying for them and asking them to pray for me. May they become your friends as well.

* * *

A word should be said about the quotations appearing at the end of each chapter of this book. Those from texts written in English are quoted exactly as they appear in the original. For those written in Greek, Latin, German, French, Spanish, and Danish, I consulted as many English translations as I could find, relied on my limited knowledge of some of those tongues, and conferred occasionally with persons fluent in them to produce what I hope are accurate translations in smooth modern English. My thanks to those who assisted me in this effort.

I am particularly indebted to Dr. Robert Davis Hughes III of the School of Theology at the University of the South in Sewanee, Tennessee, and to Father John Behr of St. Vladimir's Orthodox Seminary in Crestwood, New York, both of whom advised me in the research and writing of one or more chapters of this book. I am also indebted to the Reverend Howard Park and Helen Park of Chesterfield, Missouri, and to my colleague at Forward Movement Publications, the Reverend George C. Allen, who read all the chapters and suggested clarifications in the thought and expression. My thanks to them for the help they gave me.

I am most grateful to my friend Dean Mosher of Fairhope, Alabama, for the splendid drawings which enhance the pages of this book. When I could find photographs, paintings, and other likenesses of the subjects of these essays, I sent them to Dean. He then drew the likenesses which appear in these pages. Nothing is known of the appearance of the earliest subjects. Francis of Assisi is the first of whom an actual likeness survives, and Martin Luther is the second. With the exception of Jean Pierre de Caussade, the drawings of everyone from Luther on are based on surviving likenesses. How did Dean decide how to depict the others? He researched their ethnic backgrounds, where they lived, and what clothing they would likely have worn, and then chose a model from among his friends. Several of these models, he tells me, were Episcopal clergy from south Alabama who came to his mind as he read particular essays. Thank you, Dean, for the gift of your creativity and skill.

Richard H. Schmidt
Cincinnati, Ohio
February 2, 2008

Chapter 1

IRENAEUS

C. 130–C. 200

Early Christian Spirituality

THE ANCIENT ROMANS faced a smorgasbord of spiritual fare from which to pick and choose — Gnosticism, Stoicism, Epicureanism, neo-Platonism, Aristotelianism, Judaism, Christianity, and a range of other cults and philosophies. The typical Roman took part in several groups, either simultaneously or in sequence. Most saw no conflict in paying homage to more than one god.

Among these various spiritualities, Gnosticism was the most wide-ranging. The Gnostics were a diverse lot with many variations of belief and practice. All Gnostics shared the conviction that spirit was good and flesh was evil — the very existence of the material world, including the human body, they deemed a tragic mistake. Because God was spiritual, he would never have created the material universe. It must therefore have been the work of some lesser being, and to be saved was to rise above it and commune with God in the purely spiritual realm. By making the key to this ascent a special knowledge shared only among the chosen few, Gnosticism was divisive. Moreover, believing that spirit was incompatible with flesh, the Gnostics found unthinkable the idea that God had become incarnate (the word means "enfleshed") in the person of Jesus Christ. Paradoxically, the belief that the flesh was worthless led some Gnostics to refuse to gratify desires of the flesh, while others took it as permission for sexual license.

Irenaeus (pronounced eye-re-NEE-us) battled this many-headed opponent. With incisive reason, citations from apostolic sources, wit, and sarcasm, he defended the church against Gnostic influences. Irenaeus was the Christian church's first great theologian, often called the "father" or "founder" of Christian theology. A native of Asia Minor, as a young boy he had heard a sermon by Polycarp, the famed martyr and bishop of Smyrna who had known the apostles. Irenaeus wrote once to a friend that "childhood learning grows up with the soul and is united to it," and that he had heard the preaching of Polycarp "eagerly," recording it "not on paper but in my heart." As an adult, Irenaeus defended the faith that he had been taught as a child in Asia Minor and that he later heard expounded in Rome and the West. (Alexandria, the other great center of early Christian learning, was more sympathetic to Gnostic views.)

Archaeological remains point to a migration from Asia Minor to Gaul in the second century. These migrants took their Greek culture with them, and Irenaeus undertook to become a missionary to the region, perhaps sent by Polycarp. He settled in Lyons and is said to have become bishop of the city after its bishop, Pothinus, was martyred. Gregory of Tours, writing four centuries later, relates that Irenaeus converted virtually the entire city of Lyons and was himself martyred there sometime later. There is no contemporary evidence to support this, but a severe persecution of Christians is known to have occurred in Lyons in the late second century, and Irenaeus's martyrdom may have been part of it. At the very least, this tradition reflects the esteem in which later Gaulish and French Christians held their first great thinker and witness to the faith.

By the late second century, not only the apostles but Polycarp and everyone else who had known them were no longer alive to be consulted on disputed points. What was the true Christian message? How was one to know? Irenaeus sought to identify Gnostics and other false teachers in the church and to protect the church from them. His major work *Against the Heresies* offers both a detailed account of their teachings and a seminal, systematic statement of Christian theology.

If Christ had a higher, secret knowledge to impart to the chosen few, Irenaeus said, surely he would have shared it with his apostles. Yet the apostolic writings gave no hint of a secret knowledge. Moreover, the bishops of the church, who were successors to the apostles charged with preaching the faith the apostles handed down to them, spoke of a salvation freely available to all. For Irenaeus, the bishops are the key people in guaranteeing the authenticity of Christian teaching; he makes much of the fact that the bishops of his day were all in agreement. But what if a difference among the bishops should arise? Irenaeus advised consulting the bishop of Rome, not because the see of Rome was entitled to primacy (that idea would come much later), but because the Roman congregation was among the oldest and the purity of its tradition could be assumed. Polycarp had been among those who had visited and taught in Rome.

Ecclesiastical authority was exercised informally in Irenaeus's day. The Greek word *episcopos*, usually translated *bishop*, did not refer to a lordly figure dressed in cope and miter and presiding over a diocesan budget, divers boards and agencies, and a staff of archdeacons, all buttressed by layers of canon law. A better translation of *episcopos* might be "overseer" or "supervisor," and it appears from Irenaeus's writings and those of other Christians of the day that the offices of bishop and priest had not yet been clearly distinguished. Nonetheless, Irenaeus's understanding of the teaching office of the bishop laid some of the groundwork for the gatherings of bishops in the fourth and fifth centuries that hammered out the creeds, the imperial papacy of the eleventh century, and the promulgating of the doctrine of papal infallibility in the nineteenth century.

Irenaeus recognized that, as important as it was, the office of the bishop alone would not guarantee that the church would hold firm to apostolic teachings. He saw the need for an authoritative Christian body of scripture. There was no New Testament as we know it today. Apostolic writings circulated freely, with no agreed-upon list of authoritative texts. The books that Irenaeus accepted (because of their apostolic origin) are fewer than comprise our New Testament but are largely identical to it. The creeds were also developed later, but several times in his surviving writings Irenaeus offers summary statements of the faith, which he calls "rules of faith" or "rules of truth." These resemble the later creeds and were intended not as binding statements or supplements to Scripture but as guides in the interpretation of Scripture.

If the incarnation of the Son of God was anathema to the Gnostics, to Irenaeus it was the key to everything. To understand Irenaeus, we must recognize that modern Westerners, especially Americans, think in terms of the individual, whereas the ancients took a more corporate view of humanity. The individual is central in our understanding — individual voters, individual consumers, individual rights, individual decisions. Even in the religious sphere, we often focus on the individual's private relationship to God. The ancients, however, though not oblivious to the importance of individuals, tended to look upon humanity as a whole. When the early Christians pondered the significance of Christ's presence in the world, they thought mainly about its implications for the human race rather than for individual believers. When one was baptized, the individual's decision was important precisely because the newly baptized would be embraced by the Christian community. Modern Westerners think, as it were, of soloists who may now and then choose to play music together, whereas the ancients thought of an orchestra comprised of individuals who might occasionally play solos.

Irenaeus called his understanding of the Incarnation "recapitulation" or "summing up." Humanity had "fallen" by rebelling against God and was therefore cut off from God. Christ had "recapitulated" all of humanity in himself. Through his obedience and death he restored the human race to union with God, not merely putting us back on the right track, but gathering us up into the loving arms of God. Christ also "recapitulated" in himself all the earlier disclosures of God given to the Hebrew people and recorded in their scriptures.

The key player in this cosmic process was the divine *logos,* usually translated "Word." The idea of the *logos* derives from the Jewish notion of a pre-existing messiah and was taken up by Philo, an Alexandrian Jewish philosopher who lived at the time of Christ. Philo saw the *logos* as the pre-existent mind or reason, the creative power that fashions the world, and the intermediary between God and humanity. The author of St. John's Gospel uses the *logos* concept in identifying Christ — *logos* made flesh — and calls the *logos* "God." The *logos* was the central idea in Irenaeus's spirituality, and ferreting out its implications would soon become a driving force in the spirituality and theological debates of the church at large. The idea of the *logos* helped the early Christians wrestle with the nature and identity of Christ. That Christ had walked on earth and appeared to be human, none would have denied — but some held that he only seemed to be human. Few early Christians would have said that Jesus was merely a good man, for their experience of him had suggested that he was more than human — but in what sense? Eventually, the doctrines of the two natures of Christ and of the Trinity would emerge out of these debates, but not before many alternative understandings were put forth, examined, and discarded.

As the second century drew to a close, these questions remained unresolved. Christian spirituality was fluid, with many ideas circulating more or less freely. The outcome was far from certain. The task of refining the nuances of Christian faith would fall to other great thinkers and spiritual masters in the centuries that followed, but the questions that concerned Irenaeus have never gone entirely away, and no resolution of them has ever satisfied all who claim the name of Christ. No sooner do they seem answered than a new generation of Christians asks them again, in a different context and in new terms, and new interpreters arise who, like Irenaeus, call the church back to its roots.

IN HIS OWN WORDS

Note: All quotations are from *Against the Heresies.*

False teachers

Some people are tossing out the truth in favor of deceitful myths and endless genealogies. The apostle Paul says this promotes idle speculations and does not promote godly training in the true faith. By specious arguments craftily patched together, they mislead the innocent and unsuspecting and trap them by falsifying the Lord's own words. They become wicked misinterpreters of genuine words. By pretending to knowledge, they bring ruin upon many people, leading them away from him who established and adorned this universe, as if they had something more sublime and excellent to put forth than the God who made heaven and everything under it.

Preface

The Incarnation

In his immeasurable love, he became what we are to make us what he is.

Preface

Methods of heretics

Their system is one which the prophets did not preach, the Lord did not teach, and the apostles did not hand down. They loudly boast that they know more about it than others, citing non-scriptural documents. As it is said, they attempt to braid ropes out of sand. They try to adapt the Lord's parables, the prophets' sayings, and the apostles' words to their own sayings to make them believable, that their fabrications not seem to lack for reliable witnesses. They disregard the pattern and connection of the scriptures and, as far as they can, rip up the truth part by part. They move and rearrange passages, making things seem contrary to what they actually are and deceiving many by their poorly conceived fantasies and adaptations of the Lord's words.

1.8.1

Apostolic faith

Although it is spread throughout the world, even to the ends of the earth, the church received from the apostles and their disciples the faith in one

God the Father Almighty, Creator of heaven and earth and the seas and all that is in them; and in one Jesus Christ, Son of God, who was incarnate for our salvation, and in the Holy Spirit, who preached through the prophets. . . . This preaching and faith which the church has received, it carefully guards as if it lived in but one house. The church likewise believes these things as with one soul and one heart. It preaches, teaches, and hands them down harmoniously, as if with but one mouth.

1.10.1

Love is better than knowledge

It is better and more advantageous to be uneducated and ignorant and to be brought close to God by love than, thinking oneself learned and wise, to be found a blasphemer against God.

2.26.1

God is Creator of all

Only the Creator of all things is God. He alone is omnipotent, the Father who made and created all things, visible and invisible, things impinging both on the senses and upon the mind, things in heaven and on earth, by the Word of his power. He adapted and arranged everything according to his wisdom. He contains everything and is himself contained by nothing. He is Creator, Maker, and Fashioner. He is the Molder and Lord of all. Neither is anything above or next to him.

2.30.9

Authority of the apostolic witness

We learned the plan of our salvation from those through whom the gospel came to us. What they preached they later handed down to us in the scriptures, by the will of God, as the foundation and pillar of our faith. Some say the apostles preached before attaining complete knowledge, then brag that they have revised and improved upon the apostles. This is entirely wrong, for after our Lord rose from the dead, the apostles were filled with the power of the Holy Spirit, who came upon them from above. They attained complete knowledge and went to the ends of the earth to proclaim the blessings that are ours from God, announcing the peace that is from heaven.

3.1.1

Successors to the apostles

If anyone wants to know the truth, he may find it in the tradition of the apostles, clear and available in every church throughout the whole world. We can list those whom the apostles appointed as bishops in the churches, to be their successors in our day. These men have never known or taught anything like the foolish doctrines which some people espouse. Had the apostles possessed secret mysteries to be taught privately to the perfect few, surely they would have entrusted them to those in whose charge they placed the churches.

3.3.1

Truth found with the church

We have plenty of proofs, so there is no need to ask around concerning the truth. It may be easily obtained from the church. The apostles brought the full and complete truth to the church and lodged it with the church as if in a bank, so that anyone who wishes may draw the water of life from the church. This is the entrance to life; all others are thieves and robbers.

3.4.1

Heretics deny Incarnation

Not one of the heretics believes that the *logos* was made flesh. Examine their creeds carefully and you will find that they invariably present the *logos* of God as having no flesh and incapable of suffering, as "the Christ who is above." Some claim he revealed himself as a transfigured man but was not born a human being or made actual flesh. Others deny that he took human form at all, saying he descended in the form of a dove, on the [human] Jesus born of Mary . . . and that after he had announced the "unknown Father," he went up again.

3.11.3

Same words, different meanings

[The heretics] say the same things believers say, but with different meanings. Their meaning is in fact contrary to ours. It is blasphemous and destructive. They beguile people with terminology similar to ours. It is like inoculating them with poison, as if someone gave them gypsum mixed with water, which looks like milk but will actually kill them.

3.17.4

The suffering of Christ

If [Christ] did not truly suffer, no gratitude is due to him since there would have been no Passion. In that case, when he tells us to endure the blows and turn the other cheek when we suffer, he would be deceiving us for he would not have first suffered himself. If we had borne what he himself never bore, we would be superior to the Master.

3.18.6

Why the Incarnation?

[Christ] caused human nature to cling to God, to be one with God. For had not a man banished the enemy of humanity, that enemy would not have been justly defeated. And on the other hand, had salvation been granted by anyone other than God, we would never have been sure of it. And if humanity had not been joined to God, humanity could never have shared in incorruptibility. It was necessary therefore that the Mediator between God and human beings be kin to both, to restore friendship and concord to both, presenting humanity to God and revealing God to humanity.

3.18.7

United to incorruption and immortality

There was no way for us to receive incorruptibility and immortality except to be united to incorruptibility and immortality. But how could that be unless incorruptibility and immortality first became what we are, the perishable absorbed into the imperishable, the mortal putting on immortality, so that we might be adopted as sons?

3.19.1

The church

Where the church is, there is the Spirit of God, and where the Spirit of God is, there is the church and every form of grace, for the Spirit is truth.

3.24.1

Knowing God

No one whom God has made knows of his grandeur, for no one has ever scaled the heights of God, neither people long ago nor people today. But as for his love, God is eternally known through the One through whom he made all things. This is his *logos,* our Lord Jesus Christ, who in these last days became a human among humans, to join the end to the beginning, humanity to God.

4.20.4

FOR REFLECTION AND DISCUSSION

How does modern Western pluralism compare with the pluralism of the Roman Empire, and how does the church's response to it compare to the church's response in Irenaeus's day?

Unanimity of belief among church leaders was assumed in the early church. What might today's church learn from the teachings of Irenaeus on unity? What in his teachings is applicable today?

Compare how controversies over authority were handled in the early
church to how they are handled today.

Do you agree that the apostles handed down a faith that must be preserved as they left it, or is Christian faith something that grows and
evolves over time?

How important is it that Christians agree on doctrinal matters?

Where today do you see a survival of Gnostic beliefs and practices?

Chapter 2

ORIGEN OF ALEXANDRIA

C. 185–C. 254

Alexandrian Spirituality

THE MAN WIDELY regarded as the most creative thinker of the early church is largely unknown today outside academic circles. Origen of Alexandria was a man of profound devotion who produced a large and diverse body of writings, attracted many disciples, exerted a huge influence on later Christian biblical interpretation, and developed an understanding of the Christian gospel embracing the entire universe. Yet he is not "Saint Origen." No churches or schools have been named for him. No feast day is observed in his honor. Origen is strangely invisible today and has been for nearly sixteen hundred years. It is as if he stands in the shadows, ever present, ever observing, ever praying for us, though banished from our sight.

Origen was born to devout Christian parents who gave him a good literary education. When he was seventeen years old, persecution broke out in Alexandria, and his father was imprisoned and martyred. The young Origen wrote to his father in prison, urging him to stand firm, and he would have shared his father's fate had not his mother intervened by hiding his clothes. For Origen, martyrdom became the ultimate act of Christian commitment, and it was never far from his mind, perhaps accounting for his occasional acts of extreme self-denial. Origen became a famous Christian teacher in Alexandria and traveled widely. He was ordained in Palestine in midlife, and then moved to Caesarea in Palestine, where he continued to teach and wrote most of his biblical commentaries. Approaching old age when the emperor Decius began persecuting Christians in 250, Origen was imprisoned and brutally tortured. The persecution ceased when Decius was killed in battle just one year later, but Origen's health had been broken, and he died shortly thereafter, probably from wounds suffered during his imprisonment.

The outlines of Christian teaching were still fluid in Origen's day. All the great Christian thinkers of the first three centuries entertained ideas both rejected and accepted by the later church. Of no one is this more true than of Origen, who was declared a heretic after his death, but whose devotion, biblical interpretations, and understanding of the nature and mission of Christ continue to inform the Christian church to this day.

For Origen, the universe begins and ends with Christ. Perhaps no one has held a loftier understanding of Christ. When Origen refers to Christ, he does not mean merely, or even primarily, the historical Jesus who lived and taught in ancient Judea, but a cosmic figure, beginning not on earth but in heaven, not in time but in eternity. This was the eternal Son of God, the divine *logos* (an idea already developed by Irenaeus and others). Origen speaks of the Son as the "spotless mirror" of the Father and as the way to the Father. The Father and Son are distinct for Origen but never separated. He occasionally seems to suggest that the Son is subordinate to the Father, a notion rejected by the later church, but Origen's concern is to preserve the transcendence of God the Father, not to demean God the Son. He was a thoroughgoing monotheist who contributed to the emerging understanding of the Trinity by insisting that the relationship of Father and Son is not a physical or temporal one, but part of who God eternally is. The Father's begetting of the Son is a continuous act of the divine will. It was this cosmic Christ who assumed bodily form in the person of Jesus.

The cosmology within which Origen made sense of the Incarnation seems strange to many modern readers. Origen believed in disembodied rational souls that had been created to enjoy and adore God but that had grown bored or distracted and thereby fallen away from God. They then received bodies appropriate to their fallen state. These souls are journeying back to God, a process beginning in this life and continuing after death. The goal is the restoration of the original harmony of all things with God. Origen was a universalist — all, even the devil himself, would be saved in the end, for Origen could not conceive of God creating beings destined for oblivion. Origen agreed that sin brings punishment, but for him, punishment is not everlasting but remedial, its purpose to satiate the sinner with his sin, to re-educate him, moving him to return to God. Punishment is therefore a redemptive act of grace. This in no way diminishes the freedom of created beings, Origen says, for in the end all will be educated through their punishment and will freely choose reunion with God.

The divine *logos* was one of these souls, except that it did not fall from its original state of adoring God, but clung to righteousness, never changing, until "what formerly depended upon the will was by the influence of long custom changed into nature." In speaking of the Incarnation of the *logos*, Origen uses the analogy of a piece of iron thrust into the furnace that "receives the fire in all its pores and all its veins and becomes completely changed into fire" so that the heat and the iron are one thing. So was the divine *logos* united to human nature. The *logos* assumed humanity, and humanity was assumed into the *logos*, the human and the divine natures becoming interwoven. Christ thereby became the pattern or model for other souls on pilgrimage toward restoration and reunion with God.

Origen did not arrive at his understandings through mystical visions or philosophical speculation, but by searching the Scriptures. If no one has held a loftier understanding of Christ than Origen, neither has anyone held a loftier view of the Bible. It is in his understanding of the Scriptures that he made his most lasting mark. Origen taught that Christ opens for us the meaning of the Hebrew scriptures. Only by reading the Old Testament through the lens of Christ, Origen says, do we discern Scripture's deepest meanings. He sees the Scriptures as an extension of the Incarnation — the divine *logos* is embodied in the written word of Scripture just as he was embodied in the person of Jesus Christ. The *logos* is further embodied in the church, Origen says, giving his understanding of the Incarnation a threefold focus: the person of Christ, Scripture, and the church.

Two key beliefs about Scripture moved Origen to develop his method of interpretation. Both derive from his understanding of Christ in Scripture — and many modern readers find them perplexing. The first is that every word of Scripture is divinely inspired. Origen did not see biblical authors as mere secretaries, taking down by dictation what God said — they wrote what they chose to write, but God had clarified their thinking, and Scripture is therefore without error.

Origen's second belief about Scripture is that it is a unified whole. The Bible has for Origen but one theme throughout — every verse of the Bible is about Christ, and any verse can be used to illustrate or amplify the meaning of any other. Christ "sojourned spiritually" with Old Testament authors, and they therefore wrote under his inspiration and of him, though often under "the veil of the letter," that is, the literal meaning. The discerning reader looks behind this veil to discern the deeper truth about Christ. Passages can therefore complement one another, but never conflict.

Origen devoted his life to studying Scripture. He explains his theory of biblical inspiration in his major theoretical work *On First Principles,* but it is in his biblical homilies and commentaries that we see his theory in practice. Over three-fourths of Origen's surviving writings are expositions of Scripture, and he routinely cites an array of Scripture passages to support or illustrate a point. One of his major works, the *Hexapla,* is a meticulous, word-for-word comparison of six versions of the Jewish scriptures, intended as a study tool to help the student ascertain the exact wording of any text. Establishing the exact wording of Scripture was important for Origen because of his understanding of Scripture as incarnate *logos.*

This understanding of Christ's presence in the Scripture led to Origen's famous allegorical method of interpretation. It made sense out of many a difficult passage (though producing "meanings" that seem far-fetched to many modern readers). Philo of Alexandria and others had already pioneered in the allegorical method, and it was widely accepted among religious believers of the day. Origen enlarged upon it. He was hardly a literalist, referring derisively to those who took a literal view as "friends of the letter." The literal sense of Scripture is useful to those unable to probe deeply, he felt, but if Scripture appears untrue or ridiculous, it must carry a deeper message not apparent to the cursory reader. Origen sought the "deeply hidden meaning of the Spirit of God, concealed under the language of an ordinary narrative which points in a different direction." Only the diligent student will discern this hidden meaning. If everything were plainly explained, the ignorant and impious would trample the truth, Origen says. He speaks of three levels of interpretation and relates them to body, soul, and spirit. The body corresponds to the literal meaning, helpful for simple believers, and the soul to the moral meaning, helpful to those who have begun to make progress. The diligent and wise, however, discern the spiritual or mystical meaning, secret mysteries concealed or wrapped "under cover of some historical record or account of visible things." Some passages may lack a literal meaning entirely.

Origen was often the center of controversy. His method of scriptural interpretation was widely appreciated, but the ideas he derived from Scripture raised eyebrows. Hans Urs von Balthasar refers to Origen's "massive cosmic consciousness." Origen's mind was of the sort that traveled to lofty esoteric realms, speculating about matters beyond human understanding. It was this itch to speculate that got him into trouble. It led him to such unusual (and ultimately rejected) views as his belief that there are pre-existing souls, that all souls will eventually be saved, that the created order is eternal, and that the Son is subordinate to the Father. Knowing that he dealt with perplexing enigmas, Origen maintained a modest attitude toward his more abstruse conjectures, never calling attention to himself and often introducing an idea with the comment that he was not sure about it and was merely putting it forth for discussion. But he did not see such speculations as idle or pointless, believing that God would lead the persistent inquirer to the truth.

Controversy over Origen's views swirled even more fiercely after his death. Three centuries later, in 553, the Fifth General Council condemned Origen — no longer would Origen be quoted as a reputable authority in orthodox circles. Nothing would have grieved him more. Origen had once written, "I wish to be a man of the church, not the founder of heresy. I want to be named with Christ's name and bear the name which is blessed on earth. I wish to do this in deed as well as in spirit."

IN IIIS OWN WORDS

Constant prayer

To pray "without ceasing" [1 Thess. 5:17], unite your prayer with the necessary actions and your actions with prayer. Virtuous acts and the commandments are fulfilled and included as part of prayer. The only way we can receive the injunction to pray "without ceasing" as a real possibility is by saying that a saint's entire life, taken as a whole, is one great prayer. What is usually called prayer then becomes a part of this prayer.

On Prayer, 12.2

Saving our souls

If we want to save our soul in order to receive it back as better than a soul, let us lose it by our martyrdom. If we lose our soul for Christ's sake and cast it at his feet by dying for him, we gain true salvation for it.

Exhortation to Martyrdom, 12

Martyrdom

Do not be surprised if the great blessedness of the martyrs, which will be one of deep peace, calm, and tranquility, must begin in such a seemingly gloomy and, so to speak, wintry way. . . . Remember that you cannot hear "the winter is past" [Song of Songs 2:11] but by entering into the contest of this present winter with all your strength. When the winter is past and the rain is over and gone, flowers will appear, planted in the house of the Lord and flourishing in the courts of our God.

Exhortation to Martyrdom, 30

Why hold back?

The human mind maintains a relation to things intelligible and to God, who transcends the intelligible order. Why do we then hold back, hesitating to shed the perishable body, the earthly tent that hampers us, weighs down the soul, and burdens the thoughtful mind? Why do we hesitate to burst our bonds and leave behind the stormy bellows of the life of flesh and blood?

Exhortation to Martyrdom, 47

Apostolic tradition

We maintain that only what in no way conflicts with the tradition of the church and the apostles is to be believed as true.

On First Principles, Preface, 2

The Fall into bodies

If they are negligent, all rational creatures who are incorporeal and invisible will gradually sink lower and assume bodies suitable to the regions into which they have descended. That is to say, they begin with ethereal bodies, then assume aerial bodies, and then, as they draw near to the earth, are enclosed in grosser bodies. Finally, they are bound to human flesh.

On First Principles, 1.4.1

The eternity of creation

Since wisdom is eternal, surely if all things have been made in wisdom, then the things which later assumed substantial existence have always existed in wisdom, by a pre-figuring and a pre-formation.

On First Principles, 1.4.5

Human limitations do not nullify God

Divine providence is not nullified, especially for those who believe it rightly, merely because its works and operations are beyond human comprehension. Similarly, the divine inspiration extending through the whole body of holy scripture is not to be questioned merely because our understanding is too weak to discover the obscure meanings hidden in every single sentence. This is because the treasure of divine wisdom is hidden within the lowly, humble vessel of words, as the apostle points out when he says, "But we have this treasure in earthen vessels" [2 Cor. 4:7] so that the strength of divine power may shine all the more brightly. . . .

On First Principles, 4.1.7

Difficulties in Scripture

Divine wisdom has placed [in Scripture] certain stumbling blocks and interruptions of the narrative meaning by inserting impossibilities and contradictions into the text. This is so that the very interruption of the narrative will block the reader, as it were, and convince him to proceed no further along the road of scripture's ordinary meaning. Then, when we are blocked from proceeding further, it calls us back to the beginning and to a different way. Then we enter again, by a narrow footpath, and gain a higher road, opening up for us the immense breadth of divine knowledge.

On First Principles, 4.2.9

The soul's journey

Try to understand, if you can, the pilgrimage of the soul during which it laments, groaning and grieving that it has been on its pilgrimage for so long. We understand these pilgrimages only faintly and darkly while they last. But when the soul has returned to its rest, to the fatherland in paradise, it will be taught and understand more truly what its pilgrimage meant. . . . Therefore the stages are those by which the soul journeys from earth to heaven.

Homily on Exodus, 1.4

Mystery in Scripture

Believing in the words of my Lord Jesus Christ, I think even an iota or a dot is full of mystery. . . .

Homily on Exodus, 1.4

The outer darkness

"Cast him into the outer darkness" [Matt. 22:13] so that, living in the outer darkness, he may grow thirsty for the light and cry out to God, who can help him and set him free.

Homily on Exodus, 3.3

Punishment

It is a terrible thing, the very worst thing, when we are no longer punished for our sins, no longer corrected for our faults.

Homily on Exodus, 8.5

Multiple manifestations

The Savior became "all things to all" that he might either gain all or make them whole: he became a human being to humans and an angel to the angels.

Commentary on John, 1.34

Secure in the Lord

Our salvation can never be more secure than when it is from the Lord. May he be my ground, he my house, he my mansion, he my repose, and may he be the place where I dwell.

Homily on Psalm 36, 5.7

"Chastise me"

Every son whom you accept you chastise [Prov. 3:12; Heb. 12:6]. I beg you, then, chastise me as well. Do not place me among those not chastised. . . . If you want to inflict me with bad health and make me sick, I will patiently bear it. For I know it would only be right for me to pay for my sins by getting sick, but I want to be purified by every affliction so long as I am spared eternal sufferings and punishment. . . . If it is your pleasure that I lose all my faculties, I let them go, so long as I do not lose my soul in your eyes.

Homily on Psalm 37, 2.5

Unity of Scripture

The person who does not know music does not understand the theory of musical harmony. He hears the different strings of a psaltery or lyre, each producing a particular sound apparently unlike the sound of another, and thinks them dissonant because of their dissimilarity. Even so, they who do not know how to hear God's harmony in his holy scriptures think there is discord between the Old and New Testaments, or between the prophets and the law, or between the different gospels, or that the apostle Paul is out of harmony with the gospel, or with himself, or with the other apostles. But when a man trained in the music of God arrives, a man skilled in deed and word, . . . he shall produce the sound of God's music, knowing from his art how to strike the strings in time. . . . He knows that all scripture is the one perfect and attuned instrument of God, producing from its various notes a single sound of salvation for those willing to learn, a sound that silences and checks every activity of an evil spirit.

Commentary on Matthew, 2

FOR REFLECTION AND DISCUSSION

How does your understanding of prayer compare to Origen's?
Do you believe in a multiplicity of supernatural spiritual beings? What difference does such a belief make in one's understanding of God and of human existence?

Assess Origen's teaching about remedial punishment and universal salvation.

Reflect on Origen's "massive cosmic consciousness." What aspects of it speak to you?

Is martyrdom something to avoid at all costs, something to accept only if forced, or something to look forward to? How does your view differ from Origen's?

Is every word of Scripture divinely inspired? If so, how do you account for apparent contradictions, untruths, and irrationalities in Scripture? If not, then is it inspired at all?

Is it legitimate to look for references to Christ in the Jewish scriptures?

Chapter 3

ANTONY

C. 251-355

The Desert Fathers

23

THE CHRISTIAN CHURCH was radically transformed in the year 313. The Emperor Constantine issued the Edict of Milan in that year, ending the persecution of Christians and inaugurating an era of church patronage. Martyrdom was now but a memory as Christians assumed control of the imperial government and the church accepted power and prestige from the state. Church membership became politically expedient, and thousands suddenly came forward for baptism. Christians had formerly seen themselves as removed from, even opposed to the dominant culture, but now the church was beginning to look more like that culture, which many believed corrupt and worldly. Some early Christians had actually welcomed martyrdom as an opportunity to make the ultimate witness. What form would a serious Christian witness now assume? Where could those hungering for a deeper obedience now turn?

Many Christians at this time began to pull away from the conflicting loyalties and ambitions of the suddenly friendly empire to devote themselves to a simpler and more disciplined life for the sake of spiritual growth. Such people are found in most religions and are called ascetics. The origins of Christian asceticism are unknown, but Eusebius, the first church historian, writing in the early fourth century, says there were Christian ascetics even in apostolic times. While some doubt such an early date, Christian ascetics are known to have been scattered through the eastern parts of the Roman Empire by the late second century. There was no established pattern. Some ascetics lived alone as hermits, while others gathered in informal communities.

The first great flowering of Christian asceticism occurred in the fourth century, spurred on by the Edict of Milan and subsequent events. These ascetics, mainly (but not solely) in Egypt, sowed the seeds of Christian monasticism, seeds eventually producing the great monastic movements that to this day provide models of the spiritual life to both the Eastern and the Western churches.

By far the most famous of the Egyptian ascetics was Antony, who was over sixty years old when the Edict of Milan was issued and had already spent forty years as a hermit in the desert. His fame is largely due to the colorful biography of him written by Athanasius, perhaps a few months after Antony's death. That work proved immensely popular, and its dramatic tales of demonic confrontations became a favorite subject for later artists and devotional writers. Perhaps because of his renown, Antony is often called the "Father of Christian Monasticism," but this cannot quite be true, since he visited an old religious hermit prior to setting out on his own vocation and entrusted the care of his younger sister to a community of virgins already in existence. But Antony's story, as related by Athanasius, provided the major inspiration for subsequent monastic life, both in Egypt and beyond.

Most of our biographical information comes from Athanasius's *Life of Antony*. Born to Coptic Christian parents in a small village in the upper Nile valley, Antony lost both parents when he was around twenty years of age. They left him a considerable estate in rich farmland. But when Antony heard the words "If you would be perfect, go and sell all that you have and give the money to the poor, and you will have treasure in heaven; then come and follow me" (Matt. 19:21), he took them as meant for himself. Antony liquidated his estate, gave away the proceeds, and took up residence in a solitary place near his village, sleeping on a mat or the bare ground.

This solitude soon proved inadequate, however, so Antony retired farther out into the desert, into an old tomb. Tombs were important to Coptic Christians as the portals to everlasting life. But this, too, eventually proved inadequate, so after sixteen years in the tomb, Antony moved deep into the desert, to an abandoned fort on a mountaintop, which he made habitable by driving away the jackals, scorpions, and reptiles. After twenty years there, Antony, now fifty-five years old, retreated to his last earthly home, still farther away, three days' journey into the desert, a desolate, naked rock jutting up from the desert floor, overlooking the Red Sea. He loved the place from the moment he saw it, and he remained there another fifty years, until he died at the age of 105, in full possession of his faculties, just after addressing a group of disciples and appearing, in Athanasius's words, "like one sailing from a foreign city to his own."

Antony spent all this time "daily being martyred by his conscience," in prayer, fasting, and reciting Scripture passages. According to Athanasius, Antony spoke only Coptic and did not read, memorizing long passages from the Bible by listening to others read aloud — "in him the memory took the place of books." He usually ate once a day, sometimes less often. He did not bathe. Athanasius's picture of Antony is one of harmony, tranquility, purity, and stark simplicity, but hardly one of isolation, since disciples and admirers often visited him, bringing food, seeking counsel, and asking him to mediate disputes. Antony became famous, even beyond Egypt, and by the end of his life thousands of would-be hermits were hastening into the desert to follow his example. The desert became a city of monks, Athanasius comments. While that cannot have been the literal truth, it was not far from it. Only twice did Antony return to settled territory, according to Athanasius — once to comfort Christians facing persecution, and once to defend orthodox theology (that is to say, the theology espoused by Athanasius — and some have suggested that the hermit could not have been as involved in those controversies as Athanasius suggests, that his biographer had his own reasons for portraying Antony as a champion of orthodoxy).

Antony's fame rested on his rigorous asceticism and his recurring battles with the demons who invaded his desert hermitages. The demons assumed an astonishing variety of forms — visible and invisible, terrifying and comforting, human and animal, sensuous and repulsive, all seeking to dissuade Antony from his discipline and devotion. Antony defeated the demons at every turn, explaining in a long speech in the *Life* (which takes up fully a fourth of the text) that "a great weapon against them is a just life and trust in God." It is the Lord who masters demons, Antony says, and since they are in fact powerless, he has learned to pay them no heed. To despise the enemy, he advises, contemplate the things of the Lord, and the enemy will disappear like smoke. Athanasius's accounts of Antony's encounters with demons, besides being vivid and colorful, are often spiritually and psychologically nuanced, which may account for the continuing popularity of the work.

Two additional sources provide information about Antony. Each source offers its own portrait of him, and the three portraits are not easily reconciled. The *Sayings of the Desert Fathers* is a loose collection of short aphorisms and anecdotes that exists in many versions and fragments, in four ancient languages. It provides information about Antony and over a hundred other desert hermits of the day. The hermits' sayings resemble those of the Zen Buddhist masters, Indian yogis, and Hassidic rabbis — they are pithy, poignant, earthy, and often mystifying. They can baffle modern readers accustomed to discursive writing. Antony and the other desert fathers (and a few mothers) come across as reclusive, humble, disciplined, otherworldly, nonjudgmental, and sometimes whimsical figures. Although Antony and his disciples have sometimes been viewed as fanatical, the *Sayings* reveal them as down-to-earth men and women, with a commonsense approach to life. They aspire to silence and simplicity. Antony's approach to God is often simply to be still and say nothing. The Antony of the *Sayings* does, however, interpret Scripture to those who ask him for guidance — he is not, it would seem, the uneducated figure presented by Athanasius. Some believe the *Sayings* give a more authentic picture of the desert hermits than Athanasius's *Life of Antony*, but others point out that the *Life* was written nearer to Antony's own time than the *Sayings*, which went through many editions and revisions.

Our third source is a collection of seven letters that most scholars believe to be from Antony. Here we meet a well-educated and self-confident teacher who seems to know the work of Clement of Alexandria and Origen. The letters (unlike Athanasius's *Life* but like the *Sayings*) rarely mention the person of Christ. They focus on self-knowledge as the means of regaining the use of sound reason, which is seen as a part of human nature as God first created it, but now lost. In the letters asceticism seems primarily intended to purify the body and soul to re-establish this natural harmony with God, whereas in the *Life*, its purpose seems to be to drive away demons.

It is impossible in this short essay to deal fully with the differences among the three sources of information about Antony. I think it likely that each preserves an authentic aspect of his life and teaching and that their differences are at least partly due to the fact that they were written or compiled for different audiences and for different purposes. In any case, Antony and his fellow hermits posed a bold and uncompromising challenge to a culture increasingly absorbed with the pursuit of power and material goods — a challenge to which thousands responded.

Antony's influence continued to grow as others took his ideas and modified or elaborated upon them. While Antony was still living, Pachomius (c. 290-346), another Egyptian, gathered groups of hermits into monasteries along the upper Nile, where they lived in community under a common rule of life. This became a second model for the monastic life alongside Antony's solitary model. Basil of Caesarea (330-379) wrote a rule for monastic houses under his jurisdiction in Asia Minor that established the structure and ethos which has characterized Eastern monasticism ever since. And John Cassian (360-435) wrote two books on what he had observed on an extended visit to Egypt and founded two monasteries near present-day Marseilles, thereby introducing Egyptian monastic practices into the West.

IN HIS OWN WORDS

Desire possessions of real value

Let no one among us yearn to possess things. What is the point of possessing things we cannot take with us? Is it not better to have things we can take with us — things like prudence, righteousness, temperance, courage, understanding, love, compassion for the poor, faith in Christ, freedom from anger, and hospitality? If we have these things, we shall find them running ahead of us to lay out for us a hospitable reception in the land of the meek.

Life of Antony, 17

The virtuous soul

Where the soul maintains its intellectual capacity according to its nature, there is virtue. The soul holds its nature when it remains as it was made, and it was made beautiful and straight. . . . As for the soul, it is straight when its intellectual capacity accords with nature, when it is what it was created to be. But when it turns from its course and twists away from what it is by nature, that is what we call the vice of the soul.

Life of Antony, 20

Why demons fear ascetics

A just life and trust in God are great weapons against [demons]. Demons fear ascetics for several reasons: for their fasting, vigils and prayers, meekness and gentleness, contempt for money, lack of vanity, humility, love of the poor and of almsgiving, freedom from anger, and most of all for their devotion to Christ.

Life of Antony, 30

Judgment

None of us is judged for what he does not know, any more than he is considered blessed on account of his learning and knowledge. Judgment is rendered, rather, on whether someone has sincerely kept the faith and obeyed the commandments.

Life of Antony, 33

Fear

When a soul cannot shake off fear, it is because enemies are present.

Life of Antony, 37

When Satan told the truth

Someone once knocked at my cell door. When I went outside, I saw someone who appeared huge and tall. I asked, "Who are you?" and he said, "I am Satan." I said, "What are you doing here?" He replied, "Why do the monks and all Christians censure me for no reason? Why do you torment me every hour?" I said, "Why do you torment them?" He replied, "I am not the one tormenting them. They disturb themselves, for I have become weak. Haven't they read that 'the enemy is finished, in perpetual ruin; their cities ploughed under' [Ps. 9:6]? I no longer have anything, no place, no weapon, no city. Everywhere there are Christians, even the desert is full of monks! They should mind their own business and stop censuring me for no reason!" I was struck by the grace of the Lord and said to him, "You are a perpetual liar and never tell the truth, but this once, even if you did not mean to, you have told the truth. For when Christ came, he rendered you a weakling. He threw you down and left you defenseless." When Satan heard the Savior's name, he could not endure it, for it scorched him. He then became invisible.

Life of Antony, 41

The real marvel

Do not regard it as a marvel if a ruler writes to us, for after all, he is a man. Marvel instead that God wrote the law for human beings and has spoken to us through his own Son.

Life of Antony, 81 (in response to a letter
from the Emperor Constantine)

"Keep your attention on yourself"

Abba Antony thought about the deep judgments of God and asked, "Lord, why do some die young while others drag on into extreme old age? Why are some poor and others rich? Why do wicked men prosper while the righteous go wanting?" He heard a voice answering him: "Antony, keep your attention on yourself. These things lie in the judgment of God, and it would do you no good to know about them."

Sayings of the Desert Fathers

The cell

Abba Antony said, "Just as fish die if stranded on dry land, so do monks lose their determination to persevere in solitary prayer if they stay away from their cells or dwell among the people of the world. Therefore, as fish should return to the sea, so we must return to our cells, lest remaining outside, we forget to attend to our inner selves."

Sayings of the Desert Fathers

Temptation

Antony said: "No one who has not been tempted can enter into the Kingdom of Heaven. Without temptations, no one can be saved."

Sayings of the Desert Fathers

Moderation

A hunter in the desert was shocked to see Abba Antony enjoying himself with the brothers. To show the hunter that it was sometimes necessary to attend to the needs of the brothers, the old man said to him, "Put an arrow into your bow and shoot it." He did so. The old man then said, "Shoot another one," and the hunter did so. Then the old man said, "Shoot again," and the hunter replied, "If I bend my bow too much, I will break it." The old man then said to him, "So it is with the work of God. If we stretch the brothers beyond their limit, they will soon break. Sometimes it is necessary for them to relax their efforts." When he heard this, the hunter was pierced with compunction and, greatly edified by the old man, went away. The brothers returned home strengthened.

Sayings of the Desert Fathers

Bearing insults

The brothers praised another monk in Abba Antony's presence. When the monk went to see Antony, Antony wanted to know how he would bear insults. Perceiving that he could not bear them at all, he said to him, "You are like a village magnificently adorned on the outside but destroyed by robbers on the inside."

Sayings of the Desert Fathers

Taking offense

Abba Antony taught Abba Ammonas, saying: "You must advance further in the fear of God." He took him out of his cell, showed him a stone, and said: "Go and insult that stone and beat it without ceasing." When Ammonas had done this, Antony asked him whether the stone had answered back. "No," replied Ammonas. Then Abba Antony said, "You must reach the same point, where you no longer take offense at anything."

Sayings of the Desert Fathers

The way of not knowing

Some old men went to see Abba Antony. Among them was Abba Joseph. To test them, the old man quoted a scripture text and asked them what it meant, beginning with the youngest. Each gave an opinion as he was able. But to each the old man said, "You have not understood it." Finally, he said to Abba Joseph, "How would you explain this saying?" Abba Joseph replied, "I do not know." Then Abba Antony said, "Abba Joseph has truly found the way, for he said, 'I do not know.'"

Sayings of the Desert Fathers

Madness

Abba Antony said: "There will come a time when people will go mad, and seeing someone who is not mad, will attack him and say, 'You are mad because you are not like us.'"

Sayings of the Desert Fathers

Seeing is enough

Three priests used to go to visit blessed Antony every year. Two of them discussed their thoughts and the salvation of their souls with him, but the third never said a word. Much later, Abba Antony said to him, "You often come here to see me, but you never ask me anything." The man replied, "It is enough for me to see you, Father."

Sayings of the Desert Fathers

Knowledge of self and of God

Truly, I write to you as to reasonable men, my beloved, as men capable of knowing yourselves. Anyone who knows himself knows God, and anyone who knows God is worthy to worship him in the right way. My beloved in the Lord, know yourselves. Those who know themselves know their time, and those who know their time can stand firm and not be bandied about by various tongues.

Epistle 4

Laughing at the devil

Don't you know what the many schemes and arts of the devil are like? Evil spirits envy us because they know we try to recognize our disgrace and to flee from what they would do with us. Not only do we try to reject the evil counsels which they sow among us, but many of us even laugh at their schemes.

Epistle 6

Danger of pride

Many pursued asceticism for their whole lives but were killed for lack of discernment. Truly, my children, I am not the least surprised that, if you neglect yourselves and do not discern your works, you fall into the hands of the devil. When that happens, though you think you are near to God and expect the light, darkness overtakes you. Why did Jesus gird himself with a towel and wash the feet of his inferiors but as an example for you, to teach those who turn to him about their own beginning? For their motion originated with the pride which came at the very beginning. That is why you will never inherit the Kingdom of God except by greatly humbling your whole heart, mind, spirit, soul, and body.

Epistle 7

FOR REFLECTION AND DISCUSSION

Compare Antony's understanding of Christian living to yours. What accounts for the difference?

Write a few sentences expressing what you think Antony would say about a typical night of network television today.

What do you think Antony was seeking, and why was it important to him?

Identify modern persons or movements that embody the values of Antony.

Where might one turn today to find the contentment and solitude that
the desert afforded the ancient Egyptians?

Chapter 4

GREGORY OF NYSSA

C. 335–C. 395

The Cappadocians

HIGH ATOP THE MOUNTAINS in central Turkey lies a vast volcanic plateau known since ancient times as Cappadocia. It is dotted with vineyards and orchards and features humpbacked rock formations that produce an eerie, otherworldly landscape. Inhabitants of the region still reside in homes chiseled out of the soft rock over two millennia ago. In ancient times, Cappadocia was a Roman province known for its remoteness and its primitive, unlettered populace. But a colony of Jews had long resided in Cappadocia, and the region soon became a Christian center as well (and remained so until the creation of modern Turkey in the twentieth century). In the fourth century Cappadocia produced three Christian spiritual masters whose thought retains its appeal to this day, especially in the East. The three were close friends (two were brothers) and valued each other's work, though each had his distinctive abilities and insights. All three were from families of means who had been Christian for several generations. They afford us our earliest example of the fruits of a stable, financially secure, and intellectually attentive Christian home. They are known as the Cappadocian fathers.

The first of the three to make his mark was Basil (c. 330-379), bishop of Caesarea (modern Kayseri), the leading town of Cappadocia. We remember Basil today chiefly as the author of two influential monastic rules and for the Liturgy of St. Basil. In his day, however, Basil was known as a gifted administrator and shrewd ecclesiastical politician. He contested for the full divinity of Christ against the emperor Valens, an Arian who viewed Christ as a created being. To this end, Basil needed the support of sympathetic bishops, and so in 372 (the precise date is uncertain) he created two new dioceses in nearby small towns, naming his friend Gregory of Nazianzus (329-389) as bishop of Sasima and another Gregory, his younger brother, as bishop of Nyssa.

Reflective and retiring by nature, neither Gregory wanted to be a bishop, and neither was suited for the office. For a time, both were furious at Basil for having foisted it upon them. Gregory of Nazianzus was elevated to the post of archbishop of Constantinople in 381, from which he resigned within a year when the tangled political intrigue surrounding his appointment refused to die down. A man of extraordinary literary talent, he returned to his home in Nazianzus and spent the rest of his life writing bold sermons, letters, hymns, autobiographical poems (often carping in tone when discussing his experiences as bishop), and orations. His five orations on the Trinity earned him the title "The Theologian," by which he is still known in the East today.

The most original and spiritually evocative of the Cappadocians, however, was Gregory of Nyssa. "Less brilliant and prolific than his great master Origen, less cultivated than his friend Gregory Nazianzen, less practical than his brother Basil, he nonetheless outstrips them all in the profundity of his thought," says Hans Urs von Balthasar.

We know little of Gregory's life and must guess at some features of his personality and character from hints found in his writings and those of his two colleagues. Gregory was born in Caesarea, into a family of ten children, five brothers and five sisters. The family was devout, but as a young man Gregory seems to have been a casual Christian at best. Over his family's objections, he pursued a secular career, studying and teaching rhetoric for several years (perhaps accounting for the stylized rhetorical flourishes found in some of his writings). In addition to his brother Basil, whom Gregory came eventually to see as a mentor and whom he called "father" and "master," Gregory's sister Macrina seems to have been especially dear to him. He wrote her biography and a dialogue with her on her deathbed, called *On the Soul and Resurrection,* composed after he sat at her side during the last few days of her life. Gregory was almost certainly married, the only one of the three Cappadocian fathers to take a wife (the other two were monks), though he seems at times to have regretted marrying, referring to marriage as a "sad tragedy" and a union that produces a "dead body." There is some suggestion that after his consecration as bishop he may have continued to live with his wife, but celibately.

Gregory of Nyssa's experience as a bishop was, if possible, unhappier than that of Gregory of Nazianzus. He thought of Nyssa as a wilderness and only reluctantly took up his duties as bishop of the place. He was soon able to leave, though not on terms he might have chosen. Trusting, naïve, and with no head for figures, Gregory was not given to careful financial oversight. When funds disappeared from the diocesan treasury, he was falsely accused of having squandered them. He was deposed and carried off to prison, but soon escaped. For two years he seems to have wandered from town to town, lodging with friends. It was probably during this time that Gregory was won over to his brother Basil's theological campaign for the full divinity of Christ, which he supported and tried to complete in his later writings. Then, in 378, the death of Valens, who may have had a hand in formulating the charges against Gregory, enabled him to return to Nyssa and resume his duties as bishop, to great acclaim. Basil died the following year. Perhaps now able to emerge from his brother's shadow, Gregory came into his own. He delivered major addresses in Constantinople in 381 and 386 and seems to have traveled to Palestine and Arabia to mediate ecclesiastical disputes. After 386, Gregory drops from view.

Gregory of Nyssa saw God as shrouded in mystery and unknowable. This was not due to any inadequacy of the human mind, but to the very nature of God — an infinite God is *essentially* unknowable. For Gregory, the spiritual journey is not from darkness into light (as Origen and the other Gregory had described it), but from light into an ever-deepening darkness. The closer we draw to God, the deeper the darkness. We are sometimes bewildered, giddy, even terrified as the divine night surrounds us and God leads us further into the darkness and discloses himself there. This divine disclosure is never complete, however, for a complete disclosure would be impossible, given that God is utterly different from his creatures. God gives the faithful soul joy in the darkness by continuously manifesting his love for the soul, and the soul responds in kind. This love is *eros* — erotic love, a theme strikingly developed in Gregory's sermons on the Song of Songs. The ancients were, in fact, far more likely to see *eros* in a soul's relationship to God than in the relationship of man and woman (accounting in part, perhaps, for Gregory's refusal to rhapsodize about the joys of married life). But the soul is never fully satisfied, for God is always greater, always more, ever ahead of us. Gregory speaks of a "seeing that is not seeing." He envisions not a turning back of the clock to restore what had been before sin and rebellion entered the world, but a "perpetual journey." We always long for more, and the soul is always rising higher, always on the way, throughout eternity, never resting, never arriving, moving ever deeper into the darkness.

This idea of perpetual journey is Gregory's greatest departure from the conventional thinking that was much in the air around him. Most assumed that to attain perfection was to reach a place of rest and changelessness. Not so, said Gregory. Changing, growing, ascending — it is in these very things that perfection consists. Gregory's greatest literary work, his *Life of Moses,* is an allegorical reading of Moses' life in which Gregory sees his subject as the great exemplar of the continual journey. He speaks of "constant change," "perpetual movement," "perpetual ascent," and being "constantly born again." Having seen God face to face, Moses wanted to see still more of God, but he was never satisfied, nor could he have been, for God was always beyond him, wooing him further into the darkness.

Like Origen, Gregory was a universalist. He thought all things, even the devil, would be drawn to God in the end. It was inconceivable to him that God's plan would remain forever thwarted. No creature would be capable of resisting the divine overtures throughout eternity, and when God eventually became all in all, evil would no longer exist. This would in no way compromise human free will, for all creatures would in the end return to God — by choice. Like Origen, Gregory saw punishment not as retribution, but for the purpose of healing and restoration.

All three of the Cappadocians explored the implications of the doctrine of the Trinity, an idea being hammered out at the great church councils of the time. An early version of the Nicene Creed had been written fifty years before, but had left some questions unresolved. Everyone agreed that God was One and that Jesus was the divine Son or *logos* (a theme earlier explored by Irenaeus, Origen, and others). But making these two affirmations raised other perplexing questions. Was God totally encompassed in the person of Jesus? If so, did that not compromise God's omnipotence and changelessness? And what of the Holy Spirit? Groups of bishops met and produced creed after creed, seeking to clarify or modify the Nicene statements. Accusations of heresy flew in every direction. The hands of all three Cappadocian fathers can be seen in the final draft of the Nicene Creed, which probably came from the Council of Constantinople in 381. (Some scholars think it dates from a few decades later.)

At the heart of the Christian understanding of God as Three in One and One in Three lies the belief that God is *relationship*. Ancient philosophers understood God as existing in splendid solitude and absolute simplicity, invisible, eternal, self-sufficient, and beyond understanding. The third-century thinker Plotinus had referred to God as "the One" and "the Alone." Gregory of Nyssa and his two colleagues affirmed much of this, but saw God not in terms of splendid isolation, but as a communion of persons. Aloneness is replaced by relationship as the defining characteristic of God. Relationship implies movement, energy, giving and receiving, and at least the possibility of love, all of which are foreign to the impersonal God of the philosophers. But to the Cappadocians, that is who God is — moving, giving, loving.

In defending the equality of the Father, Son, and Holy Spirit, Gregory of Nyssa argues that the three persons share the same divine nature as three human beings share the same human nature. That shared divine nature is eternal, uncreated, and essentially incomprehensible. This analogy was faulted by some for seeming to suggest that there are really three gods. Gregory adds a second analogy, that of the rainbow, which is one light yet comprises several colors. Elsewhere, Gregory offers a psychological exposition of the Trinity, comparing it to the human soul, which was commonly believed to have three parts: reason, passion, and the appetites. Augustine would later develop this idea at great length.

IN HIS OWN WORDS

Free will

People live differently. Some live virtuous lives while others slide into vice. It is hardly reasonable to account for these differences in people by some divine constraint residing outside themselves. Each person has the power to make his own choice. . . . If someone does not acknowledge God, God does not protect him and delivers him up to passion. The reason he is pulled down into a life of passion and dishonor is that he does not acknowledge God. It is as if someone does not see the sun and falls into a ditch and then blames the sun for causing his fall. We do not say that the source of light angrily pushed someone into a ditch when that person has paid no heed to the light. It is more reasonable to say of the man who does not see that it was his failure to participate in the light that caused him to fall into the ditch.

Life of Moses, 74-76

Seeing that is not seeing

Progressing by an ever more perfect diligence, the soul comes to appreciate the truly real. As it draws closer to this vision, it comes to see that the divine is by nature invisible. Then it leaves behind all surface appearances. The true knowledge which we seek is a seeing that is not seeing, an awareness that our goal lies beyond all knowing and is everywhere cut off from us by the darkness of incomprehensibility.

Life of Moses, 162, 163

Moses the pilgrim

Moses was always moving forward and never stopped climbing upward. He set no limit to his rise to the stars. . . . He was constantly moving on to the next step, continually moving higher, because he always found another step beyond the highest one he had reached. . . . Although raised to great heights, he is still restless, desiring, less and less content, thirsting for what had already filled him to the fullest. He still begs God to give him more, as if he had received nothing at all. . . .

Life of Moses, 227

The hungering soul

Hope is always drawing the soul away from the beauty which it sees to what lies beyond, ever kindling the desire for the hidden by means of what is continually perceived. Someone who deeply loves beauty receives what he sees as an image of what he longs for and he still longs to be filled with the very imprint of the archetype.

Life of Moses, 231

Truly to see God

. . . to see God truly is never to cease from desiring God. . . . The true vision of God is to desire to see him and never to be satisfied in that desire.

Life of Moses, 233, 239

The path to perfection

The soul's path to perfection is to develop continually towards what is good.

Life of Moses, 306

From glory to glory

The best thing about our mutability is that it is always possible to grow in what is good. This ability to improve is what transforms the soul, changing it more and more into the divine. . . . Do not be distressed when you consider this tendency in your nature, but let us change in a way that brings continual evolution towards what is better, that we may be changed from glory to glory [1 Cor. 3:18].

On Perfection

Inadequacy of human speech

Human speech cannot express the reality that transcends all thought and concept. That reality is what the soul severed from evil always seeks, with which it longs to be united once it finds it. Anyone who obstinately insists on expressing this in words offends God without meaning to. For we believe in One who transcends the universe; surely he also transcends speech. Anyone trying to use human speech to get a handle on the infinite no longer acknowledges that the infinite is transcendent. If he acknowledged that, he would not equate God with his speech.

Commentary on Ecclesiastes, Sermon 7

Contemplating God

Essentially and by its very nature, the divine lies beyond every act of comprehension and knowledge. Human speculation cannot approach or reach it. . . . As with human works of art, the mind can in a certain sense perceive the author of the artifact that lies before it because the artist has expressed his artistry in his work. But notice that we see merely the artistry which the artist has impressed in his work, not the artist himself. . . . This is how we contemplate God: it is God's goodness, not God's essence, that we know.

On the Beatitudes, Sermon 6

Perfection

[God] has endowed your nature with this perfection: an imitation of the perfections of his own nature he has imprinted upon its structure, just as one would impress on wax the outline of an emblem. But your perfection has been obscured and rendered useless by the wickedness that has been viciously poured all over this divine imprint. With virtuous living you must wash off the dirt that has come to cling to your heart like plaster. Then your divine beauty will shine forth once again.

On the Beatitudes, Sermon 6

Grasping the magnificence

The soul rising upwards must leave behind everything it has already attained because it falls so far short of what the soul longs for. Then and only then will it begin to see something of the magnificence that is beyond the stars.

On Virginity

Prayer to the Good Shepherd

Where do you graze your sheep, O Good Shepherd, you who carry all your sheep on your shoulders? The single lamb you lifted up [Matt. 12:11-12; John 10:14] is the whole human race elevated on your shoulders. Show me this grazing place. Disclose to me the still waters. Lead me to the good grass. Call me by name so that I, your sheep, may listen to your voice. And may your call be the gift of eternal life.

On the Song of Songs, Sermon 2

The grandeur of humanity

Your Creator has honored you above all other creatures. He did not make in his own image the heavens, the moon, the sun, the beautiful stars — nor anything you see in the created universe. Only you are made in the likeness of that nature which passes all understanding. You alone resemble the eternal beauty, a receptacle of happiness, an image of the true Light. If you look up to him, you become what he is. You will imitate him who shines within you, whose glory is reflected in your purity. Nothing in all creation can equal your grandeur. The whole heaven, the earth, the sea — all fit into and are measured by the palm of his hand. You alone can embrace him who is so great that he grasps all creation in his palm. He resides within you and pervades your entire being, yet is not cramped. He says, "I will dwell in them and walk among them" [2 Cor. 6:16].

On the Song of Songs, Sermon 2

The open field

He who is moving upwards can always rise still higher, and the open field of the divine course is never exhausted for anyone running to the Lord.

On the Song of Songs, Sermon 5

Growing in eternity

We receive great graces at every point in our continual participation in the blessed nature of God, but the path beyond our immediate grasp is still infinite. This will always be true of those who share in the divine goodness. Throughout eternity, they will enjoy an ever greater and greater participation in grace.

On the Song of Songs, Sermon 8

FOR REFLECTION AND DISCUSSION

State what the doctrine of the Trinity means to you. Can you identify times when you have experienced God as beyond you (the object of prayer), within you (inspiring your prayers), and before you (in whose likeness you are being formed as you pray)?

What does the doctrine of the Trinity say about how God relates to us?

When someone turns to God, is it because of an innate longing always present within her, or is it because her old self has been transformed?

What do you feel Gregory would say if confronted with modern secularism?

Can God be known? If so, how and to what extent?

Does perfection consist in resting in God or in striving for God?

If life is a "perpetual journey," what kind of journey is it? A climb? A sprint? An obstacle course? A walk in the dark? A peaceful stroll?

Chapter 5

AUGUSTINE OF HIPPO

354-430

The Birth of Western Spirituality

AUGUSTINE OF HIPPO towers over Christian spirituality in the West. Apart from Jesus and the biblical authors themselves, no one has exerted greater influence over how Western Christians understand their relationship to God. Even today and even among his detractors, Augustine's influence remains unsurpassed, for it was Augustine — pondering, searching, praying, contending, never flinching from the difficult question — who defined the issues on which Western Christian history has turned for the past sixteen hundred years.

Augustine was the great champion of grace, the power of God in human life, against those who sought to make a place for human willpower. The chief advocate of willpower was a British monk named Pelagius, then living in Rome. The two men carried on a spirited debate through their writings for nearly twenty years. To understand the debate, imagine a man dangling over the side of a cliff. Far below him is a rocky ravine. He clings to a bare branch, the only thing saving him from certain death. Someone then descends on a rope — but why does this savior come, and what does he do? Does he come on his own initiative, then clasp his arms around the man and carry him to safety? Or does the man reach for his cell phone and call for help, in response to which the savior comes to tell him where to place his hands and feet so as to climb to the top? The former view would have been that of Augustine, the latter that of Pelagius.

The question is not as simple as it seems. Pelagius's position sounds reasonable enough. He believed humanity was in trouble but that sin was voluntary and resistible — human perfection was at least possible. Pelagius had a place for divine grace, but as instruction or enlightenment from God, to enable people to improve themselves. The real power still lay with human beings. Against this position, Augustine believed sin was universal and incapacitating, holding everyone prisoner. No amount of enlightenment or human effort could overcome it because sin warps even the human intellect. It is therefore solely by the grace of God, according to Augustine, that anyone is saved. But Augustine also affirmed the freedom of the human will. Grace precedes the will and attracts it, he says, but does not cancel it out, achieving the consent of the will without coercion. Grace is irresistible but not constraining; it does not overpower the will, but perfects it.

If Augustine's view sounds like a contradiction, then so be it. Call it paradoxical. Persons recovering from an addiction can perhaps understand the paradox of grace better than most. Many a recovering addict has been told, "I admire the way you faced up to your addiction." They are quick to respond, however, that their recovery is a gift and that had they relied on their own willpower or determination, they would still be in the throes of their disease. Yet addicts do make a decision — to acknowledge their powerlessness, give up control, and ask for help — and it is a free decision. Many recovering addicts will testify that even that decision, however, was not their own, but that God had been rattling around in their souls unbeknownst to them, creating the pain that would bring them to their senses and to him. This is pure Augustine.

Augustine was born to a Christian mother and a pagan father in a small town in what is today northeastern Algeria. He seems to have been a normal child, tempted by small vices such as stealing pears, but unusually introspective. As a young man, he studied rhetoric, pursued a teaching career in Rome, formed close friendships, and lived faithfully with a mistress for fifteen years. But he was restless and unsatisfied, hungering to know the meaning of life and the nature of the good. Augustine pursued his questions among several philosophical and religious groups and eventually settled with the neo-Platonists, whose high-minded philosophy continued to influence his thinking even after his conversion to Christianity. That conversion came in the year 387, when Augustine was thirty-three years of age, as a result, according to his own account of it, of his mother's prayers and the preaching of Ambrose, bishop of Milan. He had discovered at last where true happiness is to be found — in God. Augustine was then baptized and returned from Italy to his native North Africa, where, nine years later, he became bishop of the bustling seaport of Hippo (today Annaba), a post he held until his death.

Augustine's works are vast in scope; we have more from his pen than from that of any other ancient author. This short essay does not allow for a full account of his enormous contributions, but several features of his thought (in addition to his understanding of divine grace) have helped shape the spirituality of Christians in the West. A word must be said about several of these:

- Disagreements between doctrinal and/or moral rigorists and those willing to make allowance for backsliders have often troubled the church. In Augustine's day, the issue was joined by a group called the Donatists, who held that ordination at the hands of an unworthy bishop was invalid. Augustine argued for a broader, more inclusive

48

church. The grace of God does not depend, he said, on the character of the minister, for the sacraments are not the personal property of those administering them. It is God who validates them, not the celebrant.

- In his writings against the Donatists, Augustine developed an understanding of the church that has been hugely influential over the centuries but that modern people who breathe the air of secularism and pluralism find hard to grasp. He sees the church as an institution, founded by Christ, to be the visible and authoritative dispenser of God's saving grace. Augustine acknowledges that there is grace outside the church, for he recognized that God had been moving in his own life prior to his baptism. But it is through the church and its sacraments, Augustine felt, that Christians are bound together and set apart from the world. Through his dispute with the Donatists, Augustine came to see four distinguishing characteristics of the church: it is one, united by the love of Christians one for another (the Donatists scorned those not of their view); it is holy, set apart from the world by God (the Donatists held that the church's holiness lay in the character of church leaders, not in God); it is catholic or universal (Donatism was largely confined to North Africa); and it is apostolic, or faithful to the teaching of the apostolic writings as interpreted by the bishops (virtually no bishop endorsed the Donatist position). It is no coincidence that these four characteristics of the church are also those named in the Nicene Creed, which was written during Augustine's lifetime.

- Augustine's monumental book *City of God* also arose from his view of the church. It provides the first comprehensive Christian understanding of history. Surveying the history of the world from Creation to Judgment Day, Augustine sees God shaping and guiding events amidst the turmoil and confusion caused by human sin. He envisions two cities, one heavenly, the other earthly, each defined by what it loves. History is a struggle between these two cities. Although in places Augustine seems to denigrate the imperial Roman establishment and to identify the City of God with the Christian church, his distinction between the two cities is actually quite subtle, and he sees their lives intertwined in this world. Within the visible institution of the church, Augustine insists, will be found citizens of both cities.

- Augustine was not fluent in Greek (he spoke and wrote in Latin), but he was certainly familiar with the main outlines of the Cappadocian teaching about God as relationship. Augustine was concerned to demonstrate that the idea of Three in One and One in Three is not mere gobbledygook. In his book *On the Trinity,* he takes the Cappadocian understandings in some new directions. Since human beings are created in the image of God, Augustine expects to find an imprint or traces of God in the human soul. To this end, he offers a series of analogies based on human psychology. He knows they are all inadequate, but he sees in these analogies pointers to the reality of God. The human soul, for example, exists, knows, and wills — three activities or manifestations of the soul, and yet the soul is one. In another place, Augustine refers to the soul's love of itself in terms of lover, beloved, and the love that unites them — all this within the one soul. Elsewhere he refers to memory, intelligence, and will within the one soul. Many Christians in later times, meditating on the nature of God, have found suggestive Augustine's psychological analogies and his discerning of traces of God within the individual soul.

• All Augustine's writings are drenched with a sense of eternity. Our true identity resides not in the world we see, but in a higher realm. We search in vain for happiness if we seek it among the pleasures and rewards of the world. This Augustine learned from his life prior to his conversion, as told in his *Confessions,* written ten years after his conversion. Intensely personal, ruthlessly honest, and psychologically penetrating, the *Confessions* is Augustine's most popular work. The purpose of the *Confessions* is to show forth or "confess" the goodness and greatness of God, using Augustine's own life as a case study. We see him as a restless, wandering youth whom God loves and woos, leading eventually to his conversion and his discovery of true joy. The work is cast in the form of an extended prayer. The first nine of the *Confessions'* thirteen books are autobiographical, while the last four contain reflections on memory, creation, and eternity that provide the theological framework within which the first nine books are to be read. Augustine's *Confessions* is the mother of all spiritual autobiographies, the first — and many would say the greatest — work of the genre. Its admirers are legion even today, but those who read it merely for its psychological insights miss its point, for the *Confessions* is not really about Augustine at all — it is about God. The same could be said of all Augustine's writings and of the man himself — for Augustine, everything was about God.

IN HIS OWN WORDS

Bear with the wicked

The catholic church holds that unity must be maintained; the church of God must not be divided. God will judge the good and evil ones later. It is impossible today to separate the good from the wicked, and it is therefore necessary to tolerate this for now.

Commentary on Psalm 119 (120)

Pleasing God

The one who pleases himself pleases a fool, for in pleasing himself he is a fool. Only he who pleases God pleases without danger. Who pleases God? The one who is pleased with God. God cannot displease himself; may he please you so that you may please him.

Commentary on Psalm 122 (123)

The form of love

If you want to see God, you should consider that God is love [1 John 4:8]. What is the face of love? What is its form, its height, its feet, its hands? No one can say — and yet love has feet, for they lead to the church; it has hands, for they minister to the poor; it has eyes, for through them the needy become visible.

Homily on the First Epistle of John

A prayer

O God, founder of the universe, grant that I may ask the right things of you, then conduct myself so that I am fit to be heard by you, and finally be saved by you.

Soliloquy

Miracle

If you try to explain it, it is no longer wonderful; if you look for other examples, it is no longer unique. Let us allow God the power to do what we are powerless to fathom, the only explanation for which is the power of the doer.

Letter 137

The Trinity

To understand something of [the Trinity], consider memory, understanding, and will. We mention these three things separately, one after the other, but we never use one of them or even mention it without using the other two as well.

Letter 169

Love of God and neighbor

Love of God is the first commandment mentioned [Matt. 22:38-39], but love of neighbor is the first one you obey. He who gave you these two commandments to love would not, of course, put your neighbor first and God second — no, God is first and neighbor second. But you cannot yet see God. It is in loving your neighbor that you grow worthy to see God; only by loving your neighbor can you polish your eyes to see God.

Homily on the Gospel of John

The two cities

The two cities have been made by the two loves: the earthly city by love of self, even to the exclusion of God, and the heavenly city by the love of God, even to the exclusion of self. The first exalts itself; the second exalts the

Lord. The first seeks the praise of men, while for the second, God's witness to its conscience is its greatest praise. The one holds its head high in its own glory, the other says to God, "You are my glory, and it is you who raises my head" [Ps. 3:3].

City of God, 14.28

The heart finds rest

You are great, O Lord, and greatly to be praised. Great is your power and your wisdom infinite. Man would praise you. Man is but a particle of your creation, whose mortality is witness to his sin, testifying that you resist the proud — yet this man, a mere particle of your creation, would praise you. You awaken and stir us so that only in praising you can we be content. You have made us for yourself and our hearts are restless until they find their rest in you. Grant me, Lord, to know whether praying to you or praising you comes first, and whether knowing you or calling to you comes first. For who can call on you without knowing you? For we might call for help to something else, mistaking it for you. Or do we pray to you and come to know you through our praying?

Confessions, 1.1

Calling upon God

How shall I call upon my God when I am asking my Lord and my God to come into myself? Where in me can my God come? What chamber have I to receive the God who made heaven and earth? Is there in fact in me something fit to contain you, Lord my God? Can even heaven and earth, which you made and in which you made me, contain you? Or since nothing that exists could exist without you, does this mean that whatever exists contains you in some sense? If this is so, since I too exist, why do I ask you to come into me, I who would be nothing if you were not already within me?

Confessions, 1.2

His soul

My soul is like a very small house. Enlarge it so that you may enter.

Confessions, 1.5

A smiling God

Do my questions make you smile at me and bid me simply to acknowledge you and praise you for what I do know?

Confessions, 1.6

Infant sin

If babies are innocent, it is not for lack of will to do harm, but for lack of strength.

Confessions, 1.7

Augustine's sin

My sin was that I looked for pleasure, beauty, and truth not in [God] but in myself and his other creatures. That search led me instead to pain, confusion, and error.

Confessions, 1.20

God the pursuer

You follow close on the heels of your fugitives, first a God of vengeance, then of mercy, calling us back to yourself in ways beyond our understanding.

Confessions, 4.4

God the helmsman

I was tossed by every wind, but you guided me as a helmsman steers a ship, by routes I did not know.

Confessions, 4.14

Loving God

But what do I love when I love you, Lord? Not the loveliness of the body or of passing time, not the brilliance of earthly light, so welcome to our eyes, nor the beautiful melodies of song; not the fragrance of flowers, perfumes, and spices; not manna or honey; not limbs such as the body delights in embracing. None of these do I love when I love my God. And yet, when I love him, I do love a certain kind of light, a voice, a fragrance, a food, an embrace; but I love them in my inner self, where there shines a light not bound by space, where my soul hears a sound that never fades away and breathes a fragrance the wind cannot disperse, tastes food not consumed by the eating and welcomes an embrace that satisfies my desire but never grows slack. This is what I love when I love my God.

Confessions, 10.7

Pursued by God

You called, you shouted, you burst through my deafness. You shone upon me; your radiance enveloped me and you banished my blindness. You spread your aromas about me; I breathed and now I gasp for your sweet fragrance. I tasted you, and now I hunger and thirst for you. You touched me, and I burn for your peace.

Confessions, 10.27

Grace and commandment

Give me grace to do what you command, and command me to do what you will.

Confessions, 10.37

God's terms

Together with you I wanted to possess a lie. . . . And in this way I lost you, because you do not deign to be possessed together with a lie.

Confessions, 10.41

Sorry state

Poor me! I don't even know what I don't know!

Confessions, 11.25

The Trinity

There are three things, all found in man himself, which I propose for consideration. They are far different from the Trinity, but I speak of them and how they exercise themselves to show how great this difference is. The three things are existence, knowledge, and will. I am, I know, and I will. I am an existing being who knows and wills; I know both that I am and that I will; and I will both to be and to know. In these three — being, knowledge, and will — consists one whole and indivisible life. I am one life, one mind, one essence: the three are distinct yet inseparable. . . . In God, too, there is a Trinity.

Confessions, 13.11

The power of grace

It is grace that enables us to know what we should do and grace that enables us to do it. By grace we both believe what should be loved and love what we believe.

On the Grace of Christ, 13

To be truly free

We shall be made truly free when God has fashioned us, formed us, re-created us, not as human beings (he has already done that), but as good human beings. His grace is doing that right now, that we may be a new creation in Christ Jesus. . . .

The Enchiridion, 31

Constant progress

I do not want anyone to accept all my opinions so as to follow me blindly, except where he is truly convinced I am right. That is why I am now writing books, revising what I wrote earlier, to show that even I do not follow myself on every point. The way I see it is that God has helped me, by his mercy, to write books that constantly make progress. I was by no means perfect when I began, and if now, in my old age, I were to claim perfection, to be writing without error, it would not be the truth, but a sign of my conceit.

Gift of Perseverance

FOR REFLECTION AND DISCUSSION

Would you describe yourself as a Pelagian or an Augustinian? Why does it matter?

Comment on an experience of your own that illustrates the paradox of grace and free will as Augustine understood it.

Where do you see successors to the Donatists in the modern church?

Does Augustine's idea of two opposed but overlapping cities, each defined by what it loves, make sense today?

Tell of a time when you felt God was pursuing you.

Write a short prayer in the style of Augustine's *Confessions.*

How do you feel God would answer the questions Augustine poses to him in the opening two chapters of Book I of the *Confessions,* quoted above?

Chapter 6

PATRICK

c. 390–c. 460

Celtic Spirituality

58

R OUNDING A CURVE in Ireland today, travelers often confront a large
stone cross rising up out of the ground. These crosses can be as high
as fifteen feet and have been there for over a thousand years. They are of
peculiar design — a circle, suggesting eternity without beginning or end, is
superimposed over a cross, two lines with distinct beginnings and ends,
pointing to an event in history. The design of this cross binds opposites together — time and eternity, earth and heaven, darkness and light, sin and
redemption.

Ancient Irish Christians worshiped at these crosses, often beginning in
the church building, then processing outside and around the stone cross in
the churchyard, where additional prayers and psalms were recited. Some
say these crosses represent a holdover from Ireland's pagan past, when the
druids worshiped the circle of the sun. Others find in them a link to ancient Egyptian or Roman religious symbols. The earliest such crosses are
decorated with interlacing linear spirals, which, like the circle itself, seem
to have no beginning or end. Similar patterns can be found in decorated
religious books of the day, such as the famous Book of Kells, now at Trinity
College in Dublin. Later crosses tell the story of salvation with carved pan-
els depicting biblical scenes and covering the sides and arms of the cross.

A cross of this design is called a Celtic cross. The word *Celtic* is difficult to define. It refers to a group of peoples of Indo-European extraction
who once inhabited much of northern Europe. By Christian times, they
were largely confined to Ireland, Scotland, Wales, and Brittany. No one
knows when the Christian gospel was first preached in Britain, but
Tertullian, writing less than two hundred years after the Resurrection,
mentions Christians in parts of Britain that the Romans had not reached.
We shall never know the names of the early evangelists who traveled to
these far reaches of the known world, but the Celtic church developed and
grew on its own in the centuries that followed, largely untouched by the
controversies that shaped the church elsewhere. This led to two important
developments. First, the Celtic understanding of the Christian gospel
evolved in ways different from those prevailing on the European continent.
And second, when the Vandals sacked the Christian centers of Europe in
the fifth century, destroying much of what they found, Christian learning
was preserved in Ireland and the remote parts of Britain, from which missionary expeditions would eventually spring forth to convert the Vandals'
descendants in northern Europe.

Unlike the continental Christians, who carefully distinguished between true and false beliefs, between orthodoxy and heresy, the Celts made no radical break with the past, retaining much of their pagan heritage, which they saw as a kind of preparation for the Christian gospel. They continued to worship in their ancient holy places and kept many symbols of the past (including the circle, now superimposed on the cross). The Celts saw conversion more as a process of mutual enrichment than of displacement of one belief system by another. One reason may be that Christian living among the Celts centered more on concrete relationships — to one another, to animals, to the earth, and to God — than on metaphysical speculations. Another may be that women played a more prominent role in Celtic religious leadership than elsewhere. Also, the diocesan bishop with his doctrinal and juridical concerns was a minor figure in the Celtic church, where life centered more on the monastery and its abbot, whose concerns were often more spiritual in nature. The dualism that saw flesh and spirit as opposed, so prominent among the Mediterranean Christians, found no place among the Celts, who viewed the physical world, including the human body, as the theater in which God discloses himself and therefore as holy. Every planet and star, every rock and stream, every animal and plant, every human being and every part of the human being were subject to divine influence. As a result, Celtic spirituality was immediate, earthy, and intimately bound up with daily living.

No figure is more identified with Celtic spirituality in the popular mind than Patrick, patron saint of Ireland. Most of what we know of Patrick comes from an autobiographical essay, usually called Patrick's "Confession," and a letter from Patrick to a group of soldiers, seeking mercy for persecuted Christians. These are our two earliest authenticated documents from the British church. Beyond that, we must rely on later biographies of Patrick — the earliest of them was written two hundred years after his death — that make up in colorfulness for what they often lack in believability. Among the tales associated with Patrick are that he used the shamrock to illustrate the Trinity, drove all the snakes out of Ireland, and single-handedly converted the entire island.

Patrick was born in Great Britain to Christian parents. At the age of sixteen, he was kidnapped by Irish marauders, taken to Ireland, and sold as a slave to one Milchu, who owned an estate, probably in western Ireland. Patrick spent the next six years largely alone on the hillsides, tending his master's sheep. At that time, Patrick says, he was "not a believer in the true God nor had I ever been," and he "did not yet know what I should desire and what I should avoid." His time as a slave "nearly defeated" him, but he "fiercely sought" the Lord while in captivity and later came to see that this experience had benefitted him by preparing him for his later work as an evangelist among the Irish. No doubt Patrick learned the language of the Irish and their druidical religion during those six years, but he also learned to pray as a Christian. "I prayed many times every day," he says, "and the love and fear of God and my faith grew more and more, until in one day I would say up to a hundred prayers, and a similar number at night."

One night Patrick heard a voice telling him that a ship was ready to take him back home. He escaped from his captor and fled two hundred miles, presumably to a port on the east coast of Ireland, where he found a ship ready to sail for Britain. He was initially denied passage, but when he began to pray, one of the crew shouted to him to return to the ship, and he was allowed to board "on good faith." Three days later the ship docked somewhere on the British coast. Patrick wandered "through the desert" for twenty-eight days. When Patrick finally found and was reunited with his parents, they entreated him never to go anywhere again.

But Patrick was not to remain at home. He studied for the priesthood during that time, and soon had a vision in the night in which a man named Victoricus, who appeared to be coming from Ireland, brought many letters to Patrick, begging him to return to Ireland. Several more night visions followed until Patrick consented to return as a bishop and Christian evangelist to his captors. The date of his return to Ireland may have been around 430 or somewhat later. (All dates in connection with Patrick are guesses.) For the next thirty years or so, Patrick traveled through Ireland, mainly in the north, preaching, baptizing (hundreds at a time, it was said), ordaining clergy (reputedly including 350 new bishops), adjudicating quarrels among the local gentry, and founding monasteries. His usual method was to approach the local nobility and preach to them, knowing that when they were baptized, others would follow. Patrick was not the first Christian to set foot in Ireland, but nothing survives of the earlier Irish church, and it is not without cause that Patrick is seen as the founder of Irish Christianity.

Patrick's "Confession" gives a vivid picture of his personality. His sense of call and his determination to honor it stand out, along with his seemingly endless energy. Although he had studied in preparation for the priesthood after his return home and was able to write in Latin, Patrick writes that he was not "a student like others who have delved equally into both law and the scriptures." He makes frequent reference in the "Confession" to his lack of learning and polish and seems to have regretted for the rest of his life what he regarded as his inadequate education. His humility and modesty are evident throughout.

The best-known text associated with Patrick's name was probably written some time later, but it captures several features of Patrick's spirituality and may include some material from Patrick himself. It also illustrates Celtic Christian spirituality generally. The hymn is known as "St. Patrick's Breastplate" and is one of several "breastplate hymns" (or *lorica*) to come down to us from the Celts. This may be a pagan prayer form brought into the church, and echoes of the Celts' pre-Christian past can almost certainly be heard in the lines of "St. Patrick's Breastplate." Living as close to nature as they did, the Celts were keenly aware of the dangers surrounding them. They liked litanies and composed many of them, summoning God and the lesser powers subject to him, including the forces of nature, to guide and protect them. These hymns were to serve as shields or breastplates in battles both spiritual and temporal. According to legend, Patrick sang his breastplate hymn when he was ambushed, with the result that he and his companions were transformed into wild deer and thereby escaped. It is still sung today, usually on Trinity Sunday and at ordinations.

Perhaps the most striking feature of Celtic spirituality, evident in "St. Patrick's Breastplate," is the Celtic sense of the nearness of the spiritual world. The story of Patrick's escape from bandits by being turned into a deer may sound like a childish magic tale to the modern ear, a manipulation of the divine by means of artful praying. But the principle underlying the tale is hardly magic or manipulative — that God is nearby, actively working in his world to accomplish his purposes, and that divine power can be tapped. The Celts found God all around them, not in some far-off realm destined to supercede this world. While not denying that Christ had died on the cross to save sinners, they had little interest in abstract arguments about the Atonement. Rather, their piety centered on the doctrine of creation, on God's nearness and his breathing life into every living thing, even every rock and cloud. It may be that this sense of divine immanence was part of the Celts' druid past that they later "baptized." Nor has it entirely vanished from Celtic lands today. "Heaven lies a foot and a half above the height of a man," Esther de Waal reports hearing an old Irish woman say.

The sense of divine immanence meant that for the Celts, God was intimately present in the ordinary, mundane activities of daily living. "St. Patrick's Breastplate" is a hymn to the Trinity. It is perhaps surprising that the Celts so eagerly embraced the doctrine of the Trinity, which suggests to others an abstract and transcendent deity. The Celts, however, saw the three persons of the Trinity as daily companions. They summoned the power of the Triune God and saw evidences of it everywhere, even in places and activities having no obvious spiritual significance. They composed short litanies and other prayers to the Trinity to say when dressing, washing the dishes, walking down a lane, hoeing a field, drinking a glass of ale or mead. The Celts believed in two worlds, the heavenly and the earthly, and in an array of heavenly beings subject to God's authority, but the heavenly and earthly worlds were hardly separated from each other. Rather, the border between them was permeable, and they were woven together, an understanding suggested in the interlocking lines of Celtic artistic designs.

Following the Synod of Whitby in 664, when the Celtic church submitted to the authority of Rome, its distinctive understandings began to decline. But they never quite died out. In many parts of the world today, technology and distance have caused the human and natural relationships celebrated by the Celts to become arid. Spiritualities such as those of the ancient Celts challenge these understandings, and many Christians are finding the ecological, egalitarian, and earthy spirituality of the ancient Celts (and Native Americans and modern Africans) once again relevant and appealing.

IN HIS OWN WORDS

Patrick's humility

I am Patrick, a sinner, the least sophisticated of people and the least among all Christians.

"Confession" (opening sentence)

The Lord's tender care

[The Lord my God] looked at my lowliness and took pity on me because of my youth and ignorance. He watched over me before I knew him or had gained the wisdom to know good from evil. He protected and consoled me as a father protects and consoles a son.

"Confession"

How to give thanks to God

It would be wrong for me not to speak of the many blessings and graces which the Lord gave me in the land where I was a slave. I speak of them because that is the way to thank God for them. After we are disciplined and learn to recognize the Lord, we give him glory and speak of his great works to every people under heaven.

"Confession"

Patrick's statement of belief

There is not now and never has been any but the one God. There was none before him and will be none after him. This one is God the Father — unbegotten, without beginning, from whom everything else originates and who sustains it all. This we have been taught.

And there is his Son Jesus Christ. He exists eternally with the Father and was with the Father spiritually before time began. Before anything existed, he is begotten of the Father, a reality beyond our capacity to describe. Through him all things, visible and invisible, were made. He was made human, overcame death, and was received into heaven to the Father, who has given to him all power over every name in heaven, earth, and under the earth, so that every tongue shall confess that this Jesus Christ in whom we believe is Lord and God. We look for his coming again in the near future, when he will judge the living and the dead and render to each according to his deeds.

And the Father has lavishly poured his Holy Spirit upon us as gift and pledge of immortality. The Spirit makes the faithful and obedient into sons of God and fellow-heirs with Christ. This is who has been revealed to us and whom we worship and adore: one God, in the Trinity of sacred name.

"Confession"

Patrick's thanksgiving

I never cease to thank God for keeping me faithful during the time of my testing so that I can offer my soul to Christ my Lord today, with confidence as a living sacrifice. Who am I, Lord, and what is my calling, that you have appeared with such power to me? It is through your power that I today exalt and praise your name among every people, wherever I go, in good fortune and in bad. I accept whatever comes my way, good or ill, and I always thank God for demonstrating to me that I can trust him in all things and forever.

"Confession"

Patrick's early reluctance

I should always give thanks to God, for he has often forgiven my stupidity and negligence. More than once he refused to grow angry with me when, though named his helper, I refused to do what the Spirit urged and accept what he had shown me. The Lord showed me mercy a million times because he saw within me that though I was ready and willing, I still had no idea what to do with my life. All the while, many people were trying to keep me from my mission, whispering about me behind my back: "Why is this fellow risking his life among enemies who know nothing of God?" This was not from malice, I know, but because they thought it wrong that a bumpkin like me should undertake such a mission. I myself couldn't see the grace within me either, but now I know I should have acted sooner.

"Confession"

St. Patrick's Breastplate

I rise and bind to myself today
the strong virtues of the Trinity,
the Three in One and One in Three,
Creator of the universe.

I rise and bind to myself today
the strong virtues of Christ's birth and baptism,

65

his crucifixion and burial,
his rising and ascending,
his descending to judge at the last day.

I rise and bind to myself today
the strong virtues of the love of cherubim,
the obedience of angels,
service of archangels,
prayers of ancestors,
predictions of prophets,
preaching of apostles,
faith of confessors,
innocence of holy virgins,
and deeds of righteous souls.

I rise and bind to myself today
the power of heaven,
the sun's brilliance,
the moon's radiance,
the splendor of fire,
the flashing of lightning,
the speed of wind,
the depths of sea,
the immovable earth,
and solid rock.

I rise and bind to myself today
the power of God to hold me,
his hand to guide, his eye to guard,
his ear to hear me, his word to speak for me,
his shield to shelter me, his army to deliver me
from the snares of demons,
from the seductions of vices,
from the temptations of nature,
and from all who wish me harm,
far or near, many or few.

These strong virtues I call to my side today,
against every cruel and merciless force

that would attack my body and soul,
against the incantations of false prophets,
the black laws of pagans,
the false laws of heretics,
the deceits of idolaters,
the spells of witches,
and all that corrupts and binds the human soul.

Christ protect me
against poison and burning,
against drowning and wounding,
that I may receive an abundant reward.

Christ with me, Christ before me,
Christ behind me, Christ within me,
Christ beneath me, Christ above me,
Christ to my right, Christ to my left,
Christ in my lying, in my sitting, in my rising,
Christ in the heart of all who think of me,
Christ in the mouth of all who speak of me,
Christ in the eye of all who see me,
Christ in the ear of all who hear me.

I rise and bind to myself today
the strong virtues of the Trinity,
the Three in One and One in Three,
Creator of the universe

FOR REFLECTION AND DISCUSSION

List the things about Celtic spirituality that you find appealing or helpful
    and those you do not find appealing or helpful.
Do you see conversion as a process of mutual enrichment or one in which
    one belief system displaces another?
Think of a time of adversity in which now, in retrospect, you can see that
    God was preparing you for something else.
Do you see God primarily as distant or close at hand? What difference

does it make in day-to-day living? Are the two views of God mutually exclusive?

How did Patrick give thanks to God? How do you give thanks to God?

What powers beyond yourself do you trust to protect and guide you? Write a "breastplate hymn" of your own, summoning them to your aid.

Chapter 7

BENEDICT OF NURSIA

c. 480-547

Western Monasticism

FOR SIX HUNDRED YEARS, from roughly 700 to 1300, spirituality in Western Europe meant just one thing — living in accord with a modest little tract written in the sixth century on a mountaintop in central Italy. Benedict of Nursia had no thought of writing a classic or best seller. He sought merely to "establish a school for the Lord's service" and to jot down a set of guidelines for those living in community as part of that school. These guidelines are known as the "Rule of St. Benedict," or the "Benedictine Rule."

Benedict lived in turbulent, frightening times. Internal decay and external invasions had been undermining the authority of Rome for a century, and the last Roman emperor in the West had died just four years before Benedict's birth. Stable government was now a mere memory; certainties once taken for granted were now wiped away. Chaos loomed on the horizon. The Benedictine Rule offered one possible avenue to a life of stability and assurance.

We have only two sources of information about Benedict. The one on which any biography must be based is the second of a group of writings known as the *Dialogues of Gregory the Great,* long thought to have been written by that great pope some forty years after Benedict's death. Recent scholarship has challenged the Gregorian authorship of the *Dialogues,* however, thereby casting doubt on their reliability. Moreover, the *Dialogues* are not biographies in the modern sense. Their purpose was to demonstrate that Italian saints were capable of great miracles, and the Benedict of the *Dialogues* is therefore a dazzling wonder-worker. He causes a vial of poison to shatter by making the sign of the cross over it and an axe head to rise of its own accord from the bottom of a lake and re-attach itself to its wooden handle. Such tales strike most modern readers as unedifying and hokey. Nonetheless, it is to this dubious source that we must turn if we are to learn anything at all of Benedict's life. The following biographical outline is — perhaps — credible.

Benedict was born to distinguished parents in the town of Nursia, seventy miles northeast of Rome, and was sent to Rome as a young man to be educated. Disgusted by the vice of some of his friends there, he turned his back on further studies to pursue the life of a hermit. For three years he lived in a cave near the town of Subiaco, where he faced demons and temptations similar to those encountered by Antony in Egypt. As his sanctity became known, a community of monks asked Benedict to become their abbot, and he reluctantly agreed. Their laxity did not mesh well with Benedict's strictness, however, and the monks soon had second thoughts and tried to poison Benedict. (It was at that point that he caused the poisoned vial to shatter.) He returned to his solitude, but soon began to found monasteries of his own, each comprised of twelve monks. Eventually Benedict found his way to Monte Cassino, midway between Rome and Naples, where he founded another monastery, lived for twenty years until his death, and wrote his Rule. Benedict and his sister Scholastica are buried at Monte Cassino. That monastery has been destroyed and rebuilt five times — the most recent destruction was in 1944 — and it remains the principal monastery of the worldwide Benedictine order.

Our other source of information about Benedict is the Rule itself. It is in part a compilation and adaptation of earlier rules and writings, but Benedict imparted to this material a new tone and flavor. The Benedictine Rule is noted for its brevity and common sense. It appears that Benedict did not write it at one time but compiled it from notes and instructions that he jotted down at various times and perhaps revised more than once. There is no overarching design or pattern to the work, suggesting that Benedict may have produced chapters as circumstances called for them. While the Rule gives no facts about the life of its author, it does afford us a picture of his spirituality; in outlining how to run a monastery, Benedict discloses his vision of the holy life.

Perhaps the most notable feature of the Benedictine Rule, and one reason it has retained its popularity over the centuries, is its flexibility. Benedict was no "control freak." Each monastery he founded was entirely autonomous; he created no centralized authority to monitor or enforce compliance, and the Rule is more a set of guiding principles than laws. Moreover, Benedict's keen observations of human nature and appreciation for the differences in persons led him to suggest that local circumstances and individual needs might require adaptations of his Rule. He was especially sensitive to the weakest persons in the community and sought to make certain they were never embarrassed or made to feel unworthy. Regarding food rations, for example, Benedict recommends that the kitchen provide "two kinds of cooked food because of individual weaknesses. In this way, the person who cannot eat one kind of food may partake of the other . . . and if fruit and vegetables are available, a third dish may be added."

This illustrates another feature of the Rule, its moderation and balance — "nothing harsh, nothing burdensome," as Benedict says. There would be no gluttonous consumption in the monastery, no lavish buffets, but neither would there be heroic fasts. Benedict sought a spirituality that was moderate, practical, and doable even for the beginner. Holiness was to be found in performing the ordinary tasks of daily living as acts of obedience. This included forgiving and making allowance for brothers who might be weaker, hardheaded, or disagreeable. The monks' daily schedule was a carefully designed balance of prayer, study, work, and rest. Benedict expected his monks to attend to the common duties of living, but not compulsively or selfishly, and never to allow them to crowd out other important pursuits. The goal was a serene and contented acceptance of life's realities, without resentment, anger, or bitterness.

Benedictine monks take a threefold vow of "stability, conversion of life, and obedience." The vows of poverty and chastity, standard monastic vows in later times, are not explicitly required by the Rule, though they are implied.

Stability includes faithful adherence to the Rule, day in and day out, over a lifetime, in a particular community. Brothers do not normally transfer from one house to another, but learn to live together and make allowance for one another's idiosyncrasies. Novelty is not prized.

Conversion of life means allowing oneself to be shaped by the community rather than asserting one's own opinions and wishes.

The vow of obedience is the key to faithful living in the Benedictine model. Benedict urges his brothers to submit to one another, but obedience is mainly due the abbot. Each monastery is modeled after a family, with the abbot as head of household. A Benedictine house chooses its abbot, but once an abbot is chosen, his power is nearly absolute. The abbot is to be obeyed without question or grumbling. He is enjoined to be Christlike in character, to teach by example as well as by word, realizing that he "has undertaken to care for the sick, not to tyrannize the healthy," and so to arrange the affairs of the monastery "that the strong have something to yearn for and the weak nothing to run from." The abbot is to be chaste, temperate, and merciful, able to coax and threaten, to be stern and tender according to circumstances. In keeping with the Rule's emphasis on moderation, the abbot must "avoid extremes; otherwise, by rubbing too hard to remove the rust, he may break the vessel." Benedict instructs the abbot to listen to the other brothers and ponder their counsel, especially the younger ones, for "the Lord often reveals what is better to the younger."

Humility is one of the major themes of the Benedictine Rule. This is the end to which obedience is meant to lead, and Benedict devotes his longest chapter in the Rule to a discussion of it. Benedict understands humility as the release from the drive for self-assertiveness and self-fulfillment, culminating in "the perfect love of God which casts out fear" (1 John 4:18). Using the story of Jacob's ladder in Genesis 28, he develops the metaphor of a twelve-step ladder of humility, each step drawing the faithful closer to the goal of perfect love.

Benedict stresses hospitality as well. The monks are to share freely with those on the outside, especially pilgrims and the poor who knock at the monastery door, receiving them as Christ, meeting visitors "with all the courtesy of love," and welcoming them with prayer.

One of the most striking features of Benedictine life is that the brothers own no private property. All things are held in common and given by the abbot to the brothers as needed. So insistent is Benedict on this that he authorizes the regular search of brothers' beds to uncover anything hidden there and instructs that when receiving small gifts from family members on the outside, brothers inform the abbot, who will then decide whether that brother or someone else has greater need of the gift. This communal regimen is meant to encourage humility and thankfulness among the brothers and discourage competition and a preoccupation with material things.

At the heart of Benedictine spirituality are the daily offices, structured services of Scripture reading and prayer in which all the brothers participate. Seven of these offices are spaced throughout the day, beginning with Vigils at the midpoint of the night and ending with Vespers in the evening. This is the one area on which Benedict offers more than general guidelines, giving detailed instructions — how many psalms and canticles to sing at each office, when "Alleluias" are to be added, what to do differently on Sunday, how to modify the times and length of the offices for the changing seasons, how to deal with brothers who doze or skip an office, and so on. Yet Benedict gives no advice on how to pray. One can imagine his responding to a young monk asking for instructions on prayer by saying, "Just *do* it!" — the regular, faithful, attentive recitation of the offices would in time shape and fill the soul with the mind of God.

If the daily offices are the heart of Benedictine spirituality, the Psalter is the heart of the offices. According to Benedict's scheme, the community reads through (more likely, sings through) the entire book of Psalms every week. The monks are therefore exposed (unlike many modern worshipers) to all the despairing, doubtful, bitter, vindictive, jingoistic, nationalistic, and seemingly racist passages in the Psalter. It is not that every sentiment expressed by a psalmist is admirable, but that in praying the Psalms, we confront ourselves as we really are. The Psalms are a reality check to keep prayer from becoming sentimental, superficial, or detached from the real world.

In addition to the Scripture heard during the daily offices, Benedictine brothers are to set aside about four hours each day for *lectio divina,* or holy reading, in private. *Lectio divina* is more than merely reading sacred books. It is reading in order to listen to God and listening in order to respond to God, which means reading slowly and meditatively. Periods of silence are therefore common in a Benedictine monastery.

The Benedictine Rule was not an immediate sensation. Not until over a century after Benedict's death did it begin to replace other monastic rules in the Western church. This was due in part to the popularity of the biography of Benedict in the second *Dialogue,* which began to circulate in the mid-seventh century. By the early ninth century, Charlemagne and his successor, Louis the Pious, made the Benedictine Rule the norm in all the monasteries of their realm, which by that time included most of western Europe.

Benedict's medieval successors departed from their founder's norms by adding rubrics, responses, and seasonal variations to the daily offices until Benedictine prayer became quite complicated. Moreover, reading the daily offices came to be seen as *the* way to a holy life, even for those outside the monastery, with the result that prayer came to be seen as a specialty of the clergy and ordinary laypeople were discouraged from attempting a life of prayer. Benedict would have deplored this development had he foreseen it. Both Benedict himself and most of his brothers had been laypeople, and he was skittish about admitting clergy to his monasteries lest they expect special privileges.

Today, in keeping with the flexibility of Benedict's Rule, a number of expressions of Benedictine spirituality continue to attract men and women throughout the world, among Roman Catholics, Anglicans, and Protestants. Thousands have taken full monastic vows and live in a cloistered community, but many people outside the cloister have also affiliated themselves with a Benedictine abbey. While living in the secular world, they stay in touch with the abbey, make an occasional retreat there, and maintain a discipline of stability, conversion of life, and obedience as outlined in the Benedictine Rule.

IN HIS OWN WORDS

Introducing the monastic life

My son, pay attention to what the master says. Listen with the ear of your heart. Welcome this advice and carry it out diligently. It comes from a father who loves you. You have drifted away from him through sloth and disobedience. Diligent obedience will bring you back. This message from me is for you if you are ready to abandon your own will, once and for all, and fight for the true King, Christ the Lord, with the strong, noble weapons of obedience. . . .

We plan to establish a school for the Lord's service. We want nothing harsh, nothing burdensome in its regulations. The common good, however, may prompt us to a bit of strictness, to amend faults and preserve love. Don't be intimidated and run off the road leading to salvation, for it is bound to be narrow at the outset. But as we move along in this way of life and in faith, we shall soon be running on the road of God's commandments, our hearts bubbling over with the unspeakable joy of love. Never swerving from his instructions and faithfully following his teaching in the monastery all the days of our life, we shall patiently share in the sufferings of Christ that we may be found worthy to share in his kingdom.

Rule, Prologue

Obedience

The first step of humility is unhesitating obedience. This comes naturally to anyone who cherishes Christ above all. . . . Such persons quickly lay aside their own concerns, abandon their own will, and put down unfinished whatever they are holding in their hands. Walking readily the way of obedience, they obey the voice of authority in everything. As soon as the master gives an instruction, the disciple quickly puts it into practice, fearing God. Instruction and obedience occur together, as if a single action.

Rule, 5

Silence

There are times when, out of respect for silence, even good words are not spoken.

Rule, 6

Humility

Brothers, if we want to attain the height of humility, if we would move quickly to that exaltation in heaven which humility in this life enables us to reach, we must erect and climb the ladder on which Jacob dreamt of angels descending and ascending [Gen. 28:12]. There is no doubt that this dream shows that we descend by exaltation and ascend by humility. . . .

[The twelve steps of humility are these:]

1. A person keeps the fear of God before him and never forgets it. . . .

2. Rather than love his own will and enjoy satisfying his desires, a man imitates by living out this saying of the Lord: "I have come not to do my own will, but the will of him who sent me" [John 6:38].

3. A person submits to his superior in all obedience, for the love of God, and imitates the Lord, of whom the Apostle says: "He became obedient even unto death" [Phil. 2:8].

4. A person quietly embraces suffering, enduring it without wavering, never trying to escape from it, obeying even under hard, unfavorable, and unjust circumstances. . . .

5. A man humbly confesses all to his abbot, concealing neither sinful thoughts which may have entered his heart, nor any wrong committed in private. . . .

6. A monk is content with the meanest and most menial treatment, regarding himself as a poor and worthless laborer, no matter the task assigned to him. . . .

7. A person not only admits out loud but is inwardly convinced that he is inferior to everyone else. . . .

8. A monk does only what is endorsed by the common rule of his monastery and the example of his superiors.

9. A monk bridles his tongue and keeps silent, except when asked a question. . . .

10. He does not laugh quickly. . . .

11. A monk speaks gently, without laughing, seriously and with becoming modesty, briefly and reasonably, but without raising his voice. . . .

12. A monk always displays humility in his bearing as well as in his heart, so that it is evident in the Work of God [daily office], in the oratory, the monastery, the garden, on a journey, in the field — everywhere. Sitting, walking, or standing, his head must be bowed and his eyes lowered. . . .

Having ascended all these steps of humility, the monk will soon arrive at that "perfect love" of God which "casts out fear" [1 John 4:18]. Through this love, things he once did with dread he now will begin to do with no effort at all, as though naturally, from habit, no longer out of the fear of hell, but out of love for Christ, good habit, and delight in virtue. All this the Lord will graciously show forth by the Holy Spirit in this workman who has been cleansed of vices and sins.

Rule, 7

Prayer

Prayer should be short and pure, unless perhaps prolonged under the inspiration of divine grace. Communal prayer, however, should always be short, and when the superior gives the signal, everyone should rise in unison.

Rule, 20

Private ownership

Above all, this evil practice [private ownership] must be uprooted and banished from the monastery. Unless the abbot so orders, no one may presume to give, receive, or keep anything as his own, nothing at all — not a book, a writing tablet, a pencil — in short, not a single thing, for even their own bodies and wills do not belong to the monks to do with as they choose. They are to look to the father of the monastery for the supplying of their needs and are allowed only what the abbot gives and permits. Everything is possessed in common, by everyone, so that no one presumes to call anything his own [Acts 4:32].

Rule, 33

Distribution of goods

Whoever needs less should thank God and not be upset, and whoever needs more should feel humbled because of his physical weakness or behavior, not puffed up due to the kindness shown him. In this way, all the brothers will be at peace. First of all, let there be no word or sign of the evil of grumbling, no manifestation of it for any reason at all.

Rule, 34

Summary of monastic life

"They should each try to be the first to show respect to the other" [Rom. 12:10], supporting with great patience one another's weaknesses, both of body and behavior, and eagerly competing with one another in obedience. No one is to pursue what he thinks is better for himself, but only what he deems better for someone else. The brothers demonstrate pure love to one another, loving fear to God, sincere and humble love to their abbot. Let them prefer nothing whatever to Christ, and may he bring us all together to everlasting life.

Rule, 72

FOR REFLECTION AND DISCUSSION

What insight of Benedict to you feel is most needed in today's world?
What insight of Benedict do you feel you personally need most? What do you need to do about it?
Make a list of "ordinary tasks of daily living" that can become for you acts of obedience. What needs to change for them to become acts of obedience?
How do you respond to Benedict's views about private property in the monastery?
Do you see any dangers or inadequacies in Benedict's program for holy living?

Select a Bible passage and spend thirty minutes reading and rereading it, very slowly and reflectively. Jot down the thoughts and insights that come to you.

What does the word *humility* mean to you? Compare that to what it meant for Benedict.

Chapter 8

SYMEON THE NEW THEOLOGIAN

949-1022

Experiencing the Spirit

A s THE SECOND MILLENNIUM of the Christian era dawned, the power of the Byzantine empire and the splendor of its church were unexcelled anywhere on the planet. It was an age of political stability (Emperor Basil II ruled from 960 to 1025), economic prosperity, and artistic excellence. Neither pillaging Crusaders nor conquering Turks were yet visible on the horizon, and the centuries-old order seemed immutable, even God-ordained. Church life centered on Constantinople's cavernous Cathedral of Hagia Sophia (Holy Wisdom), where the Orthodox liturgy was celebrated with reverence and grandeur. Not surprisingly, church authorities had little use for reformers, even if (as reformers often do) they called for a return to forgotten elements of the tradition. Such a man was Symeon, who worshiped for much of his life at Hagia Sophia but who seemed oblivious to ecclesiastical authority and to tradition as the authorities understood it.

Symeon's spirituality sprung from a different source. His theological views were solidly orthodox — he knew, revered, and often quoted the Bible and the church fathers — but Symeon looked to them less to define Christian faith than to validate his personal experience of God. It was a question of authority. The church was hierarchical, formal, conventional, and — in Symeon's view — often lifeless. Order was prized over spontaneity. One did and believed what one was told to do and believe. For Symeon, however, Christian living was intuitive and charismatic, relying less on official teachings (faithful though Symeon was to them) than on inner revelations. The conventional understanding was that such revelations had ceased after the apostolic era and that only in heaven would later Christians gaze upon God. Not so, said Symeon. Citing Jesus' remark in the Sermon on the Mount that the pure of heart shall see God (Matt. 5:8), Symeon wrote, "If he said that God will be seen by the pure of heart, then obviously, where such purity is found, the vision will follow. If you had ever purified your heart, you would know that what is said is true. But you have paid no attention to this, not even believed it. You have despised that purity, so naturally you do not see the vision." Symeon was not one to temper his comments.

Symeon was born into a noble family in Paphlagonia, a province of Asia Minor on the Black Sea. At the age of fourteen, he was introduced to a lay monk at the famous Stoudion monastery in Constantinople. The monk's name was Symeon (the younger man eventually took the elder's name), and this relationship would change the younger man's life. Young

Symeon wanted to enter the monastery immediately, but the elder Symeon put him off for thirteen years, during which young Symeon pursued other careers and committed "numerous offenses," "actions beyond all forgiveness," including murder, adultery, sodomy, and slaying infants, as he later wrote (and exaggerated?) in his *Hymns of Divine Love*. At the age of twenty, Symeon received a divine revelation, the first of many, which he describes in his Discourse 22 (referring to himself in the third person as "George"). He continued his worldly ways for several years, but when he finally entered the Stoudion, at the age of twenty-seven, his zeal and devotion to his spiritual father Symeon were irrepressible — so much so, that he was asked to leave after a few months. Symeon the elder then arranged for his young friend to enter the nearby monastery of St. Mamas. By this time, young Symeon had apparently amended his ways, for after just three years, he was elected abbot of St. Mamas. For the rest of his life he continued to revere his mentor Symeon and advocated training under a mature spiritual guide.

Symeon's twenty-five years as abbot of St. Mamas were productive but stormy. The place had apparently fallen on hard times, but Symeon managed to rebuild it by attracting other committed young Christians to the community. But as with many monasteries of the day, not all who entered did so for the purest of reasons. This required Symeon to teach his charges about the spiritual life and enforce sometimes unpopular disciplinary measures. His *Catechetical Discourses* are mainly sermons given to the monks at St. Mamas but are hardly dry lectures on how to behave in the cloister. The *Discourses* comprise an original and provocative work, redolent with Symeon's lively personality and testimonies to his mystical encounters with Christ. They also disclose Symeon's unwavering commitment to authentic and thoroughgoing devotion — those looking for a tepid profession could look elsewhere. At one point, some of his charges at St. Mamas staged a revolt, but it died down when the patriarch of Constantinople declined to support it.

Chief among Symeon's opponents was a certain Stephen, on the staff of the patriarch of Constantinople. Stephen accused Symeon (no doubt truthfully) of continuing to promote the unauthorized veneration of his mentor, the elder Symeon, and of railing against the church hierarchy in favor of a more personal, charismatic authority. As a result, Symeon was exiled from Constantinople in 1009. The exile was rescinded the next year, but Symeon chose to remain where he had lived during his exile, in a small town on the Asiatic side of the Bosphorus. He built a small monastery there, where he lived the rest of his days in solitude with a few disciples.

Symeon's other major literary work is his *Hymns of Divine Love,* a series of fifty-eight poems, some running several hundred lines, written during the latter years of his life. The work has been sometimes compared to Augustine's *Confessions,* but the similarity is limited. Both works lay bare their authors' souls, but unlike the *Confessions,* Symeon's *Hymns of Divine Love* give virtually no information about events, people, and places in his life. The events related in the *Hymns* take place entirely within Symeon's soul. The reader may dip into the *Hymns* at any point, for themes recur according to no apparent pattern. These are the same themes addressed in the *Catechetical Discourses,* but here Symeon is less analytical and didactic, plunging tearfully into penitence, then soaring in exalted adoration. His flights of adoration are particularly distinctive and suggestive. Symeon describes, often in erotic, sensual terms, his mystical encounters with and love for Christ. His words seem almost to explode off the page.

Symeon insists that he is passing on what he has experienced, direct personal encounters with the risen Christ, not something learned from a book or heard secondhand. This theme — the importance of speaking and writing about what one has actually experienced and refraining from commenting where one lacks experience — is a major one throughout Symeon's work. His opponents, lacking actual experience of Christ, also lacked credibility, he said.

Symeon experienced Christ as light. The light imagery in his writing is stunning in its variety. The divine light is bright and warm, dazzling sunshine and blazing fire. It is a shimmering pool, a sea of glory, an infinite ocean, a foretaste of the world to come, embracing the entire universe. It purifies the soul from sinful passions and inspires virtue. It emboldens the Christian and enables him to speak with God as friend to friend. The divine light is both the desire for God and the presence of God. It is not mere human reason (as for the "Enlightenment" philosophers of a later time), but the presence of Christ, formless, shapeless, beyond human speech and thought, but utterly real. Symeon sees the face of Christ in the light — inwardly, not with the eyes.

This experience of Christ is not just for the ancients or the next life, Symeon says. Nor is it merely for the spiritually advanced. The vision of the divine light is for everyone, right here and right now, even the spiritual beginner. If you want to see it, begin with repentance. Symeon's own expressions of penitence, especially in the *Hymns*, are intimate and revealing. Penitence is not for him a onetime thing, but a lifelong orientation of the soul, accompanied by tears. Tears, both sorrowful and joyful, are a sign of true penitence for Symeon.

Repentance leads to dispassion, or detachment from worldly cares. Symeon's spiritual father, the elder Symeon, expressed dispassion in an odd and disconcerting way, by gazing unfazed upon naked human bodies and walking about naked himself (one reason, perhaps, that the younger Symeon's devotion to his mentor was frowned upon). For the Stoics, dispassion had meant a calm lack of emotion. But in Christian usage (including Symeon but beginning much earlier), dispassion is the balancing of human appetites, emotions, and reason, opening a space for the cultivation of virtues such as love and humility.

The Holy Spirit does this, Symeon says. It does not result from human initiative. In a foreshadowing of modern Pentecostalism, Symeon writes of a "second baptism," the baptism with the Holy Spirit. Baptism with water must be fulfilled by growth in grace, Symeon says. Those baptized in infancy often "fall away" from the grace given in baptism by failure to obey the commandments, rendering their baptism an empty type or symbol. God does not abandon those who have fallen away, however, but gives a second baptism, not of water but of the Holy Spirit. Although he never says it explicitly, Symeon seems in places to imply that this second baptism is more important than baptism with water and that grace must be consciously and intentionally appropriated to be effective. In any case, it is clear that for Symeon, the holy life, though initiated by and dependent on the power of God, requires willing cooperation on our part.

All of this leads to our deification or divinization, an understanding central to Symeon and to Orthodox spirituality generally. It was Athanasius in the fourth century who articulated this idea most succinctly when he said, "God became human in order that humans might become gods." Similarly, Symeon asked at one point, "My God, is it you?" God replied, "Yes, I am he, God, who for your sake became man; and look, I have made you, as you see, and shall make you, god." We must not suppose that human beings become the essence of God. This could never be, for God is by nature unapproachable and inaccessible, says Symeon. Yet God has come to us and united himself to us. In joining himself to human flesh, God has also elevated that flesh, for once joined to God, human flesh can never again be other than divine. In a surprising passage from Hymn 15,

Symeon says that we become members of Christ and Christ becomes our members, then names parts of his body, including his genitals, as places of Christ's habitation — we are deified totally, physically as well as spiritually. Symeon sees this deification as a lifelong process continuing into the next life. Nor will it ever end, he says (echoing Gregory of Nyssa) — because God is infinite, our union with God will never cease growing deeper and fuller.

Symeon said little that had not been said before, but he expressed the tradition in powerful new ways. The word "new" when first applied to him may have been meant to dismiss his work as trendy or newfangled, but the title "theologian," with which it was soon linked, is the highest honor the Orthodox Church can bestow.

IN HIS OWN WORDS

Resurrection

Let us look carefully, if we wish, at the mystery of the resurrection of Christ our God which occurs mystically in us at all times. Let us see how Christ is buried within us as in a tomb and how he unites himself to our souls and rises again, raising us with himself. . . . The resurrection of Christ occurs in every one of us who believes, and not just once, but every hour, as it were, when Christ the Master arises within us, arrayed in splendor and flashing with the lightnings of incorruption and divinity.

Catechetical Discourse 13

Baptism in the Holy Spirit

Only the Holy Spirit opens what is sealed and closed, unseen and unknown by human beings. Once unveiled, it becomes knowable to us. So how can those who admit to never having known the Holy Spirit's presence, radiance, illumination, and his coming to dwell within them, how can they know, perceive, or even think about those things? How can such mysteries be understood by people who have in themselves never been recast, renewed, transformed, reshaped, and regenerated by him? How can they who have not yet been baptized in the Holy Spirit know the change that takes place in those who have been baptized in him?

Catechetical Discourse 24

God is light

We testify that "God is light" [1 John 1:5]. Those who have been allowed to see him have all seen him as light. Anyone who receives him receives him as light because the light of his glory precedes him and there is no way he can appear apart from light. . . . If someone does not enter rightly into the light, it is because he has not rightly passed through the gate of repentance. Had he done so, he would have been in the light.

Catechetical Discourse 28

Soul as lamp

God is fire . . . and every human soul is a lamp. A lamp, though full of oil or tow or other flammable material, remains quite dark until it receives and is kindled with fire. The soul is like this. It may appear to be adorned with all virtues and still not have received the fire. That is to say, it has not received the divine nature and light; it remains unkindled and dark, its works uncertain. Everything must be tested and revealed by the light. If the lamp of one's soul remains in darkness, untouched by the divine fire, he needs a guide with a shining torch to discern his actions.

Catechetical Discourse 33

Deification

Glory to your mercy and your divine plan,
because you, God by nature, became human,
without change or confusion, evermore God and man.
And glory to you who made me, by nature mortal, into a god,

a god by adoption, a god by your grace and the power of your Spirit.
You who are God miraculously joined the two extremes.

Hymn 7

Invisible beauties

I have attained some knowledge
    of what the mind cannot understand,
and I now contemplate invisible beauties from afar,
light inaccessible, glory unbearable.
It stirs me up; I am utterly afraid.
It is just a simple drop of the abyss that I contemplate,
but as a mere drop is enough to disclose
    everything about water,
with its quality and appearance,
as the whole texture is known by the tip of the fringe,
or as the proverb states, "The lion is known by its paw,"
so, in just that way, I embrace and consider the whole in a single
    particle:
I adore him in person, my Christ and my God.

Hymn 11

Christ within me

. . . He himself is found within me,
radiating in the interior of my miserable heart,
illuminating me on every side with his immortal splendor.
He is completely intertwined with me, totally embracing me.
He gives himself to me, the unworthy one,
and his love and beauty fill me.
I am utterly satisfied and overwhelmed by the divine delight and
    sweetness.
I share in the light and participate in the glory.
My face shines like that of my Beloved
and all my members carry the light.

Hymn 16

Light and fire

You, my God and Creator, are beyond nature,
utterly beyond all essence.
But the reflection of your divine glory
permits us to see it as a simple, gentle light.
Light reveals itself. I think it
unites itself completely with us, your servants,
light that we contemplate in spirit, from afar,
light suddenly become visible within us,
light springing up like water, burning like fire
in the heart when it truly possesses it.
It is by this light that I have known, my Savior,
that my lowly and pitiful soul has been seized,
burned, and consumed.
When fire takes hold of something like dry wood,
will it not burn? Will it not consume it?
Will it not inevitably bring sufferings with it?
But allow me to say, my Savior, that after it has burned me,
this fire displays a splendor beyond words, adorable in its loveliness.
It delights me and produces a flame of desire
that I cannot bear. Indeed, how shall I bear it?
How shall I suffer fully? How shall I endure
or express this great wonder
which has happened to me, the prodigal?

Hymn 24

I see

I no longer want to see the light of this world,
not even the sun itself or anything in the world.
For I see my Master. I see my King.
I see him who is true light and the Creator of all light.
I gaze upon the source of all good things.
I see the cause of all things.

Hymn 28

The chase

When he ran, I ran after him.
When he fled, I pursued him,
like a hound chasing a rabbit.
And when the Savior went far from me and hid himself,
I did not lose hope,
as if I had lost him.
I did not turn back,
but sat and groaned,
right there where I was.
I wept and cried out to the Master who was hidden from me.
Then he appeared to me, even to me, who had rolled in the dust, and
cried out.
He drew near to me.
When I saw him, I leapt to my feet
and threw myself at him, to grasp him.
But he quickly fled.
I ran hard, and often as I ran,
I managed to grasp the fringe of his clothing.
He paused — and joy filled me.
Then off he went again,
with me in pursuit.
He would disappear, then return;
hide, then show himself.
But I never turned back,
never gave up the chase. . . .
Then — when he saw that I regarded everything as nothing,
that I was deeply convinced in my soul
that everything in the world,
even the world itself, was nothing to me, did not even exist,
that this conviction kept me separate from the world —
then he appeared totally to me,
he who has totally united himself to me,
who is outside the world
and who supports the world
and everything in it,
who holds them in his one hand,

the visible and the invisible.
Then he — listen closely! — he meets me
and reveals himself to me.
Where and how he came, I do not know.

Hymn 29

Incarnation and deification

Dwelling changeless in his divinity,
the Word became human by taking on flesh.
Preserving his humanity changeless in his flesh and soul,
he made me completely god.
He assumed my condemned flesh and endowed me with complete
    divinity.
As a baptized person, I have put on Christ,
not in a sensible way, but entirely spiritually.

Hymn 50

Incarnation

I came down from on high.
Being totally invisible,
I assumed the heaviness of flesh
and acquired a soul.
I, God, the changeless One,
I, the Word, became flesh.
By taking on flesh, I received a beginning.
Everyone could see me as man.
Why did I consent to do this?
For the same reason I created Adam:
to contemplate me.
But he was blind — and therefore everyone
descended from him was blind.
I did not cling to my divine glory,
thereby abandoning those whom I created by my hands
when they had been blinded by the deceit of the serpent.

No, I became like human beings in every way,
sensible to the sensible,
wishing to become one with them.
You can see the desire I had
to be seen by the people.
I wanted to become man
and be seen with human eyes.
How, then, can you say that I hide myself
from you and am not seen?
I shine with a true brilliance, yet you do not see me.
Pay attention to this mystery!

Hymn 53

FOR REFLECTION AND DISCUSSION

List the images (note especially the verbs) Symeon uses to refer to his relationship to Christ.

Is Christian faith based mainly on the testimony of the apostles and others or on the believer's personal experience of God? What is the relationship between the two?

How are human beings "deified"?

How do you think Symeon would respond to a modern Westerner who said to him, "But what practical difference does this make?"

Chapter 9

ANSELM

1033/4-1109

Medieval Spirituality I

B ORN IN THE MOUNTAINS of northern Italy, Anselm of Canterbury was the child of a devout mother who died when he was still a youth. By the age of fifteen he was thinking of taking monastic vows, but the local monastery did not accept him, apparently due to his father's opposition. He and his father grew increasingly estranged until, at twenty-three, Anselm fled across the Alps to France. In Normandy, he looked up the renowned scholar Lanfranc, prior (second in authority after the abbot) at the Benedictine abbey at Bec, and began studying under him. Anselm professed monastic vows at Bec in 1060 and after three years succeeded Lanfranc as prior there. In 1078, he was unanimously chosen abbot.

Anselm was always happiest in the monastery. Understanding God was a passion throughout his life, and the discipline of the monastery gave him long hours to unsnarl knotty theological dilemmas. His fervent *Prayers and Meditations* and the famous *Proslogion* come from this time. Anselm often wrote of the joy he found in the monastic life, seeking God through unquestioning obedience, stability, and prayer. Even after Anselm succeeded Lanfranc a second time, as archbishop of Canterbury in 1093 (a post forced upon him against his will), Canterbury's Benedictine abbey was his first love. He disliked the administrative duties that fell to him as archbishop, and his sixteen years in Canterbury were marked by controversies with King William Rufus and with Henry I, partly because Anselm supported papal claims against the British crown. Twice he was exiled to the continent. The strain of the archbishop's office moved Anselm more than once to ask the pope to relieve him of the post because he felt it was harmful to his soul. Even as a renowned scholar and powerful prelate, he continued to see himself above all as a monk seeking to know and love God. Both in Canterbury and earlier at Bec, Anselm was deeply concerned with the spiritual welfare of other monks under his charge and earned a reputation among them as gracious, genial, affable, and unwilling to hold a grudge. It is said that he was a captivating storyteller.

It is as a theologian of startling originality that Anselm is chiefly remembered today. His theological method, though commonplace in later centuries, was revolutionary in its time. Other medieval thinkers, including Anselm's mentor Lanfranc, supported their views largely by citations from Scripture and the works of the ancient church fathers. Anselm, however, sought to affirm the truth of Christian teachings solely through rational demonstration. He must have spent long hours mulling over thorny questions until the light finally dawned in his mind — and then he would put pen to paper. But he always started from a prior position of faith. "I believe so that I may understand," he wrote in the *Proslogion*. Anselm's essays are splendid meditations on the rationale of Christian faith — always beginning with commitment and only then thinking out its ramifications. For Anselm, commitment came first because without it nothing made sense. He did believe, however, that speculative thought could draw one closer to God. That was, in fact, the whole point of theology for him. Hence Anselm's theological writings often read like devotional pieces.

The *Proslogion*, or *Address*, is perhaps the best example of this. It contains, in one short paragraph, Anselm's famous "ontological proof" for the existence of God. This is a brilliant piece of logical gymnastics — or is it merely a bit of linguistic trickery? After nearly a millennium, the ontological proof continues to attract admirers and irk critics. Some find it almost mystically compelling, while others dismiss it as a verbal sleight of hand. The argument is quite simple. It hinges on Anselm's definition of God as "that than which nothing greater can be conceived." Since to exist is greater than not to exist, he says, "that than which nothing greater can be conceived" must exist.

Fascinating as the ontological argument may be to chew over (and that's what Anselm intended people to do with it, to inspire their devotion), of greater interest to many today is the latter part of the *Proslogion*, where he comments on God's creativity, justice, and mercy. The *Proslogion* is not, however, primarily a piece of theology. It is actually one long prayer, and its most compelling passages are those where Anselm is least analytical and most impassioned, where we see a great thinker *praying* his theology, exercising his mind to kindle his heart, trying to rise above the merely logical to contemplate the splendor of God.

Anselm's other famous work, *Cur Deus Homo*, or *Why God Became Human*, was written during his later years. Here, too, he broke new ground by seeking to demonstrate from reason alone why God became human and died to redeem humanity from sin and death. The argument in *Cur Deus Homo* (which is repeated more briefly in Anselm's "Meditation on Human Redemption") is subtle and multifaceted, but the main thread of it can be summarized briefly. It hangs on Anselm's understanding of what is right, fitting, or just. He believed that God has a design for the universe and that everything, including God himself, has its proper place and way of relating to other things. Intelligent beings owe honor to beings superior to them, and every created being is to honor God above all. Anselm defined sin as dishonoring God, not giving God his due. Human beings have grievously dishonored God, throwing God's design for the universe out of balance. It is not fitting, however, that God's plan be thwarted, so things must be set right again; justice must be served. But how could this be done? Since it would be unbefitting God's dignity simply to write off humanity's debt, satisfaction must be made for our disobedience. Justice requires that a human being pay the debt, since humanity is the guilty party. But the debt is greater than any mere human could pay — only God himself could, in fact, pay so great a debt. Hence the only way to set things right would be for God himself to assume human form. It would be fitting that as man, the God-man would pay the debt, and as God, the God-man would be able to pay the debt, thereby restoring the universe to its rightful order.

Anselm's theory is often called the "satisfaction theory" of the Atonement. Later thinkers have sometimes faulted it for relying too much on a feudal understanding of order, looking at divine justice in rigidly legal terms, and portraying God as a petty tyrant jealous to protect his honor. Within Anselm's framework, however, his theory makes good sense, and it has been hugely influential in the Western church.

Anselm's *Prayers and Meditations* are powerful testimonies to his searching, passionate faith. Here he moves beyond speculating and analyzing. Anselm wrote no prayer manual, but he produced written prayers "to stir up the mind of the reader to the love or fear of God." Like his theology, Anselm's prayers and meditations strive for both clarity and spiritual purification and were in their day startling in their originality. Prior to Anselm, most prayer had been a communal exercise in monasteries, conducted according to the fixed forms of the Benedictine offices. Anselm knew these services and loved them, but his own prayers moved beyond the Benedictine norm and established what would soon become a major new prayer form. They are longer than most liturgical prayers, emotional, and deeply personal, intended to be used by individuals to spur their own private devotional life. They have about them a sense of urgency, intensity, and spontaneity, even though they are in fact carefully crafted literary compositions. Many of Anselm's prayers are gripping to read. They were widely circulated and became well known.

Anselm addresses most of his prayers to saints whom he asks to intercede for him because he feels unworthy to approach God without a good word from those more worthy than he. He speaks to the saints almost as if he knows them personally. Within a prayer to a saint, he often addresses God or Christ as well.

As was common among medieval monastics, Anselm's prayers and meditations often dwell on his sinfulness. In one paragraph in his "Lament for Virginity," for example, he calls himself a "miserable little man" and refers to "dark depths of boundless grief," "horrible darkness of inconsolable mourning," and "the whirlpool of bitterness." We would be wrong, however, to think of Anselm's prayers and meditations as unduly negative. He may seem to wallow in fear and self-reproach one moment, but a moment later he soars to the heights in praise and gratitude for God's love for him and urges his soul to hope and rejoice. Anselm's *Prayers and Meditations* comprise one of the classics of Christian devotional literature.

IN HIS OWN WORDS

From *Prayers and Meditations*

> Perfect what you have begun,
>   and give me what you have made me long for,
> not because I deserve it, but because of your kindness
>   that came first to me.
>   Most merciful Lord,
> transform my tepid heart into one that loves you ardently.
> I thirst for you, I hunger for you, I desire you,
>   I sigh for you, I covet you:
> I am like an orphan taken
>   from a compassionate father.
> Weeping and wailing, with all its heart the orphan
>   constantly clings to that dear face.

"Prayer to Christ"

> I cannot endure the interior horror of my face
>   without groaning deeply in my heart.
>   I cannot fly away from myself,
> but neither can I look at myself, for I cannot bear myself.

But then, if I do not look at myself, it is even worse,
    for then I am deceived about myself.
    The weight of this anguish is too heavy for me.
If I look within myself, I cannot endure myself;
if I do not look within myself, I do not know myself.
If I do not examine myself, I am damned.
If I look at myself, I cannot bear the horror that I see;
if I do not examine myself, I shall certainly die.

                                       "Prayer to St. John the Baptist"

    Look now and see the ailing sheep
lying at the shepherd's feet, groaning;
he comes before the Lord of both shepherd and sheep.
    The runaway returns
and asks forgiveness for his mistakes and disobedience.
To the good shepherd who can heal he shows
    the gashes of his wounds and the bites of wolves
    which he encountered when he wandered off
    and the neglected sores
    that have long afflicted him.
He begs the shepherd for mercy while there is still some life in him
and prays to the merciful shepherd
    more by laying bare his need
    than by actually asking

                                            "Prayer to St. Peter"

    Christ, my mother,
    you gather your chicks under your wings.
This dead chick of yours finds a place under those wings.
Your gentleness comforts the frightened
    and your sweet fragrance refreshes the desperate.
    Your warmth revives the dead;
    your touch justifies sinners.
    Mother, acknowledge your dead son once more,
by the sign of your cross and the voice of his confession.
    Warm your chick, revive your dead man,
        justify your sinner.

Let your frightened one receive your consolation;
despairing of himself, let him find comfort in you;
recreate him
in your full and boundless grace.
Consolation for sinners flows from you;
May you be blessed for evermore.

"Prayer to St. Paul"

Death and torment, however great,
bring no dishonor, for they are ordained.
But sin has its own unique dishonor,
    bringing eternal unhappiness.
It were better to choose eternal torment,
    which of itself brings no eternal dishonor,
    than to choose sin, which adds dishonor to eternal sorrow.
    Certainly, unhappy man,
you should steer clear of the dishonor of sin itself,
more than any torments eternity could bring.
For when you sin, you commit a most dishonorable perversion,
    preferring yourself to God your Creator,
    and nothing is more unjust than that. . . .

"Prayer to St. Nicholas"

But you, God . . .
You have created an ignorant scholar, a blind leader,
    an erring ruler:
    instruct the teacher you have set up,
    guide the leader you have appointed,
    govern the ruler you have approved.
        I beg you,
    teach me what I am to teach,
    lead me in the way I am to lead,
    rule me so that I may rule others.
Or better, teach them, and me through them,
    lead them, and me with them,
    rule them, and me among them.

"Prayer by a Bishop or Abbot"

My prayer is a cold little thing, Lord,
because it burns with so faint a flame.
But you are rich in mercy
and will not mete out to [my friends] your gifts
in proportion to the dullness of my zeal.
But as your kindness is above all human love,
so let your eagerness to hear
be greater than what I feel when I pray.

"Prayer for Friends"

You only are mighty, Lord;
   you only are merciful.
Whatever you cause me to desire for my enemies,
give it to them and give the same to me,
   and if what I ask for them is ever
   outside the rule of love,
whether through weakness, ignorance, or malice,
   give it neither to them, good Lord,
   nor to me.

"Prayer for Enemies"

Anselm's fear

I fear for my life. When I examine myself carefully, I think my whole life is sinful or sterile. If anything in it seems fruitful, it is either flawed or a fake, somehow corrupt, so that it either fails to please or actually displeases God. . . . Even if I do something helpful, it does not begin to balance the things of the body I have wasted. Does anyone pasture an animal that is not worth the cost of its feed? But you, gracious God, feed and wait for this useless creeping thing, this stinking sinner. . . . I blush that I am alive; I am afraid to die.

"Meditation on Fear"

No sin is small

Maybe you think a particular sin is small. Would that the strict judge would regard any sin as small! But, poor me, any and every sin dishonors

God because it disobeys his laws. So where is the sinner who presumes to call some sin small? How small a thing is it to dishonor God?

"Meditation on Fear"

Consider your Redeemer

Christian soul . . . think once more about the strength of your salvation and where it is found. Meditate on it; delight in contemplating it. Shake off your lethargy and start thinking about these things. Taste your Redeemer's goodness, burn with love for your Savior. Chew the honeycomb of his words; suck their flavor which is sweeter than sap; swallow their healing sweetness. Chew by thinking, suck by understanding, swallow by loving and rejoicing. Be happy to chew, thankful to suck, joyful to swallow.

"Meditation on Human Redemption"

Do what I cannot

Lord, make me to taste by love what I taste by knowledge, to know by love what I know by understanding. I owe you more than everything I am, but I have no more. Left to myself, I cannot give you what I owe you. Draw me close to you, Lord, by your boundless love. I am wholly yours by creation; make me wholly yours in love as well, Lord. My heart lies open before you. I ask, I seek, I knock [Matt. 7:7; Luke 11:9]. You who made me seek, make me receive; you who gave the seeking, give the finding; you who taught the knocking, open to my knock.

"Meditation on Human Redemption"

From the *Proslogion*

Invitation to turn aside

> Little man, come and
> turn aside for a while from your daily work,

escape for a moment from your turbulent thinking.
    Put aside your weighty cares,
    let your burdensome distractions wait,
    free yourself a while for God
    and rest for a time in him.
Enter the inner recesses of your soul,
    shut out everything but God
    and what can help you to seek him.
    Then, when you have closed the door, seek him.
Now, my whole heart, say to God,
    "I seek your face,
    Lord, it is your face that I seek" [Ps. 27:8].

Seeking the Lord

Lord, I am so bent over that I can only look downwards.
    Raise me, that I may look upwards.
    My iniquities have gone over my head,
covering me and pulling me down like a heavy burden.
    Remove this weight, this covering, from me
    lest the Pit close its mouth over me.
    Let me discern your light,
    whether from afar or from deep down.
    Teach me to seek you,
    and then, as I seek you, show yourself to me,
    for unless you show me, I cannot seek,
    and unless you show yourself to me, I will never find you.
May I seek you by longing for you,
    and long for you by seeking you;
    let me find you by loving you,
    and love you in finding you.

Faith seeking understanding

Lord, I am not trying to reach your height,
for my poor mind could not even approach it.

But I do want to understand a little of your truth
     which my heart already believes and loves.
I do not seek to understand so that I may believe,
     but I believe so that I may understand;
          and further,
I believe that unless I believe I shall never understand.

Ontological proof

Lord, since it is you who gives understanding to faith, grant me to understand as well as you think fit, that you exist as we believe, and that you are
what we believe you to be. We believe that you are that thing than which
nothing greater can be conceived. . . . And certainly that than which nothing greater can be conceived cannot exist only in the understanding. For if
it exists only in the understanding, it is possible to conceive of it existing
also in reality, and that is greater. If that than which nothing greater can be
conceived exists in the understanding alone, then this thing than which
nothing greater can be conceived is something than which a greater can be
conceived. And this is clearly impossible. Therefore there can be no doubt
that something than which a greater cannot be conceived exists both in the
understanding and in reality.

Joy

     . . . I have found a fullness of joy
          that is more than full.
This joy fills the whole heart, mind, and soul;
     it fills the entire person,
          yet there remains more joy that is beyond measuring. . . .
          God of truth,
     I ask that I may receive,
     so that my joy may be full.
Meanwhile, may my mind meditate on it,
my tongue speak of it,
my heart love it,
my mouth proclaim it,

my soul hunger for it,
my flesh thirst for it,
and my whole being desire it,
until I enter into the joy of my Lord,
who is God, triune unity, blessed forever. Amen.

FOR REFLECTION AND DISCUSSION

What part does rational thought play in the life of faith?

Is ignorance a condition to be accepted or a condition to be corrected?

What do you make of Anselm's "ontological proof" of the existence of God?

What do you make of Anselm's "satisfaction theory" of the Atonement?

How is your outlook influenced by the idea of "right, appropriate, fitting, or just"?

Choose a person from the Bible or church history and compose a short prayer to him or her.

Chapter 10

BERNARD OF CLAIRVAUX

1090-1153

Medieval Spirituality II

B ERNARD OF CLAIRVAUX was born when Anselm was approaching old age. The two never met, though Bernard knew Anselm's work and used it in his preaching and writing. Both were called to take part in the sometimes heated ecclesiastical and political disputes of their day. They consented to do so, even though their first commitment was to the monastic life and they were happiest when praying or studying in the cloister. Each has left a rich legacy of devotional writing. As a thinker, Bernard was less original and speculative than Anselm — his concern was not to uncover fresh insights but to defend Christian orthodoxy — and whereas Anselm focused largely on Christ's death and the Atonement, Bernard was drawn to the Incarnation, including the details of Christ's birth at Bethlehem and other incidents of his earthly life. Bernard was even more strongly committed to the monastic life than Anselm (if that be possible), and his writing matches or exceeds that of Anselm for warmth and passion.

Little is known of Bernard's early years. Born to a noble family in Burgundy, Bernard was twenty-one years old when he took vows as a Benedictine monk. In the six centuries since Benedict had written his Rule, much had changed in the life of a monk. Successive layers of liturgical additions had transformed Benedict's plan of simple daily prayer into a complicated scheme. Many houses were no longer autonomous but were subject to the centralized authority of a mother house. Some had acquired large estates, requiring monks who specialized in managing them and resulting in a level of opulence unknown to the simple monastics of earlier times. Bernard intentionally declined to enter one of these houses, choosing instead Cîteaux, a little known monastery that was small, poor, remote, and stark. Cîteaux was the mother house of the Cistercians, a new order that declined all revenues from feudal estates, depended entirely on the labor of the monks themselves, and was committed to the strictest interpretation of the Benedictine Rule.

Bernard chose Cîteaux because, as he said, he knew his character was "weak." Surely no one else would have described Bernard as weak. It is a testimony to his strength of character (to say nothing of his holiness of life and his captivating eloquence) that he convinced thirty relatives, including his father and all his brothers, to abandon worldly comforts and join him in the rugged confines of Cîteaux. Dozens of others soon followed. Three years later, Bernard was dispatched to found a daughter house. He chose a location in a clearing in the midst of a dense forest in eastern France and called the place Clairvaux ("Clear Vision"). The first monks of Clairvaux built a modest, even austere campus, within which Bernard insisted on occupying the least desirable room. By the time of Bernard's death forty years later, nearly nine hundred men had taken vows and resided at Clairvaux. Also, largely due to Bernard's influence, three hundred Cistercian houses had been founded throughout western Europe, most of them stemming directly from Clairvaux.

As his fame spread, Bernard was sought out by popes and kings. He became the most powerful man in Europe, a savvy political advisor, a gifted mediator of disputes, and a powerful and persuasive polemicist. Bernard almost single-handedly launched the Second Crusade (and was much abashed at the end of his life when dissension within its ranks caused it to fail). It is estimated that over his adult lifetime, Bernard spent a third of his nights away from Clairvaux, engaged in political negotiations, oratorical jousts, diplomatic missions, and theological debates (the most famous with the early scholastic Peter Abelard). Yet through it all, Bernard remained essentially a monk.

Bernard's devotional writings assure him a lasting influence. His rhetorical and literary gifts make his writings a pleasure to read, even in translation. At the heart of them is a seemingly boundless joy in the love of God, so much so that in 1953 Pope Pius XII bestowed upon him the title Doctor Mellifluus ("Doctor Flowing with Honey"). Love was much in the air in twelfth-century France, as the troubadours and trouvères traveled the country, singing of romance. Bernard found this romantic language useful in expressing his adoration for God. For Bernard, love does not begin on the human side, however, but in the heart of God. We love God, Bernard believed, because God first loved us (1 John 4:9-10). God woos the human soul, and our love for God is but a response to the love flowing from God, most fully seen in the person of Jesus Christ. Only God can satisfy the deepest human longings and desires, Bernard says (following Augustine), and when he speaks of God, his words convey a sense of rhapsody and exhilaration bordering on the erotic.

The Virgin Mary had been revered from earliest Christian times, but her rise to a place of prominence in Western Christian devotion occurred during the medieval period, and Bernard was a major force in this development. He revered her both as the Mother of God and as intercessor for sinners. "When the winds of temptation rise against you and you founder on the rocks of tribulation, gaze upon that star and think of Mary. Call upon her by name," Bernard wrote.

Bernard knew the Bible, and virtually every paragraph of his writings is sprinkled with biblical references. The modern reader must remember that ancient and medieval Christians commonly saw the Bible as an allegory with several levels of meaning, and that serious Bible students sought to ferret out the deeper sense of Scripture planted beneath the surface. For Bernard, the entire Bible was about the love of God. The sacred authors wrote under the influence of that love, and Bernard sought to uncover the message of love found in every verse of Scripture.

It is not surprising that the Song of Songs proved a rich source for Bernard. That biblical book is a series of love songs between a man and a woman and was widely viewed as an allegory celebrating the love between God and the church or the individual soul. Bernard's eighty-six sermons on the Song of Songs were not the first to be written in this vein on that text. Both Jewish and Christian authors, including Origen, Gregory of Nyssa, Jerome, and Augustine, had tapped that reservoir, called "bride mysticism," before him. Bernard's sermons on the Song of Songs range widely, offering comment on many current topics, but throughout them are woven some of the most lyrical words on divine love ever put to paper. These sermons are sensuous and erotic in places, particularly when Bernard speaks of God's love for humanity. He develops the kiss as a spiritual gesture, beginning with kissing the feet of Jesus, then the hands, and finally the lips. Some may have trouble with the physicality of this imagery, but it is actually intended to lead away from carnal passion by focusing the soul on Christ.

Human love for God progresses through four stages, Bernard says. We begin by loving ourselves only, a sterile love that produces nothing and leads nowhere. But in time we notice that we cannot survive alone and that God graciously meets our needs. We then begin to love God, but only because of what God does for us. This is the second stage of love. Gradually, as we experience God's love, our love is purified and expanded so that we are moved to love God for God's own sake, not merely for the benefits he bestows upon us. This is the third stage of love, but one final stage remains: the love of ourselves — as God loves us and for God's sake. We grow inebriated with divine love and forget ourselves, becoming like broken dishes, rushing toward God, clinging to him, becoming one with him in spirit. "To lose yourself, as if you no longer existed, to cease completely to experience yourself, to reduce yourself to nothing is not a human sentiment but a divine experience," Bernard writes. In this life, we experience this final stage of love only fleetingly, if at all. In one of his sermons on the Song of Songs, Bernard speaks of "a sudden momentary blaze of glory, so that a great flame of love is enkindled in the soul."

This is, of course, the language of mysticism. Mystics are found in all ages and in all great religions. A mystic experiences God directly, intuitively, without the aid of logical reasoning or any church, scripture, or other human mediation or testimony. Some mystics, such as Plotinus in the third century, have the sense that their personal identity is swallowed up and engulfed in the divine. For Bernard, though, the human soul retains its identity and becomes all the more alive. Others, like Gregory of Nyssa, speak of moving into a darkness where God discloses himself. Bernard, however, writes of gazing upon God in the luminous face of Christ. Bernard's mystical experience is an intense relationship of love, preceded by much prayer and longing; it is the culmination of a long, plodding ascent. When the moment passes, it leaves one craving more. It is a foretaste of heaven.

The Middle Ages produced several notable Christian mystics. Those who lived after Bernard all knew of him, harkened back to him, and borrowed from him. Most of them, however, rarely left the cloister or hermitage and shunned political and administrative tasks. Anyone wanting to consult them had to seek them out on their own turf. Bernard's active engagement in the world around him gives him a unique place among the great mystics.

The Cistercian order was largely obliterated in France following the Revolution of 1789 but has made a comeback in the past two centuries and now maintains houses in several countries, most in remote locales. Bernard's vision continues to inspire the Cistercians to live a simple life shorn of luxury and ornamentation and to devote themselves to intercession, adoration, and manual labor, with long periods of silence. The Trappists, stricter still, are an offshoot of the Cistercians.

IN HIS OWN WORDS

Limping with confidence

Despite my infirmity and my shrinking sinews, how happy I would be and how I would glory, Lord Jesus, if your virtue and humility were fully realized in me. Your grace is sufficient for me when my own virtue fails. With the foot of grace firmly planted on the ladder of humility, I would safely climb upward, painfully dragging my weak foot behind me, until, clinging to the truth, I reached love's wide plain. There I shall sing my thanksgiving hymn: "You have set my feet on a wide plain" [Ps. 31:8]. And so I step cautiously out into the narrow way, ascending the steep ladder, one step at a time, miraculously climbing to the truth, late and limping perhaps, but nonetheless confident.

"The Steps of Humility and Pride," 9

Loving God

God himself is the reason we love him, and the measure of that love is to love him without measure.

"On Loving God," 1

"Can we then love God grudgingly?"

The first thing to know is that God deserves to be loved greatly, boundlessly in fact, because he first loved us. Small and worthless though we are, God in his infinity loves us. This he does freely. Nothing requires God to love us — his love is a gift. But our love for God is not given freely, because we owe it to him. That is why I have already said that we must love God without limit. After all, how could we limit our love of the Infinite and Immeasurable? Immeasurable and eternal God, unimaginable love, boundless majesty, infinite wisdom — *God loves us!* Can we then love God grudgingly, doling out our love for him bit by bit? O Lord! My strength and support, my liberator, my most adorable all, most loving — I need and long for nothing but you. My God, I shall love you, not as you deserve or as I would, but as much as I can. I can love you only as far as my weakness allows, but I shall love you more and more, as you enlarge my capacity to love you. Yet not even then, never, shall I love you as you deserve.

"On Loving God," 6

True love

Love is a matter of the will. You cannot acquire it by transaction or contract; it is spontaneous, impulsive, free. True love is its own satisfaction; its reward is the beloved. If you think you love something, but it is because of some other thing, it cannot be true love, for true love is its own end, not something you pursue to gain something else.

"On Loving God," 7

God's love and ours

. . . God is the reason for loving God; he is both the cause of our love and its object. God offers the opportunity to love, creates the ardor, and consummates the desire. He makes himself adorable. Our love would be useless if we did not hope someday to love him perfectly. God's love prepares our love and rewards it. Since God loves us first, out of his great tenderness, we must repay his love and are permitted to hope in him with joy. He lavishly gives to all who call upon him, though he can give us nothing better than himself. . . . You, Lord, are so good to the soul that seeks you — what must you be to the soul that finds you? But most wonderful is this: no one can seek you who has not already found you. You desire to be found that you may be sought, and sought that you may be found.

"On Loving God," 7

The highest step of human love

O pure and holy love! Sweet, delightful affection! Pure and sinless intention of the will, freed from every taint of selfish vanity, still more sweet and delightful because everything in it is divine. To experience it is to become like God. As a drop of water vanishes in wine and assumes the wine's taste and color; as red, molten iron seems to lose its own nature and becomes like the fire; as air on a sunny day seems not merely bright, but light itself; so do the human affections of the saints mysteriously melt and flow into the will of God. For could God be all in all if anything survived in us? Our substance surely remains, though in a different form, a different glory, a different power.

"On Loving God," 9

Perfection

No one can be perfect without yearning to be still more perfect. We show ourselves to be more perfect by aspiring to a still higher perfection.

"On Consideration"

The Christian's danger

For a Christian, both danger and victory are defined by the disposition of his heart, not the outcome of the war. If he fights for a good reason, the result of the fight cannot be evil, nor can the result be deemed good if his reason is evil and his intention perverse.

"In Praise of the New Knighthood," 1

The song of love

Love is such that only those can sing its praises who have learned to do so by loving sweetly. It is not a matter of moving the lips, but a hymn sung in the heart. It is not uttering a sound, but flowing joy; love's harmony is one not of words, but of wills. It is not heard with the ear; it does not echo in public; only the bride and the Bridegroom, the one who sings and the one to whom it is sung, can hear it. It is a nuptial chant celebrating the chaste and delightful embraces of souls, a harmony of shared sentiment and affection. The beginning soul does not know this. The soul must have attained the ripe and perfect age, and through its virtues have grown worthy of the Bridegroom, before it can sing of love.

Sermons on the Song of Songs, 1.11

Mystical ecstasy

If one of you is drawn away for an hour and hidden in this secret place, in this sanctuary of God, undistracted by anything, untroubled by the needs of the senses, nagging problems, remorse or regret, or (still more difficult) obsessive fantasies of things sensible, when you return to us, you may well boast and say, "The King has brought me into his chamber" [Song of Songs 1:4].

Sermons on the Song of Songs, 23.16

When the moment has passed

When the Word departs, the soul can only blurt out, over and over again until it happens, its one unrelenting desire: "Come back!"

Sermons on the Song of Songs, 74.2

Holy marriage

What is more delightful than this union? What is more to be desired than this love uniting the soul to the Word and freeing it so that it dare express all its desires to him, cling constantly to him, speak to him as an intimate friend, and refer everything to him? Indeed, this is a spiritual contract, a holy marriage, an embrace in which two spirits become as one in the union of their wills.

Sermons on the Song of Songs, 79.1

The language of love

Everywhere in this song, the speaker is love. To understand what it is saying, we must love. Unless you love, do not bother to listen to love's song — you will not understand it. A cold heart cannot understand words of fire, nor can someone ignorant of Greek or Latin understand something spoken in that language. For someone who does not love, the language of love is babble. . . . Those to whom the Holy Spirit has given the grace of loving will understand this language. They know its words well and they respond in the same tongue, that is, by works of love and devotion.

Sermons on the Song of Songs, 83.3

Seeking or sought?

Do you want to return? If it is a matter of the will, why ask for help? Why beg elsewhere for what you possess so abundantly within yourself? . . . If a soul wants to return and asks to be sought, it seems to me that it is not entirely dishonored or abandoned. Where does that desire come from? Unless I am wrong, it comes because the soul has already been sought and visited, a seeking and visiting that has borne fruit by exciting the will, without which a return would be impossible.

Sermons on the Song of Songs, 84.3

FOR REFLECTION AND DISCUSSION

Do you feel comfortable using sensual imagery to describe your relationship to God?

Have you ever had a mystical experience? If so, how does it compare to Bernard's?

Where in Bernard's four stages of love would you say that you are at present? Looking back, can you see any progress from one stage to another?

Do you agree with Bernard when he says, "Unless you love, do not bother to listen to love's song"?

Has your experience been more one of seeking after God or of being sought by God?

Read Bernard's words of love to God. Then write a short paragraph or poem addressed to God, telling God how and why you love him.

Chapter 11

FRANCIS OF ASSISI

1181/2-1226

The Mendicants

The Mendicants

EVERYONE SEEMS to love Francis of Assisi. He is perhaps best known as the plaster figure with a bird on his shoulder standing in a suburban garden. After that, people think of him as the beguiling innocent who converted a hare, charmed a wolf into submission, and persuaded birds to listen to his sermons. This picture of Francis comes largely from later biographies, some of them unduly fawning, and while not unrelated to the Francis of history, it little resembles the thirteenth-century Umbrian saint. Today's Francis of the flower bed makes everyone feel good and challenges no one, whereas the real Francis infuriated many people and challenged everybody.

Nothing in the first two decades of Francis's life hinted at what was to come. The son of a prosperous Assisi merchant, Francis was a spoiled child who became a carefree, devil-may-care young man about town. He dreamt of a military career that would make him famous, but in November of 1202, he was captured and spent a year as a prisoner of war in a dungeon stinking of human sweat and urine. It was there that the future Francis began to emerge, for while other prisoners sniveled and moaned, Francis maintained a cheery disposition, poked fun at his chains, and told jokes. He befriended everyone, especially those whose bitterness had alienated them from their fellow prisoners.

That was the first of many times Francis would march to a different drummer. Upon his return home, Francis resumed his reveling, but his friends noticed a difference in him. Francis seemed preoccupied, far away. When asked about this, Francis replied he was "about to take a wife of surpassing fairness," by which he meant "Lady Poverty" — Francis had fallen in love with the poor.

This transformation came about only with effort. Lepers repelled Francis, for example, but lepers were among the most destitute people, so Francis forced himself to conquer his aversion to them. Seeing a leper beside the road one day, he dismounted his horse, pressed money into the man's rotting hands, and kissed them. Francis then circulated among the lepers of the area, distributing alms and kissing them until "what had been bitter became sweet." On another occasion, on a trip to Rome, Francis gave the clothing off his back to a tattered beggar and spent the rest of the day among the beggars outside the city's basilica.

His new lifestyle understandably disrupted Francis's life at home. In a famous incident, Francis took and sold a large quantity of dry goods belonging to his father, intending the money for the poor. Incensed and probably thinking his son had gone mad, Francis's father locked him in a dark closet for several days. Shortly thereafter, Francis's father took him to the bishop to be disciplined, whereupon Francis stripped himself down to a hair shirt in front of the bishop, folded his clothing, and handed it to his father, saying, "Until now I have called you my father on earth, but from now on I want only to say, 'Our Father who art in heaven.'"

These stories and others like them, some clearly apocryphal, portray someone who was either a saint or a self-willed lunatic. On the one hand, Francis's heart embraced the entire created order, especially the poor, and his good nature and humor became legendary. On the other hand, he stubbornly resisted compromise, however out of step he was with the rest of the world. Biographer John Holland Smith refers to Francis's "bull-dozing approach to life." Even after his witness had attracted thousands of followers throughout Europe, the tension between rigorous faithfulness to his ideal and accommodation to the world continued, both within Francis himself and in the movement he founded.

The foundational principle that moved Francis of Assisi was total commitment to the Christ-like life. What is sometimes called Francis's conversion took place when he heard the Gospel reading from Matthew 10: "You received without payment; give without payment. Take no gold, or silver, or copper in your belts, no bag for your journey, or two tunics, or sandals, or a staff." This was what Jesus had done, so Francis would do the same. "This is what I want!" he exclaimed, vowing to live precisely, literally as Jesus had lived. It was a life of artless simplicity, with no gap between theory and practice. As a result, Francis is known today as the person, more than any other in history, who most faithfully followed in the footsteps of Jesus. G. K. Chesterton, author of an engaging biography of Francis, calls him "the mirror of Christ rather as the moon is the mirror of the sun." This total identification with Christ was outwardly manifested during the last two years of Francis's life when the mysterious stigmata appeared on his hands and side, marks resembling the wounds of the crucified Christ. Others since Francis's time have exhibited such marks, but Francis was the first. He sought, unsuccessfully, to conceal them from others.

Boundless love was what Francis saw when he looked at Christ, so that's what he aimed for. This was no abstract or intellectual love, but a specific, total giving of himself to whoever was with him at the moment. Francis was courteous to everyone — the rich and the poor, his fellow friars, bishops and popes, even the Saracens, infidels, and thieves: "Come, brother robbers, we are all brothers and we have some good wine." On one occasion, when his followers were observing a rigorous fast and one brother began to wail from the pain of hunger, Francis declared an immediate feast — all the brothers were to eat lest the weakest among them feel shamed.

For Francis, poverty was the key to the loving, Christ-like life. He looked upon money as a kind of drug, addictive and lethal, to be shunned. Even minimal private property was repulsive to him. To own something, Francis believed, was to grasp for a security found only in day-to-day dependence upon God and would likely lead to divisions among people. When his bishop urged him to moderate his lifestyle, Francis said, "My lord, if we had possessions, we would need arms for our protection, for disputes and lawsuits usually arise out of them, and, because of this, love of God and neighbor are greatly impeded. Therefore, we do not want to possess anything in this world." The only time Francis is recorded as having been angry was when he heard talk of modifying the rule of absolute poverty.

Real poverty is a state of the soul, not an outward circumstance, Francis felt. It must therefore be purely voluntary, an act of love — poverty that is imposed is not an act of love. Only in complete, chosen, inner poverty is freedom found, Francis believed, for it enables people simply to be who and what they are, neither dominating nor dominated. "You could not threaten to starve a man who was ever striving to fast. You could not ruin him and reduce him to beggary, for he was already a beggar," Chesterton observes.

Humility is the sister of poverty. The rule of poverty extended even to inner possessions such as honor, knowledge, talents, and virtues. These can lead to spiritual pride and must be renounced, Francis said. Even the fact that one has renounced everything can become the cause of pride. One should seek virtue but not dwell on one's virtue, and another's virtue should give as much pleasure as one's own.

Francis is well known — and often misunderstood — for his love of nature. This reputation stems from two sources: the stories found in early biographies and his celebrated "Canticle of the Sun," one of the greatest hymns ever written. Francis composed it in 1225, just a year before his death, when his health was already failing, and recited it while walking through the fields. But the "Canticle of the Sun" is no mere paean to the beauties of nature. Each stanza begins with an expression of praise to God, the source of nature. The language makes it unclear whether Francis is praising God because of the works of nature or bidding the works of nature to join him in praising God, but either way, the focus is on God, not on nature itself.

People are often struck by Francis's praise of "our Sister Bodily Death" in the "Canticle of the Sun." Someone will say, "Praise God that we shall someday die? But I don't want to die! How could Francis have praised God for death?" For Francis, death was a natural thing, part of the universe that God created, something God had always intended. He saw the natural order, including death, as the theater in which God discloses his power, radiance, beauty, humility, and playfulness. All created things, even death, have life and personality for Francis, pointing to the life and personality of their Maker.

Francis quickly attracted followers and disciples. The orders he founded were part of a larger spiritual movement in western Europe at the time that also included the Dominicans, the Carmelites, and the Augustinians. These are called the "mendicant" orders because they supported themselves not through endowments and managing monastic estates, but entirely through alms.

Not one but three monastic orders emerged from Francis's ministry, all embodying his spirit and principles. The Friars Minor (Little Brothers) was the first, founded in 1209, followed by the Poor Clares for women, and the Third Order, which enabled persons to follow the Franciscan rule without abandoning family and career.

Organization and supervision were not Francis's gifts. In 1219 he made a preaching tour of eastern Europe and Egypt and let others take on the oversight of his increasingly varied followers. Differences about the rule of poverty and other matters continued to trouble Francis's followers until Bonaventure (1217-1274) — whose life as a young boy had been saved through Francis's intercession and who is often called the "second founder" of the Franciscans — became their minister general in 1257 and succeeded in reconciling divergent factions. Moreover, whereas Francis had written little, Bonaventure wrote several spiritual works of lasting value and gave the Franciscans a solid intellectual foundation. Franciscan spirituality today continues to appeal to many searchers hungering for something more than the consumer-driven materialism of the modern age.

IN HIS OWN WORDS

Those in authority

People placed in authority over others should glory in their position only as much as they would glory if assigned the task of washing the brothers' feet.

"The Admonitions"

The status of humanity

Be aware of the wondrous state in which the Lord God has placed you, O man, for he created you and conformed you to the image of his beloved Son in the body and to his likeness in the spirit. And yet all creatures under heaven, each in its own way, serve, know, and obey their Creator better than you do. Even the demons did not crucify him — but you, together with the demons, have crucified him and do so still today by delighting in vices and sins.

"The Admonitions"

Love of enemy

The one who truly loves his enemy is not upset at being injured himself, but is upset, out of love, because of the sin of his enemy's soul.

"The Admonitions"

Virtue and vice

Where there is love and wisdom,
    there is neither fear nor ignorance.
Where there is patience and humility,
    there is neither anger nor disturbance.
Where there is joy in poverty,
    there is neither covetousness nor avarice.
Where there is inner peace and meditation,

there is neither anxiety nor dissipation.
Where fear of the Lord guards the house,
   the enemy cannot gain entry.
Where there is mercy and discernment,
   there is neither excess nor hardness of heart.

                                    "The Admonitions"

Canticle of the Sun

Most high, omnipotent, merciful Lord,
praise, glory, honor, and all blessing are yours!
To you alone do they belong, Most High,
and no one is worthy to speak your name.

Praise to you, my Lord, with all your creatures,
especially Sir Brother Sun,
who is the day and through whom you give us light;
he is beautiful and radiant with great splendor,
and bears a likeness to you, Most High One.

Praise to you, my Lord, through Sister Moon and the stars in the
   heavens,
which you have formed, clear, precious, and beautiful.

Praise to you, my Lord, through Brother Wind,
and through the air, cloudy and serene, and weather of every kind,
by which you sustain your creatures.

Praise to you, my Lord, through Sister Water,
which is useful, humble, precious, and clean.

Praise to you, my Lord, through Brother Fire,
through whom you lighten the night.
He is beautiful and playful, robust and strong.

Praise to you, my Lord, through our Sister Mother Earth,
who sustains and governs us
and produces divers fruits, colorful flowers, and herbs.

Praise to you, my Lord, through those who grant pardon for the love
   of you
and bear infirmity and tribulation.
Blessed are they who endure in peace,
for you, Most High, shall give them a crown.

Praise to you, my Lord, through our Sister Bodily Death,
from whom no one living can escape.
Woe to those who die in mortal sin.
Blessed are they whom death will find in your most holy will,
for the second death shall not harm them.

Praise and bless my Lord;
give thanks to him and serve him in great humility.

The Eucharistic elements

With all that I am and more, I beg that when it is appropriate and it seems
profitable, you humbly entreat the clergy to revere above all else the most
holy Body and Blood of our Lord Jesus Christ and his holy written words
by which his Body is consecrated. Chalices, corporals, altar hangings — everything pertaining to the sacrifice must be of precious material. Moreover, if the Body of the Lord is poorly reserved anywhere, it should be
moved to a precious location and kept under lock and key, according to the
mandate of the church. Then it should be carried from place to place reverently and administered to people in a seemly manner. Similarly, if the
written words of the Lord are ever found in a place unsuitable for them,
they should be gathered up and kept in a more suitable place.

"First Letter to the Custodians"

The humility of God

Let all humankind tremble,
   let the whole world shake

and the heavens rejoice
when Christ, the Son of the living God,
   is on the altar
   in the hands of a priest.
O admirable heights and sublime lowliness!
O sublime humility!
O humble sublimity!
That the Lord of the universe,
   God and the Son of God,
so humbles himself
that to save us
he conceals himself in a tiny piece of bread!

"Letter to the Entire Order"

A letter of submission

Almighty, eternal, just, and merciful God: grant that we in our misery may do what we know you want us to do and do it for you alone. May we always desire what pleases you. Then, cleansed and enlightened within and burning with the flame of the Holy Spirit, grant us strength to follow in the footsteps of your beloved Son, our Lord Jesus Christ. Relying solely on your grace, may we find our way to you, Most High, you who live and reign in perfect Trinity and simple Unity, and are glorified, almighty God, forever and ever. Amen.

"Letter to the Entire Order"

A sinful brother

There should never be a brother, anywhere in the world, who sins and then, having looked into your eyes, goes away without receiving mercy, if mercy is what he seeks.

"Letter to a Minister"

For faith, hope, and love

Most high and glorious God, shine into the darkness of my heart and give me, Lord, a right faith, a certain hope, perfect love, and the sense and knowledge to carry out your holy and true commandment.

"Prayer before the Crucifix"

Anger

Let all the brothers — ministers, servants, and the others as well — be careful not to let the sin or evil of another disturb or anger them. Otherwise, the devil will seek to destroy the many through the fault of one.

"The Earlier Rule"

No contention

The brothers should be careful not to make any place their own or argue about it, whether it be a hermitage or any other place. And whoever comes to them, friend or foe, thief or robber, they should receive with kindness.

"The Earlier Rule"

Brothers' behavior

When the brothers travel about the world, they should carry nothing for the journey, neither a knapsack nor a purse, not bread, money, or a staff [Matt. 10:9-10]. And when they enter into a house, let them first say, "Peace to this house" [Luke 10:5]. Then, remaining in the house, they may eat and drink anything served to them. They should not resist evil, but if someone strikes them on one cheek, they should offer the other cheek also, and if someone takes their clothing, they should not withhold their coat as well [Luke 6:29]. They should give to anyone who asks, and if anyone takes what is theirs, they should not ask to have it returned.

"The Earlier Rule"

Brothers' preaching

Every brother should preach by his deeds.

"The Earlier Rule"

Poverty

The brothers must acquire nothing as their own property, neither a house nor a place, nothing at all. Rather, since they are pilgrims and strangers in this world and serve the Lord in poverty and humility, let them confidently beg for alms. They should not be ashamed at this since the Lord impoverished himself for us in this world. It is this summit of highest poverty that has established you, most beloved brothers, as heirs and kings of the kingdom of heaven. It has made you poor in things but exalted in virtue.

"The Later Rule"

True joy

One day at St. Mary's, Francis called Brother Leo and said, "Brother Leo, write this down. . . . Write down what true joy is. A messenger comes and says that all the great theologians in Paris have joined the order. Write down that this is not true joy. Then all the prelates throughout all the mountains, archbishops and bishops, or the kings of France and England, have done the same. Write down that this is not true joy. Then my friars go to the unbelievers and convert all of them, or I have such grace from God that I heal the sick and perform many miracles. I am telling all of you that true joy is not in any of these things. . . .

"Say that I am returning from Perugia and come here late at night, in the dark. It is the dead of winter — wet, muddy, and so cold that icicles hang from the edges of my habit and strike my legs, drawing blood. I come to the gate here, all covered with mud and cold and ice, and I knock and call out for a long time. Finally a friar comes and asks who I am. I say, 'I am Brother Francis.' And he says, 'Go away. This is a terrible time to be traveling about. You cannot come in here.' I insist once more and he replies, 'Go away, you uneducated nincompoop! Never come here again. We are important people here, many of us, and we do not need the likes of you.' But I still stand at the gate and I say, 'For the love of God, let me come in tonight.' And he replies, 'I will not do it! You go to the lepers' hospital and ask them.' I tell you that if during all this I remain patient and do not grow upset, that is true joy, true virtue, and the salvation of the soul."

"The Little Flowers of Saint Francis"

FOR REFLECTION AND DISCUSSION

What does it mean to be "poor in spirit"? Can one be poor in spirit while rich in material possessions, and if so, how?

How does the "Francis of the flower bed" compare to the Francis of history?

Had you been the father of the young Francis of Assisi, what would you have said to him?

If you were to undertake to live a totally Christ-like life, what changes would you make? What holds you back?

Write a hymn of praise around the works of nature. In addition to Francis's "Canticle of the Sun," you might look at "A Song of Creation" (*Book of Common Prayer*, 1979, p. 88), "Benedicite Aotearoa" and "Song to the Holy Spirit" (*A New Zealand Prayer Book*, 1997, pp. 63, 157), and Psalm 104.

Chapter 12

GREGORY PALAMAS

1296-1359

Hesychasm

"LORD JESUS CHRIST, Son of God, have mercy on me, a sinner."
So prayed a nineteenth-century Russian pilgrim as he trekked across Siberia to Jerusalem. His story is related in *The Way of a Pilgrim* (also published as *The Pilgrim's Tale*), an anonymous work long popular in Russia. It has also introduced Westerners to the prayer popularly known as the "Jesus Prayer."

The Jesus Prayer has a long history. Based on the publican's prayer in Luke 18:13, it seems to have been recited as early as the fifth century, as a means of living out St. Paul's injunction in 1 Thessalonians 5:17 to "pray without ceasing." Ignatius Brianchaninov, a nineteenth-century Russian monk and bishop, is typical of many writers on the Jesus Prayer. He advises beginners to recite the prayer "as often as possible," whenever the mind has a free moment, beginning with a hundred repetitions "unhurriedly and with attention," since frequent prayer eventually becomes unceasing prayer. Continuous repetition of the prayer focuses the mind on the name of Jesus and often brings a direct experience of Christ "in the heart." This happens when the person praying reaches inner stillness — in Greek, *hesychia*. That word also names the spirituality — hesychasm — which has shaped Orthodox devotion for over a thousand years and of which the Jesus Prayer is the best-known expression.

Though rooted in the teachings of the church fathers and a staple of Orthodox spirituality today, hesychasm was once controversial. The controversy began as a debate over how or whether God can be known. On one side stood Barlaam, a Greek who went to Constantinople in 1338 and won a name for himself as a philosopher. Barlaam was much taken with the thought of ancient Greece as it was being rediscovered in the West at the time. He believed that all knowledge resulted from reflecting upon sense experience and that since God is immaterial, beyond sense experience, he is therefore unknowable. On the other side were the Christian mystics who for centuries had claimed to experience God directly, often in the form of light. Was it possible to know and experience God directly, or was it not? Barlaam said no. The chief spokesman for those who said yes was Gregory Palamas.

Palamas was born in Asia Minor to a devout family of the Byzantine nobility. As a youth he studied Aristotle and other secular subjects, but at the age of twenty, Palamas decided to become a monk. Along with his widowed mother, two sisters, and two brothers, whom he convinced to pursue monastic vocations as well, Palamas set out for the "Holy Mountain."

Mount Athos, a rugged peak at the tip of a thin peninsula jutting from northern Greece into the Aegean Sea, had been, since at least the tenth century, a great center of hesychast spirituality, with dozens of large, rambling monasteries built into its cliffs. It remains home to hundreds of monks from throughout the Orthodox world today.

On Mount Athos, Palamas combined the traditional hermit and communal forms of monasticism, living alone in his hermitage for five days each week, then joining others for worship on the weekend. After ten years, Turkish raiders caused Palamas to abandon his unprotected hermitage on the Holy Mountain. He moved to Thessalonika, where he was ordained in 1326 and continued to preach and live a life of simplicity and renunciation. He soon took up the hermit's life again, on a mountain near Beroea, but after five years, raiders (this time Serbian) forced him to abandon this retreat as well. He returned to Mount Athos.

It was the dispute with Barlaam that eventually drew Palamas away from the Holy Mountain for good and plunged him into the midst of Byzantine politics in Constantinople. Palamas and hesychasm were alternately embraced and rejected by the political and ecclesiastical establishment, and Palamas was imprisoned for a time in 1343. Four years later, having regained favor, he was named archbishop of Thessalonika, the final victory of hesychasm coming in 1351, when both emperor and patriarch gave their blessing to the movement. Turks captured the ship on which Palamas was traveling from Thessalonika to Constantinople in 1354, resulting in his spending a year as their prisoner, during which he was treated kindly and entered into mutually respectful theological conversations with his Muslim captors. Palamas proved a beloved archbishop — his surviving sermons disclose a sensitive pastor in action — and is today the patron saint of the church in Thessalonika.

Perhaps the best place to begin an exploration of the several questions on which Palamas and Barlaam differed is with the human body. As a hesychast, Palamas prayed with his body as well as his mind. Regular breathing helped to quiet the mind. Palamas calls this a "spiritual sabbath" that strips "the cognitive powers of the soul of every changing, mobile, and diversified operation, of all sense perceptions and, in general, of all corporal activity." Christians today who pray the Jesus Prayer often recite the first half of the prayer while inhaling and the latter half while exhaling as a means of quieting the mind and opening it to the presence of God.

Given Barlaam's view that all knowledge comes through the intellect reflecting on sense experience and that God is irretrievably beyond the senses, it is not surprising that he rejected any attempt to be in touch with God that included seeing, hearing, touching, tasting, or inhaling, as hesychastic prayer typically does. He was scandalized by the idea that the human body could be transfixed by divine light, dismissed the hesychasts' bows, prostrations, incense, and regulated breathing, and mocked those who bowed their heads to commune with God as *omphalopsychoi* (literally "souls-in-the-navel," or, as one might say today, "navel-gazers"). The hesychasts, however, clung to the classical Christian understanding that God entered the world in fleshly form and continues to visit and empower his church through the water of baptism and the sacramental bread and wine — material things. For the hesychasts, therefore, sense experiences are among the means through which God acts and makes himself accessible. Still today Orthodox worship calls on all five senses when prayer is said (or, more likely, sung).

And yet Palamas and the other hesychasts agreed with Barlaam that God is beyond human knowing, "not only beyond knowledge, but beyond all unknowing," as Palamas says — even talk about what God is not cannot approach him. We may speak of God's uncreated goodness, eternal glory, and divine life, Palamas says, but these are merely names we have created. They do not describe God or enable us in any sense to possess or understand God. God is inaccessible not because of some deficiency or deformity of the human mind, but because God is *in his essence* beyond human thought and experience. God will always be shrouded in a cloud, hidden from our sight, not because of who we are but because of who God is.

So far, Palamas and the hesychasts are in accord with Barlaam. But Palamas goes on to say that the cloud that hides God from our sight is not an empty cloud, but places before us a Presence offering a true knowledge of God. This paradox rests on Palamas's distinction between the *essence* and the *energies* of God. In his essence, God is beyond knowing. But God is active in the world through his energies, manifest in us as we grow in godliness and do God's work. The divine energies include God's goodness, wisdom, providence, and majesty. "He makes himself present to all things by his manifestations and by his creative and providential energies," Palamas writes. These energies are truly and wholly God, not created beings or qualities separate from God himself. When we gaze at the energies, it is God whom we see, though not the divine essence that ever remains beyond all seeing. Nor is this a back door to polytheism, Palamas insists, for the energies are all manifestations of the one and undivided God.

These divine energies flow from an exercise of God's free and omnipotent will. They are not ours by virtue of our being human, as are our intelligence, virtues, and natural capacities, but are acts of grace whereby God invites human beings into union with himself — that is, with the divine energies, since union with the essence of God is impossible. God transfigures our minds and purifies our bodies, entering our hearts and changing us so that God lives within us, gazing upon himself. This is the classical Orthodox understanding of deification — when God became human, he also caused humans to become divine. We are only fully human, Palamas writes, when we are united with God.

This brings us to the central place of Christ in Palamas's spirituality. Union with God is no vague absorption into the divine, like drops of water in an ocean, but is effected through the grace of baptism, incorporation into Christ's body. It is union specifically with Jesus Christ, a historical person who was also the Son of God, the second person of the Trinity. In the first of his *Triads,* Palamas's main work defending hesychasm against Barlaam, he writes of the Son of God's "incomparable love for man" expressed by uniting himself with us "by clothing himself in a living body and a soul gifted with intelligence," thereby joining himself to "each of the faithful in communion with his body," making each of us "a temple of the undivided Divinity."

It is not primarily for his personality and life story that Gregory Palamas is remembered — little of that comes through in his writings. Nor is it for his dazzling new insights — his distinguishing between the essence and the energies of God was not an entirely new idea. We remember Palamas for the theological framework he developed affirming that God is both transcendent and immanent, both inaccessible and at hand. He did this at a time when the Renaissance, rationalism, and individualism in the West were beginning to erode belief both in a transcendent reality and in our ability to commune with that reality. The West has never entirely forgotten this belief, but in recent centuries it has often found expression more in fringe groups and sects than in mainline churches. As western Europe, and eventually America as well, turned in other directions, the Orthodox churches of the East preserved and embodied elements of Christian tradition, understanding, and experience that much of the West left behind. It is perhaps to Gregory Palamas, more than to any other single figure, that modern Christians are indebted for the preservation of this spiritual tradition.

"Lord Jesus Christ, Son of God, have mercy on me, a sinner."

IN HIS OWN WORDS

Body as temple

My brother, don't you hear the Apostle's words: "Do you not know that your body is a temple of the Holy Spirit within you" [1 Cor. 6:19]? Or again: "We are the house of God" [Heb. 3:6]? God himself says: "I will live in them and move among them, and I will be their God" [2 Cor. 6:16]. Why should any thinking person grow angry at the thought that our mind dwells in what will, by its very nature, become the house of God? How could God have caused the mind to inhabit the body in the beginning? Could even God do something wrong? That is the kind of thing heretics believe.

Triad, 1.2.1

Contemplation

Contemplation is more than abstraction and negation. It is a mystical union and a deification that cannot be described. It is from the grace of God and imprints itself on the mind after stripping away everything from here below.

Triad, 1.3.17

Unseen realities

Beyond prayer lie the indescribable vision, ecstasy in that vision, and hidden mysteries. Similarly, beyond the stripping away of beings, or rather after we cease thinking of them, not only in words but in fact, there remains an unknowing that is beyond knowledge, a darkness beyond radiance.

Triad, 1.3.18

Master the passions

If you practice true mental prayer, you must free yourself from the passions and reject all contact with things that interfere with prayer. That is how to acquire uninterrupted and pure prayer. If you have not yet attained this level but want to, you must master every sexual pleasure, completely rejecting the passions, for the body's capacity to sin must be mortified. You must be freed from domination by passionate emotions. Similarly, your judgment must defeat the evil passions that move in the realm of the mind, rising above sensual delight. If we cannot even taste mental prayer, not even with the faint touch of the lips (so to speak), and if passionate emotions control us, then we most certainly need the physical suffering that comes with fasting, vigils, and such things. That is how we apply ourselves to prayer.

Triad, 2.2.6

The body transformed

The spiritual joy that flows from the mind into the body is in no way corrupted by communion with the body. It transforms the body and makes the body spiritual because it rejects all the body's evil appetites. No more does it pull the soul down, but now it rises with the soul.

Triad, 2.3.36

All is one

Having moved beyond all other beings, this power [to see God] can only act by itself becoming completely light. It becomes like what it sees. It is united but not mixed, light itself seeing light through light. If it looks at itself, it sees light; if it looks at the object of its vision, it sees light; if it looks at the means by which it sees, it sees light. That is what union is — everything is so unified that looking at it, one can make no distinction; means, end, and object are the same. One is conscious only of being light and seeing light, as distinct from every created thing.

Triad, 2.3.36

Knowledge of God

Everyone has the natural faculties of sense and intelligence, but how can these faculties permit us to know God, since God is neither sensible nor intelligible? Surely by some way other than sense and intelligence. Those faculties are the means to know created beings but they are limited to such beings and what they may know of God is mediated through them. But persons who possess not only the faculties of sensation and intelligence, but also spiritual and supernatural grace are not limited to knowledge gained through created beings. They also know spiritually, in a way beyond sense and intelligence, that God is spirit. They have become totally God and know God in God. Hence it is by this mystical knowledge that things divine must be thought of.

Triad, 2.3.68

Deification is not fulfillment of nature

If deification merely perfects the rational nature but does not elevate those created in the form of God beyond their rational nature, if it is merely a state of the rational nature and is only activated by a natural power, then the deified saints do not transcend nature, are not "born of God" [John 1:3], are not "spirit because born of the Spirit" [John 3:6], and Christ's coming into the world has not "given the power to become children of God" to those who "believe in his name" [John 1:12]. If that were the case, deification would have belonged to everybody even before Christ came and would today belong to all people, regardless of their faith or devotion.

Triad, 3.1.30

Participating in God

We can participate in God, but God is completely beyond participating in. Hence there must be something between that divine essence that cannot be participated in and we who do in fact participate in God. Otherwise there would be no participating in God. If what exists between the participators and what cannot be participated in were removed, there would be merely a vast emptiness. That would cut us off from God, destroy the link, and create a vast, unbridgeable abyss between God on the one side and the creation and government of God's creatures on the other. Then we would have to look for a different God. . . . God presents himself to everything by his manifestations, his creative and providential energies. We must seek a God in whom we can participate in some way, so that each of us, in the way proper to us and by the analogy of participation, may receive being, life, and deification.

Triad, 3.2.24

Seeing the beyond

These divine energies are in God and are invisible to the created eye. But the saints see them, for the Spirit has helped the saints to transcend themselves. . . . Those who are united to God and deified fix their eyes on God in a way that is divine. They see not as we do, but with a sense beyond the senses and a mind beyond thinking. It is a miracle. The Spirit penetrates the human faculty with its power, enabling them to see things utterly beyond us.

Triad, 3.3.10

Abundance

If you fail to notice your suffering brothers — that is, Christ's brothers — and refuse to share your abundant food, shelter, clothing, and care with the needy, if you withhold your surplus rather than attend to their needs, then listen carefully and groan. Indeed, it is we ourselves who should listen and groan — I who speak these things stand accused. My conscience testifies that I am not entirely free of passion. While some may shiver and go without, I eat well and am nicely clothed. But even more to be mourned are those with treasures beyond their daily needs who cling to them, even seek to expand their holdings. Though commanded to love their neighbor as themselves, they have not loved their neighbor even as much as they have loved dust — for it is gold and silver that they have loved, and what are gold and silver but dust?

Homily 4

Poverty of spirit

The poor in spirit are those whose spirits (or souls) are free from boasting, vainglory, and the love of pleasure and who therefore either choose external poverty or bear it courageously when they have not chosen it. The rich and comfortable enjoy a fleeting glory, and those who would be like them yield to more harmful passions and fall into worse traps of the devil which are even harder to manage.

Homily 15

Mercy

The virtue of mercy means two things: First, it means giving shelter, protection, food, and aid to those in need. Second, it means approaching offenders with patience, forgiveness, and compassion.

Homily 36

Those who wrong us

The person who wrongs us benefits us in many ways, if we are willing. I think of him as a merchant ship filled with rich cargo that could not only pay our huge debt, but guarantee us future riches as well. We saw something in this city ourselves recently which I regard as similar in a way. Barbarians attacked us, besieged the town, and cut off our vital supplies from inland, nearly conquering us through privation. But then a ship carrying vast stores of wheat appeared and docked in our harbor, rendering the barbarians' threat null. The price of food fell and we were able to lay in a supply for the future as well. In this way, the spiritual enemy of all Christians, more savage by far than any barbarian, attacks us unseen. He cuts off the soul on all sides from everything it needs for salvation and surrounds it with a dearth of virtue. Its lack of virtuous deeds crushes the soul with despair. In this way our enemy defeats and destroys the soul. But then, by the providence of the Savior of sinners, someone arrives who has done us wrong and needs our compassion. When we have given it to him, he renders null all the devil's ill will toward us, reconciles us to God, offers us plentiful stores of mercy and salvation, and promises us eternal life.

Homily 36

FOR REFLECTION AND DISCUSSION

What does it mean to "pray without ceasing" (1 Thess. 5:17)?

How does the body contribute to the spiritual life?

How would Palamas say that God is known? How would you say that God is known?

What does Palamas mean when he says we participate in God and are united with God?

Why must the passions be subdued?

How are we benefited by the person who has wronged us?

Chapter 13

JULIAN OF NORWICH

1342–C. 1420

The English Mystics

FOURTEENTH-CENTURY ENGLAND must have been a terrifying place. Medieval society was collapsing as Europe lurched toward a new era. England's war against France, begun in 1337 over competing royal claims, would drag on for over a century and exhaust both countries. Church life was unseemly, with corrupt and worldly bishops, lazy (and often absent) clergy, and monks who spent more time hunting and feasting than praying. Worst of all, the bubonic plague, or "Black Death," took the lives of between a third and a half of the English population between 1348 and 1362.

Despite such pressing concerns, England produced four notable spiritual writers during this time: two men, one woman, and an anonymous author. They are known as the English mystics. The most prolific of the four was Richard Rolle (1300-1349). Opinionated, quirky, and acerbic, especially in his younger years, Rolle was an itinerant hermit who distrusted both the monastery and the university. Similar in some ways to Francis of Assisi, he would have been called "anti-establishment" today. His best-known work, *The Fire of Love,* is a vigorous tract including accounts of the sounds, sights, aromas, and other physical manifestations often accompanying his mystical experiences. Walter Hilton (d. 1396), an Augustinian monk and a more systematic thinker than Rolle, sought a balance between the active and the contemplative life in his treatment of the soul's spiritual pilgrimage, called *The Ladder* (or *Scale*) *of Perfection.* The anonymous author wrote several surviving works, notably *The Cloud of Unknowing,* another book about the soul's spiritual pilgrimage. It disparages the kinds of sensible manifestations celebrated by Rolle and commends a blank, empty receptivity when praying.

It is the woman in the group, however, who is today the best known and loved of the English mystics. The fourteenth century might seem an unlikely time for an English writer to proclaim the boundless goodness and love of God, but Julian of Norwich's *Showings,* or *Revelations of Divine Love* (the book is known by both titles), equals in this regard anything ever written. We know almost nothing of Julian, not even her name. (She took the name of her place of residence, St. Julian's Church in Norwich.) We know that she was born in 1342, but to whom and where we don't know. Her death is unrecorded. Some have conjectured that Julian enjoyed a happy relationship with her mother, based on her mother's presence during Julian's illness in 1373 and her tender use of the term "mother" in her writing. Others have detected a hint that Julian herself may have been married, widowed, and lost one or more children to the Black Death. Her writings disclose considerable theological learning (despite her claim that she was "unlettered"), which may point to an upbringing in a religious community. But most of this is speculation.

Julian spent the last several decades of her life in a cell built into the wall of St. Julian's Church, a space of about one hundred square feet, from which she could see the high altar of the church. She confined herself by choice, and she was not the only person of that time to make such a choice. A woman living as a hermit for religious reasons was called an anchoress (a man was an anchorite). Such persons were often sought out for counsel by people struggling with the trials and tragedies that surrounded them. Another spiritual author of the day, the bizarre (and possibly psychotic) Margery Kempe, reports having gone to Julian and been comforted by her.

The pivotal event in Julian's life began on the afternoon of May 13, 1373, when Julian, sick nearly to the point of death, received the first of a series of sixteen visions of Christ. The visions concluded the next day. Julian was apparently fully conscious and awake during the visions, which probably came to her prior to her taking up residence in her cell, and which may have inspired her to do so. She spent the rest of her life reflecting on these visions and wrote two accounts of them. The "Short Text" of *Showings*, written shortly after the fact, is brisk and immediate in tone, while the "Long Text," coming twenty or more years later, contains mature, nuanced reflections on the significance of the visions.

The visions themselves are less important than what Julian makes of them. They center on the crucified Christ and are graphic, even gory — hot red blood running down from under the crown of Christ; his dehydrated body hanging from the cross; his dry, bloodless face. Through it all, however, the Christ of Julian's visions is lavishly loving and joyful. He is no masochist, but would gladly suffer even more for humankind if that were possible. Julian's Christ is satisfied only when we are satisfied; his delight is in our holiness, joy, and bliss.

This and other key elements of Julian's spirituality are illustrated by a story she tells in chapter 51 of the Long Text. A medieval lord sends his servant on a mission. Loving and respecting his lord, the servant dashes off, eager to obey. But soon he falls into a ravine and is badly hurt. He grieves less over his wounds than over his inability now to do his lord's bidding or even to see his lord. The lord, aware of his servant's misfortune, gazes lovingly upon him. The lord's own honor requires that so beloved a servant be rewarded for his pains, even to the point of turning his falling and woe into honor and bliss. "It seemed to me that the loving regard which he kept constantly on his servant, and especially when he fell, could melt our hearts for love and break them in two for joy," Julian writes.

Julian develops this story at some length, and her entire book can be seen as an extended commentary on it. Note that the servant incurs no blame for his failure to carry out his lord's bidding. Julian saw human sin as the result of naiveté, ignorance, blindness, foolishness, and weakness — and since none of this is humanity's fault, it does not call for punishment. She sees God treating humanity as pure and blameless, as the victim rather than the doer of wrong, and even goes so far as to say that the more grievous and painful the sin, the more will it be rewarded with joys in heaven. Where Christ appears, she says, peace is received and wrath has no place — "I saw no kind of wrath in God, neither a brief nor an extended wrath." There may be anger, contention, and strife within us, but we are "all mercifully enclosed in God's mildness and in his meekness, in his gentle kindness and in his accessibility."

Julian grants (because the church says so) that humanity is guilty and sometimes deserves blame and wrath, but when she looks at God, she sees none of it. If this seems contrary to orthodox teaching, Julian is quick to say that this is merely what she saw, that she does not fully understand it, and that she trusts the church to correct any errors she may seem to introduce. Julian bowed to the teaching of the church that some will be eternally condemned to hell and asked, for purposes of instruction in the faith, for a vision of hell. All she saw, however, was the devil himself in hell, together with all the woe and tribulation he had caused. Julian was out of step with an age that often emphasized divine wrath at the expense of divine mercy.

Why does God allow sin? Julian's answer to this question is consistent with her story of the lord and the servant. The reason is that God loves us. "We need to fall, and we need to see it," she says, because otherwise we would never learn the depth of God's love for us. "Enduring and marvelous is that love that will not be broken because of offenses."

Love is the defining feature of Julian's God, and this love is no mere generalized kindliness, but personal, intimate, and passionate. She envisions God as a feudal lord in his house, full of joy and mirth, "gladdening and consoling his dear friends with himself, very familiarly and courteously." She does not ask the saints to pray for her, as was common in that day, for God much prefers that we approach him directly. "There is no created being who can know how much and how sweetly and how tenderly the Creator loves us," she says. It is our nature to "have God" and God's nature to "have us," and God wants nothing more than that we desire, know, and love him until, at the last, we shall be filled to the full in heaven.

Julian is known today for her references to God as Mother. She was not the first to explore the feminine side of God, but she developed this idea more fully than anyone before her. She refers to God as "our loving Mother," but more typically it is Jesus whom she calls "our true Mother." As a loving human mother suffers when her child is hurt or maligned, just so does a loving Jesus suffer for us, and as a human mother's love for her child remains constant even when she modifies her guardianship as her child matures, so it is with our Mother Jesus. When we grow distressed or frightened on account of our sin, we should not hold back but run to our Mother or call to her for help. "So he wants us to act as a meek child, saying, 'My kind Mother, my gracious Mother, my beloved Mother, have mercy on me.'"

We come finally to Julian's often quoted — and often misunderstood — line: "All will be well and every kind of thing will be well." She says this, or something similar, several times. Remember where and when Julian lived — these words do not convey a glib, simplistic optimism. She was aware, more than most readers of this book, that life can be brutal. Her affirmation comes from her profound conviction that God loves us and is working for us in ways we cannot fathom. The reason that all will be well is that nothing happens by chance. God does everything that is done, and everything that God does is done well. If we sometimes do not see the sunshine, it is not because the sun is not shining.

IN HER OWN WORDS

Note: All quotations are from the Long Text of *Showings*.

Thy will be done

Lord, you know what I want, and whether you want me to have it. If you do not want me to have it, do not be displeased with me, for I want nothing that you do not want.

Ch. 2

A hazelnut

He showed me a small thing, something no bigger than a hazelnut in the palm of my hand, it seemed, and it was round like a ball. I gazed at it with the eye of my understanding and wondered what it was. I was amazed that it could last, for I would have expected it to disintegrate into nothing because of its small size. Then I was answered in my understanding that it lasts and always will last because God loves it and that everything that is exists through the love of God.

Ch. 5

Clothed in God

As fabric clothes the body, skin clothes the flesh, flesh clothes the bones, and the trunk clothes the heart, so are we, both soul and body, clothed and enclosed in the goodness of God, but even more closely, for those other things vanish and waste away, but the goodness of God is always whole, and closer to us beyond comparison.

Ch. 6

Seeking and finding

This vision enabled me to see that the soul's unrelenting search greatly pleases God, for the soul can hardly do more than seek, suffer, and trust. This is achieved in every soul to whom the Holy Spirit gives it. This illumination by finding is a very special grace of the Spirit, when he wills it. To seek with faith, hope, and love pleases our Lord, and finding pleases the soul and fills it with joy. So I was taught to understand that when the Lord wishes the soul to labor, to seek is as good as to contemplate. God wants us to continue to seek until we see him, and it is by that very means that he shows himself to us, as a special grace, when he wills it.

Ch. 10

God in all things

The blessed Trinity is always and entirely happy with all its works. God revealed all this most blessedly, as if to say, "Look and see that I am God. I am all things. See that I do all things. See that I never remove my hands from my works and never shall. See that I guide everything to the end for which I ordain it, before time began, with the same power and wisdom and love with which I created it. How could anything be amiss?"

Ch. 11

Laughing at the devil

[The devil] can never do as much evil as he would like, for his power is locked in the hands of God. . . . I saw our Lord scorn his malice and disdain him as a nothing. He wants us to do the same. When I saw this, I laughed heartily, which made those near me laugh as well, and their laughter made me happy. Would that all my fellow Christians had seen what I saw. Then they would all have laughed with me. I did not see Christ laughing — but I know it was the vision he showed me which made me laugh, for I understood that we may laugh to comfort ourselves and rejoice in God, because the devil is rendered impotent.

Ch. 13

"All will be well"

In my earlier foolishness, I wondered why God, with his great wisdom and knowledge of the future, did not prevent sin. It seemed to me then that if God had done that, all would have been well. Though the impulse to think this was greatly to be shunned, I still wept and sorrowed on account of it, lacking reason and good judgment. But Jesus, who in this vision informed me of everything I need, answered as follows: "Sin is necessary, but all will be well, and all will be well, and every kind of thing will be well." . . . And so our good Lord answered every question and doubt I could raise, comforting me by saying, "I may make all things well, and I can make all things well, and I shall make all things well, and I will make all things well — and you yourself will see that every kind of thing will be well."

Chs. 27, 31

Effects of divine grace

It is contrition that made us clean, compassion that made us ready, and true longing for God that made us worthy.

Ch. 39

The Lord approaches the soul

Our courteous Lord shows himself to the soul, gladly and with the happiest smile, welcoming the soul as a friend, as if it had been in pain and imprisoned, saying, "My dear one, I am happy that you have come to me in your distress. I have always been at your side, and now you see me loving, and in this bliss we are made one."

Ch. 40

Petitionary prayer

[Our Lord said,] "I am the ground of your beseeching. First, I will that you have it, then I cause you to want it, and then I cause you to beseech it. Once you beseech it, how could you not have what you beseech?" . . . Everything which our good Lord causes us to beseech is something he has ordained for us from eternity. So here we see that our beseeching is not the cause of the goodness and grace he gives us. Rather, the cause is his own goodness. . . . Beseeching is a true, gracious, and enduring will of the soul that is united and joined to our Lord's will by the sweet, secret operation of the Holy Spirit. Our Lord himself is the first to hear our prayer, as I see it, and he is most thankful to accept it. With great joy he sends our prayer higher, to a treasure house, where he places it for safe keeping forever. There it is, before God with all his holy ones, continually received, continually ministering to our needs. And when we receive our bliss, it will be given to us as a measure of joy, with his endless and honorable thanks.

Ch. 41

Prayer and trust

God wills that our prayer and trust be equally generous. For if we do not trust as much as we pray, we do not fully honor our Lord in our praying, and we impede and hurt ourselves. The reason, I believe, is that we do not really know that our Lord is the ground from which our prayer springs and that he gives our prayer to us as an act of loving grace. If we really knew that, we would trust that our Lord will give us all that we desire.

Ch. 42

Prayer

Prayer is a witness that the soul wills what God wills. It eases the conscience and fits us for grace. Therefore God teaches us to pray and to trust firmly that our prayer will be granted, for he gazes upon us in love and wants to make us partners in his good will and work. He moves us to pray for what he wants to do, and for this prayer and good desire, which come to us as his gift, he will repay us and give us an eternal reward. . . . God showed such great pleasure and delight, as if he were in our debt for every good deed we do — even though it is he who does it. Therefore we pray to him urgently that he do what pleases him, as if he were to say, "How could you please me more than by begging me urgently, wisely, and sincerely, to do the very thing I want to do?" And so in prayer the soul is made to accord with God.

Ch. 43

"I am he"

As truly as God is our Father, so truly is God our Mother. This he has revealed in everything, especially in these sweet words which he says: "I am he. That is, I am the power and goodness of fatherhood. I am he, the wisdom and the lovingness of motherhood. I am he, the light and grace which is all-blessed love. I am he, the Trinity; I am he, the unity. I am he, the highest goodness of every kind of thing. I am he who causes you to love. I am he who causes you to yearn. I am he, the endless satisfaction of every true desire. For where the soul is highest, noblest, and most honorable, there it is also lowest, meekest, and most mild."

Ch. 59

Praying to the Trinity

. . . as truly as God is our Father, so truly is God our Mother. Our Father wills; our Mother works; our good Lord the Holy Spirit confirms. It is therefore our place to love our God in whom we exist, and to thank and praise him in reverence for our creation, mightily praying to our Mother for mercy and pity, and to our Lord the Holy Spirit for help and grace.

Ch. 59

"Supremely familiar"

Our Lord himself is supremely familiar and as courteous as he is familiar, for he is courtesy itself.

Ch. 77

FOR REFLECTION AND DISCUSSION

What do you think motivated Julian to become an anchoress? What spiritual advantages might come with such a life?

If you were to write a story about God and humanity with a lord and his servant as the characters, how would it differ from Julian's story?

How do you react to the idea that God is delighted with you?

Reflect on Julian's passage about the hazelnut. Do you agree that *everything* has being through the love of God?

Do you agree that "sin is necessary"?

How does Julian's comment that "all will be well and every kind of thing will be well" differ from glib, simplistic optimism?

Julian says "the soul's constant search" is pleasing to God. Is this a recipe for constant frustration? See the hymn "I Sought the Lord, and Afterward I Knew."

Write a prayer addressed to God as Mother.

Chapter 14

MARTIN LUTHER

1483-1546

Reformation I

W HEN I WAS A YOUNGSTER, my family often drove through the southern Appalachians, where signs painted on the sides of mountains urged the motorist to "Get right with God." I'll be sure to do that, I thought — by saying my prayers, going to church, and being good. I didn't know Martin Luther had shot down that notion of getting right with God four centuries earlier.

The medieval church had developed an elaborate system for getting right with God, based on the kind of devotional acts I had favored as a boy. The church vigorously promoted acts of piety such as taking monastic vows, saying masses, making pilgrimages to holy sites — and buying indulgences. The idea of the indulgence presupposed an understanding of God as Judge (rather like my childhood idea of God) and the belief that after death the soul goes to purgatory, where it must pay for sins committed in this life. The church taught that God would shorten the time a soul spent in purgatory in exchange for acts of penance or monetary gifts called indulgences. The church had first offered indulgences to men risking their lives in the Crusades, but by the sixteenth century the practice had degenerated into little more than a sordid commercial transaction supporting the Renaissance prelates in a life of sumptuous luxury.

Martin Luther was by no means the first to question this tawdry business, but his objection was the first to rattle the system. The Protestant Reformation is often said to have begun on October 31, 1517, when Luther nailed his famous ninety-five theses to the door of the Castle Church in Wittenberg, objecting to the sale of indulgences.

As a young man, Luther bought fully into the prevailing understanding of how one gets right with God. Born in Saxony to German peasant stock, for the first twenty years of his life Luther seems to have followed his stern but loving father's plan for him to gain an education and join the rising middle class. There was nothing exceptional in the family's religious observances. But in 1505 Luther was terrified when a lightning bolt nearly killed him during a summer thunderstorm. Two weeks later he entered an Augustinian monastery and began to devote himself to the task of getting right with God. Luther was ordained a priest in 1507. His academic gifts were soon noted, and he was named doctor of theology and Bible professor at the newly formed University of Wittenberg in 1511, a post he retained until his death.

During this time, Luther meticulously observed the rigorous spiritual disciplines of his order, seeking some assurance of God's favor toward him.

When that assurance was not forthcoming, he became afraid and despondent (a tendency he battled all his life) and turned up the disciplinary heat, resorting to lengthy chastisements, vigils, fasts, and confessions. But still he felt condemned by God, whom he perceived as uncompromising and demanding, setting a standard impossible to achieve and then punishing people for not achieving it. "My heart shivered and trembled as to how God could be merciful to me," he later wrote. He came to hate the God he was commanded to serve.

Luther's gradual disillusionment with this regimen may have begun in 1510 with a visit to Rome, where he found the pope and his advisors to be irreverent, unscrupulous, and worldly, and the lesser clergy busy rattling off mass after mass, hired to do so on behalf of wealthy patrons seeking to secure God's favor.

The ninety-five theses pertained only to the question of indulgences and were meant for discussion among theologians. But they were widely distributed, thereby opening a larger debate. During the next four years, Luther wrote several major works challenging accepted understandings of Christian spirituality. When traditionalists and papal loyalists expressed outrage, Luther responded by dashing off yet another tract. He had a gift for the vivid phrase. His opponents he called "dragons, specters, ghosts, and witches," "a pantheon of wickedness," "monsters of perdition," and "this swarm of the Roman Sodom." Not to be outdone, Pope Leo X issued a bull in 1520 beginning with the words "A wild boar has entered your vineyard, O Lord" and threatening to excommunicate Luther if he did not recant within sixty days. Luther publicly burned the papal bull. Four months later, called again to recant at the Diet of Worms, Luther refused and made this famous statement: "Here I stand. I can do no other. God help me. Amen." The Protestant Reformation was now in full sway.

More than anything else, it was his study of the Scriptures for his Wittenberg lectures that led Luther to question things. Despite the work of Erasmus, Thomas More, and others, Bible study had not yet become a staple of religious education, and Luther was startled at what he discovered in the Bible. Not only was there no reference to indulgences, but Luther found no warrant for the whole medieval scheme for getting right with God through acts of devotion. The breakthrough seems to have come when Luther was pondering Romans 1:17: "For the righteousness of God is revealed through faith from beginning to end; as it is written, 'The justified will live by faith.'" If a sinner is justified (gets right with God) through faith rather than works of devotion, what is faith, and how does one get it? And if the biblical texts are the witness of the apostles, can the pope issue edicts contrary to Scripture? Could the entire church have misunderstood the point of the Christian gospel?

Luther's study of the Bible led him to his understanding of justification by faith — and everything else in his spirituality flows from that. It may help to state first what faith is *not* for Luther. It is not something one does — showing religious devotion, loving one's neighbor, obeying the commandments. Luther had tried all that in the cloister and still felt alienated from God. Nor is faith believing that Christian teachings are true. Faith for Luther isn't belief *that* — it is belief *in*. Believing *that* something is true can make no difference in a person's life, but to believe *in* someone or something is to take a risk, to make a commitment, to trust. For Luther, faith means trusting the promises of God disclosed in Jesus Christ, even in times of doubt, despondency, and confusion. If you trust God and his promises, you are right with God; if you trust something else, you are not. "When I realized this, I felt myself born again," Luther said. "The gates of paradise had been flung open and I had entered." He was later to compare faith to the response of a plant to the sun, the opening of one's eyes, a new hope, a joyful expectancy.

For Luther, justification by faith involved a new understanding of the righteousness or justice of God. If God simply overlooks the sin of someone who trusts his promises, as a doting grandparent overlooks the misbehavior of a grandchild, how is God righteous? Luther pondered this question until, as a result of his reading of the apostle Paul, he came to see that God's righteousness is not punitive, but merciful and transforming. God reconciles us to himself while we are yet sinners solely because it is God's nature to forgive and restore. It is as if a judge, after pronouncing a criminal guilty, then commutes the sentence and enters personally into the heart and mind of the criminal to enable him to put the past behind and begin again. Luther speaks of the soul's clinging to the divine promises, being absorbed, saturated, and intoxicated by them. He speaks of "the wedding ring of faith." A marvelous exchange takes place between the divine and human natures. By it Christ unites himself to us and shares our suffering, death, and descent into hell. By it also we are united to Christ and share in Christ's victory and freedom.

Good works and acts of devotion now re-enter the picture, no longer as means of earning divine favor or diminishing the punishment due to a sinner, but to bring the sinner's life in the world into accord with his new status of being right with God. Christ dwelling in the heart of the believer transforms the believer more and more into himself — a completely free person who is yet servant of all. It is, in the last analysis, not the believer's righteousness but the righteousness of God, dwelling in the heart and soul of the believer, that effects justification.

Luther called this understanding a "theology of the cross," which finds God in humble suffering and shame. He contrasted it to the popular "theology of glory," which seeks God in human virtue and achievement. Luther simply accepts with gratitude the truth of the cross. He does not try to explain how this forsaken Christ reconciles the world to God, for he knows he cannot — at the cross one enters the realm of mystery and wonder. That the maker and ruler of the universe should come to us suffering on a cross, that Christ could be both lord and servant, is for Luther a great paradox. He accused his opponents of trying to iron out the paradox of the cross and thereby rob the Christian gospel of its mystery and power.

Luther's understanding of the church springs from all this. One gets right with God by means of faith in Christ; faith is God's gift to the sinner — and God plants this faith in the believer's heart by means of the divine Word. The Word is Christ — and is proclaimed through preaching and the sacraments. The preached word is central to Luther, and he sees it as a kind of sacrament, a means of planting and nurturing faith. Luther also affirms that Christ is truly present in the sacrament of the mass (unlike some of his more radical contemporaries, who saw it as a mere sign or reminder of Christ), but he understands the sacrament as embodied Word. "Nothing else is needed for a worthy holding of mass than a faith that relies confidently" on the promise of God, Luther says. He acknowledges that there is a priesthood, but not a special order of priests. Ordination, he says, is "nothing else than a certain rite by which the church chooses its preachers." For Luther, every baptized person is a priest, a voice through which the divine Word can speak. Moreover, nonreligious callings such as cook, tailor, and shoemaker are as holy for Luther as the call to become a priest or monk. In fact, he called for the abolition of monasteries and convents. This effectively undercut the whole superstructure of late medieval spirituality, with its special orders and quasi-magical powers over the fate of human souls.

Martin Luther lived another twenty-five years after the Diet of Worms. He left his monastic order, married in 1525, and fathered six children. But his major work had been completed by 1521. The rest of his life he spent clarifying, organizing, and refining that work and advising the new Lutheran churches springing up in Germany. Part of that time Luther spent translating the Bible into German, which opened the Scriptures to every German-speaking Christian. Many believe that Luther's Bible, with its sturdy prose style and mastery of colloquial usage, begun in 1521 and under revision until the day of his death, is his greatest contribution.

IN HIS OWN WORDS

God's love

The love of God does not find, but creates what pleases it.

Heidelberg Disputation

Sin, preaching, and grace

Preaching that tells us we are sinners instills hope, not despair. Such preaching about sin is a preparation for grace. . . . Yearning for grace wells up when sin is recognized.

Heidelberg Disputation

Good works and suffering

Only in suffering and the cross may God be found. . . . Friends of the cross say that the cross is good and that works are evil because it is through the cross that works are dethroned and the old Adam, who is greatly edified by works, is crucified. Good works will cause someone to be puffed up unless he has first been deflated and destroyed by suffering and evil, which disclose to him his worthlessness and that his works come from God, not himself.

Heidelberg Disputation

Good works and righteousness

I want the words "without works" to be understood as follows: It is not that the righteous person does nothing, but that his righteousness does not result from his works. Rather, righteousness creates works. Grace and faith are infused without our works. Works follow after they have been given.

Heidelberg Disputation

God pardons

Those who say, "God does not demand perfection" ought to say instead, "God pardons."

Heidelberg Disputation

Why a Christian does good works

A Christian who lives with this confidence in God knows everything, can do anything, ventures everything that needs doing, and does it all gladly and willingly. He does this not to accumulate merits and good works, but because it makes him happy to please God by doing these things. He simply serves God — with no thought of reward, simply knowing that his service pleases God. But the person who is not at one with God or who doubts it will worry and start looking for things to do to influence God by his many good works.

On Good Works

Faith and works

Apart from faith, no one can do this work. All works without faith are dead, no matter how glorious they appear or what grandiose names are given to them.

On Good Works

The church

The scriptures speak plainly about the church and use the word in one sense only . . . the community or assembly of all believers in Christ on earth. . . . This community or assembly includes everyone who lives in true faith, hope, and love. So it is the essence, the life, the nature of the church to be an assembly of hearts united in faith, not an assembly of bodies. . . . It is a spiritual unity. . . . But the blind Romanist makes it into an external community like any other.

The Papacy in Rome

The pope

Let no one resist the pope. Rather, let everyone bow to God's providence and honor the pope's authority, patiently enduring it, just as if the Turk ruled over us. This will do no harm. I contend for just two things: First, I will not allow anyone to set up new articles of faith and demean all the other Christians in the world, slandering them and calling them heretics, apostates, and unbelievers, merely because they are not subject to the pope. It is enough that we let the pope be the pope; we need not allow God and his saints on earth to be blasphemed for the pope's sake. Second, I will accept everything the pope says and does, provided that I first test it by the holy scriptures. He must remain subject to Christ and submit to the judgment of the holy scriptures.

The Papacy in Rome

The priesthood of all believers

A priest in Christendom is merely an officeholder. As long as he holds his office, he takes precedence, but when he leaves his office, he is a peasant or townsman like anyone else. . . . It follows that there is no fundamental difference between laymen and priests, princes and bishops, religious and secular, except in the office or work they do. It is not a matter of status. All are of the spiritual estate; all are truly priests, bishops, and popes. But not all have the same work to do.

To the Christian Nobility

The mass

What we call the mass is God's promise to forgive our sins, a promise confirmed by the death of the Son of God. . . . If the mass is a promise . . . then access to it comes not from any works, powers, or merits of one's own, but by faith alone. Where the Word of the promising God is, there must necessarily be the faith of the person accepting the promise. Clearly, then, our salvation begins with a faith that clings to the Word of the promising God who takes the initiative and offers us that Word of promise, freely and with undeserved mercy, with no effort from us. God's Word comes first. Then follows faith, and then love. And then loves does every good work.

The Babylonian Captivity of the Church

Promise and faith

God does not and never has dealt with us except through a Word of promise. We, then, cannot deal with God except through faith in the Word of his promise. . . . It is obvious that these two, promise and faith, necessarily go together. . . . Without this faith, things such as prayers, preparations, works, signs, and gestures incite impiety rather than promote devotion.

The Babylonian Captivity of the Church

All vocations are holy

The works of monks and priests, however holy and arduous, differ not one whit in the sight of God from the works of the unlettered laborer in the field or the woman doing her household chores. God weighs all works by one criterion only, and that is faith. In fact, the menial housework of a servant or housemaid is often more acceptable to God than all the fasts and other works of a monk or priest, because the monk or priest may lack faith.

The Babylonian Captivity of the Church

The promises and commands of God

God's promises give what God's commandments require; they fulfill what the law decrees. That way, everything is God's and God's alone, both the commandments and the obeying of the commandments. God alone commands; God alone obeys.

The Freedom of a Christian

What flows from faith

[A Christian] should think: "Though I am unworthy and condemned, God has given me in Christ all the riches of righteousness and salvation, with no merit on my part. This he has done as an act of pure mercy, freely given. The only thing I need, therefore, is faith to believe that this is true. Why then should I not do everything that I know is pleasing and acceptable to a Father who has overwhelmed me with his immeasurable riches, and do it freely, joyfully, with my whole heart and an eager will? I will therefore give myself as Christ to my neighbor, just as Christ offered himself to me. I will do in this life only what I see is needed, helpful, and healthful to my neighbor, because through faith I have in Christ more than enough of every good thing." From faith flow love and joy in the Lord, and from love flows a happy, willing, and free mind that serves one's neighbor willingly, oblivious to gratitude or ingratitude, praise or blame, gain or loss.

The Freedom of a Christian

Faith and love

A Christian lives not in himself, but in Christ and in his neighbor. If he doesn't, he is no Christian. He lives in Christ through faith and in his neighbor through love. Through faith, he is carried up beyond himself to God, and by love he descends beneath himself into his neighbor.

The Freedom of a Christian

FOR REFLECTION AND DISCUSSION

How does one get right with God?

Define faith as Luther understood it.

What is the place of good works in Luther's spirituality? What is the danger of good works?

How do Christians today seek to justify themselves before God by good works?

Jot down a list of the major characteristics of God as Luther understood God. What would you add or delete from the list, and why?

Luther looked only to the Bible to find God. Do you feel God communicates to his people only through the Bible?

How does Luther's understanding of the church compare to your understanding of the church?

Chapter 15

IGNATIUS OF LOYOLA

1491-1556

The Jesuits

THE ROMAN CATHOLIC CHURCH did not sit passively by as most of northern Europe deserted its ranks, but found fresh vigor even while Luther lived. What is usually called the Counter-Reformation included doctrinal clarifications, disciplinary reforms, and a new spiritual and missionary thrust launched by the one Roman Catholic of the day who ranks alongside Luther and Calvin as a spiritual master: Ignatius of Loyola.

Ignatius's life didn't start out that way. He was born to a noble family, in the castle of Loyola in the Basque country in northern Spain. As a youth he was imbued with notions of chivalry, military honor, and romantic conquests, "given to the vanities of the world; and what he enjoyed most was warlike sport, with a great and foolish desire to become famous," he wrote years later, in the opening sentence of his *Autobiography*. But Ignatius's first military encounter, a border skirmish against the French in 1517, saw a cannonball shatter one of his legs. After it was set and he recovered, he walked with a severe limp, and his vanity drove him to insist his leg be broken again and reset, despite the intense pain, because he feared the deformity would hamper his worldly ambitions.

What initiated the change in Ignatius was not his leg wound or the pain he endured, but the lack of reading material during his convalescence. When Ignatius ran through the small supply of chivalric romances at hand, he turned to the only other literature available: a life of Christ and a volume of tales about the saints. Reading both several times, he began to take delight in wondering what would happen if he lived as the saints of old had lived.

In 1522 Ignatius decided to make a pilgrimage to Jerusalem, but on his way stopped off at the small town of Manresa, intending to stay for a few days. Political considerations, however, caused him to extend his stay for ten months, and it was in Manresa that Ignatius's mature character and thought began to emerge.

Ignatius felt a sense of divine comfort during his first few weeks at Manresa, but he soon became obsessed with his sinfulness and undertook an austere program of fasting, vigils, and long hours on his knees. He refused to cut his hair or fingernails. His sense of sin intensified; he contemplated suicide. Eventually Ignatius decided to stop confessing past sins, whereupon he felt liberated and began to receive illuminating mystical contemplations. These continued throughout his life. Ignatius's contemplations had more to do with the mind and the will than the emotions, serving to clarify his understanding of earlier experiences and redirect his priorities and commitments. God was treating him, he wrote, "as a school-master treats a child." He later made his pilgrimage to Jerusalem and studied in Barcelona, Alcala, and Paris, but all his subsequent insights built upon the foundation laid at Manresa.

It was also at Manresa that Ignatius began jotting down notes on the spiritual disciplines he found helpful. These notes formed the core of his *Spiritual Exercises,* the work for which he is chiefly known. For the next twenty-five years, he revised and added to these notes until they became the book we have today. As the title suggests, the *Spiritual Exercises* is not a text to be read and digested (although some passages do bear careful meditation), but a manual for a spiritual director to assist the seeker in discerning God's will. George Ganss has said it is like a book on how to play tennis — one who reads it but does not take a racquet and go onto the court will not become a skilled player. The *Exercises* suggests ways to pray and topics for meditation, but one grows spiritually only by doing what is suggested.

Early on, even before leaving Manresa, Ignatius shared his exercises with friends. A small group formed around him. They began to think of founding a new religious order, not on the Benedictine model of daily prayer services in the cloister or on the mendicant model of living off alms among the poor, but one committed to apostolic service, to teaching the spiritual life to Christians, and to carrying the gospel of Christ to the ends of the earth. When Pope Paul III gave his approval in 1540, the Society of Jesus was born. It is popularly known as the Jesuits. Just eleven men comprised the original order; they elected Ignatius their first superior general. He drew up the *Constitutions,* a document both practical and spiritual, affording rules for administering the society and a codified picture of the apostolic life. It provides for flexibility in achieving goals and eliminates or minimizes everything, including set times for communal prayer, that might detract from the order's apostolic mission.

The heart of Ignatian spirituality is the four-week directed retreat. Spiritual seekers have always pulled away for periods of solitude and reflection, but until Ignatius there was no guide for what to do during such a time. The *Exercises* provides a purpose, structure, directions, methods, and topics for reflection. Each retreatant has a spiritual director, a Jesuit trained in the use of the Ignatian method who meets privately for an hour every day with the retreatant. Apart from that one hour, and perhaps daily worship, the retreatant maintains silence as he prays, reflects, and works through the *Exercises.* The director discusses the retreatant's progress and guides the retreatant through the *Spiritual Exercises,* tailoring and modifying them as needed for each individual and suggesting biblical passages and topics for reflection. The retreat can be condensed into shorter periods or spread over longer periods, depending on the retreatant's available time. Ignatius believed God leads each person along a path most fitting to that person, and a key feature of the *Exercises* is therefore its flexibility and adaptability.

Each week of the *Exercises* has a theme, and the themes progress logically through the four weeks. The suggested exercises are masterfully balanced, including appeals to the emotions, the intellect, the imagination, and the will. Week One focuses on the retreatant's sin, including his part in humanity's rebellion against God, the need to repent, and the sweetness that comes when the soul is purified and free to move toward God. Week Two opens with a meditation on the kingdom of Christ, followed by reflections on the Incarnation and Christ's public ministry, with the goal of helping the retreatant become more Christ-like in his priorities and decisions. During the third week the retreatant is drawn into the sufferings and passion of Christ, and then in the fourth week into the joy and victory of his resurrection.

Throughout this progression, various methods of prayer are introduced, and a number of themes are suggested for meditation. Each is seen as a means to an end — to draw the retreatant into a life of faithful service. Although one may make an Ignatian retreat at any time, those facing a major life decision (or "election," as it is called) such as marriage, ordination, life vow, or new career, often find the retreat most helpful. Again and again Ignatius poses the question of how one orders one's life and priorities so as to glorify God and save his soul. Several other features of the *Exercises* and of Ignatius's spirituality should be noted:

- Ignatius taught an activist form of devotion — Jesuits are called to *do* something, not merely to *be* something. They preach, teach, and travel to far places when so ordered. Whereas Luther and Calvin downplayed good works lest the believer think they earned him salvation, Ignatius emphasized human free will and cooperation with God in the process of salvation. Related to this was his positive view of the created order, including the human person. Ignatius was keenly aware of human sin and the need for repentance and amendment of life, but he saw the world not as a lost or degraded place, but as the theater in which God draws sinners back to himself.

- The faithful Christian should adopt an attitude of indifference toward the things of the world, Ignatius says. This does not mean he ceases to care about them, but that he is equally willing to possess or not to possess, to be honored or not to be honored, to be alone or to be among people. Indifference is less a stoic willingness to endure than a commitment to seek God's glory in all things, making every choice on that basis.

- Ignatius calls on the imagination and the five senses in his use of the Bible. He has little interest in the Bible as the source of church dogma, seeing it instead as a means of elevating the retreatant's imagination. He typically retells a Bible story, visualizing the scene, inhaling the odors, and listening to the sounds, all to bring the story to life in the retreatant's imagination. The retreatant enters into the story, watching and listening, and is enabled to make his decision for the greater glory of God. This gives opportunity for a colloquy or conversation in the retreatant's imagination, which is made "in the way one friend speaks to another, or a servant to one in authority."

- Ignatius's goal in all things is to glorify God, which includes acts of both praise and service. The phrase "the greater glory of God" appears so often in Ignatius's writings that it can be considered almost his motto. Facing a decision, he invariably asked which choice would be to the greater glory of God — indeed, everything suggested in the *Exercises* is a means to assist the pilgrim to glorify God. Christ was Ignatius's model, and the many meditations on the life of Christ in the *Exercises* are designed to move the retreatant to glorify God as Christ did.

The Society of Jesus began growing immediately. By the time of Ignatius's death, people the world over were doing the *Exercises,* and there were over a thousand Jesuits living in houses or colleges in Portugal, Spain, Italy, France, Germany, India, and Brazil. Within the next 150 years, the Jesuits grew to encompass 612 colleges, fifteen universities, and over a hundred seminaries throughout the world. Today, Jesuit houses and colleges are a major presence on all continents, and not only the Jesuits themselves but many others as well, both Catholic and Protestant, make the time to go into solitude, seek out a Jesuit director, and work through the *Exercises* "to the greater glory of God."

IN HIS OWN WORDS

What is a spiritual exercise?

By the term "spiritual exercises" we mean every method of examining our consciences, meditating, contemplating, praying both out loud and silently, and other such spiritual activities as will be mentioned later. For just as there are physical exercises such as taking a walk, traveling on foot, and jogging, so are there spiritual exercises, methods to prepare and dispose our souls to free themselves from all disordered tendencies and attachments, and then to seek and find God's will for managing our lives and saving our souls.

Spiritual Exercises, 1

Principle and foundation

Human beings are created to praise, revere, and serve God our Lord, and by this means to save their souls. Everything else on the face of the earth was created for human beings, to help us pursue the end for which we are created. Therefore we should use these things to the extent that they help us toward our end, and rid ourselves of them to the extent that they hinder us from it. To do this, we must make ourselves indifferent to all created things that are not forbidden to us, where we are free to say yes or no. This means we should not seek or prefer health to sickness, wealth to poverty, honor to dishonor, a long life to a short one, and so on in all other things. We should seek and prefer only what will most help us attain the end for which we are created.

Spiritual Exercises, 23

General examination of conscience

There are five points: First, give thanks to God our Lord for benefits received. Second, ask for grace to know our sins and rid ourselves of them. Third, ask an account of our souls from the moment we rose to this present examination, considering first our thoughts, then words, then

deeds. . . . Fourth, ask pardon of God our Lord for our failings. Fifth, re-
solve, with his grace, to amend them. Close with the Lord's Prayer.

Spiritual Exercises, 43

Offering

Eternal Lord of all things, I make my offering with your grace and help, in
the presence of your infinite goodness and the presence of your glorious
Mother and of all the holy men and women in your heavenly court. I wish
and desire, it is my deliberate choice — provided only that it is for your
greater service and praise — to imitate you in bearing all injuries and af-
fronts, both actual and spiritual poverty, if your most holy Majesty wishes
to choose me for such a life and state.

Spiritual Exercises, 98

Making a decision

In every good decision, insofar as it depends on us, we should focus our attention on just one thing, the purpose for which we are created, namely, to
praise God our Lord and to save our souls. Whatever we choose should
help us fulfill that purpose.

We ought not to drag the end into subjection to the means, but subject
the means to the end. Sometimes, for example, people choose first to
marry, which is the means, and only then to serve God our Lord in their
marriage, although the service of God is the proper end of marriage. Similarly, others first seek to possess benefices, and only afterwards to serve
God in them. These persons do not go straight to God, but want God to
come straight to their disordered attachments. As a result they make a
means of the end and an end of the means, seeking first what they should
have sought last.

We should first aim at desiring to serve God — that is the end — and
only then to take a benefice or to marry, if that be the suitable means for us
to attain that end.

Finally, nothing should move us to choose a means or to decline it except one thing, the service and praise of God our Lord and the eternal salvation of our souls.

Spiritual Exercises, 169

Indifference

I must keep as my objective the end for which I am created, to praise God our Lord and save my soul. Moreover, I should remain indifferent, that is, with no disordered affection or attachment, so that I am not more emotionally disposed to accept the thing proposed than to reject it, nor more inclined to reject it than to accept it. Instead, I should find myself in the middle of a set of scales, ready to follow the course I perceive to be more to the glory and praise of God our Lord and the salvation of my soul.

Spiritual Exercises, 179

Love

Love is a mutual communication between two persons. The one who loves gives and communicates to the beloved what he or she has, or a part of what one has or can have, and the beloved does the same in return to the lover. If the one has knowledge, he gives it to the other who does not. The same is true of honors and riches. Each shares with the other.

Spiritual Exercises, 231

Prayer

Take, Lord, and receive all my liberty, my memory, my understanding, my will — all that I have and possess. You, Lord, have given all to me. I now give it back to you, O Lord. All is yours. Do with it as you will. Give me only your love and your grace, for that is enough for me.

Spiritual Exercises, 234

Spiritual desolation

I use the term desolation to refer to times when we are bogged down in spirit, in mental darkness or turmoil, inclined to earthly things, restless and agitated with temptation. This leads to loss of faith, hope, and love. One is completely listless, tepid, and unhappy, and feels separated from our Creator and Lord. . . . One should never make a change during a time of desolation. Instead, hold firm and constant to any resolution and decision made the day before the desolation, or to a decision made during a previous time of consolation. For just as the good spirit guides and counsels us in times of consolation, so it is the evil spirit who guides and counsels us in times of desolation. We will never reach the right decision by following his counsels.

Spiritual Exercises, 317-318

Purpose of the Society of Jesus

The Society of Jesus seeks to assist its members and their neighbors to attain the end for which they were created. In addition to the life one lives, sound learning and a method of teaching it are also necessary to achieve this purpose. . . . To this end, the Society operates colleges and some universities.

Constitutions, 307

True obedience

The command to obey is fulfilled in the execution when the thing commanded is done. It is fulfilled in the will when the one who obeys also wills what is commanded. It is fulfilled in the understanding when he forms the same judgment as the one issuing the command and regards the commandment as good. Obedience is incomplete where there is not, in addition to the execution, an agreement in the will and in the judgment between the one who commands and the one who obeys.

Constitutions, 550

166

The bond of unity

The main thing uniting the members one to another and to their head is, on both sides, the love of God our Lord. When the superior and the subjects are closely united to his divine and supreme Goodness, they are easily united among themselves. That same love will descend from the divine Goodness and spread among everyone, and especially within the body of the Society.

Constitutions, 671

Learning from illness

[God our Lord] intends [illnesses] to provide us a fuller knowledge of ourselves, to root out the love of created things from us, and to make us more conscious of the brevity of our lives so that we will prepare ourselves for that other life that never ends. I also think he visits with these afflictions those whom he dearly loves. Through an illness, a servant of God acquires half a doctorate in how to direct and order his or her life to the glory and service of God,

Letter to Isabel Roser, 10 November 1532

Sometimes move cautiously

Sometimes we restrain our enthusiasm for speaking of the things of God our Lord. At other times, we speak with greater enthusiasm or energy than we actually feel. When the enemy tries to make us either exaggerate or diminish the communication we have received, we must consider the good of other people over our own desires. We must move cautiously to help others, as one does when fording a stream. If I find a solid footing or a prospect of producing some good, I proceed. But if the ford is rough or my well-intentioned words could lead to scandal, I always hold back and seek a better time or occasion to speak.

Letter to Teresa Rejadell, 18 June 1536

FOR REFLECTION AND DISCUSSION

Where in the world today and in your own life do you see indifference practiced, and where do you see it denied?

Why do you think would-be retreatants are advised against trying to work the *Spiritual Exercises* on their own?

Identify the elements in Ignatius's teaching that would be helpful to someone facing a major decision.

Choose a biblical story (such as Jesus' birth narrative in Luke 2 or the marriage feast at Cana in John 2) and then take a few minutes to place yourself in it by imagining what will impact each of the senses. Where do you find yourself in the scene? Who speaks to you? What do you reply?

Chapter 16

JOHN CALVIN

1509-1564

Reformation II

S EEN IN HIS OWN DAY as fresh, audacious, and daringly liberal, John Calvin is often today dismissed as cold, tedious, and rigidly conservative. That's because we usually look at Calvin through the lens of subsequent events and confuse later Calvinists with the man himself. While it is true that *The Institutes of the Christian Religion,* Calvin's major work, is intellectually demanding and uncompromising, it also contains powerful passages of joy and hope. Moreover, Calvin himself was a contented and happy man who enjoyed lively and enduring friendships.

Our knowledge of Calvin's early years is sketchy because he rarely wrote about his personal life. This was due both to his retiring nature and to his theological convictions — he shrank from drawing attention away from God. Calvin was born in Noyon, fifty miles north of Paris, into a religious family. His father was a commoner, the son of a boatman, but managed to win the patronage of the local bishop for his obviously gifted son. The young Calvin was tutored in the household of a prominent family, then sent to Paris, where he learned grammar and rhetoric. Calvin's father seems to have vacillated between a career in law and a career in the church for his son, and Calvin therefore studied both jurisprudence and theology at several schools, ranging from the austere Montaigu College in Paris to the liberal-minded school of law in Orleans. During this time, Calvin acquired a love of learning and of language. His favorite moments were spent alone with books.

The ideas of Martin Luther and other Protestant reformers were percolating in the French church during this time. The young Calvin could not have been unaware of this ferment, but his own early religious convictions are unclear. His conversion to "evangelical" Christianity, as Protestant understandings were commonly called, seems to have occurred around 1530. Central to it, and to his later life and thought, was the conviction that God had "subdued" him, "led me about by different turnings," and "made me play my part" — Calvin himself was not the active party in his conversion; it was an act of God. Much debate has centered on Calvin's conversion. He wrote of it just once, in his *Commentary on the Psalms,* where he says it was "sudden," but neither gives a date for it nor tells what precipitated it. Calvin apparently continued his studies under the patronage of the church for some time thereafter, but in 1534 he resigned his benefice and the income it afforded him, formally breaking with the Roman Catholic Church. He moved from place to place for several years, during which he published the first edition of *The Institutes.* In 1540 Calvin married a widow with two children. Their one child, a son born in 1542, died in infancy, and when his wife died in 1549, Calvin took on the care of her two teenage children by her former marriage.

It is with the city of Geneva that Calvin's name will forever be associated. He took up permanent residence there in 1541 and hardly left Geneva again. Calvin's Geneva is often misunderstood. He was not the ruler of the city, nor could he have been had he wished it. Calvin was pastor and preacher, and civil affairs were handled by a town council with whom Calvin often tangled. His primary goal was to structure the church so as to inspire the citizens of Geneva with the evangelical faith. To this end he persuaded the town council to enact his Ecclesiastical Ordinances, detailing the church's ministries and the responsibilities of church and state, anticipating that they would work independently, each supporting the other. Because of Calvin's personal integrity, mental vigor, and pastoral skill, he quickly became Geneva's leading and most renowned inhabitant, with considerable personal and moral authority even over affairs outside the province of the church. Although there were always those opposing his work, it is not a total exaggeration to say that under Calvin's influence, Geneva became a model evangelical community, a kind of "Protestant convent."

It was his *Institutes*, however, that made John Calvin a celebrity among evangelical churchmen of his day and for which he has been revered ever since. The first edition of *The Institutes*, published in 1536, was just six chapters in length, written to defend evangelical Christianity on the grounds that it, not Roman Catholicism, is the legitimate successor to the apostolic church. Calvin continued to pore over the work and enlarge it throughout his lifetime, adding new topics and expanding on ones addressed in earlier editions. *The Institutes* covers virtually the entire scope of Christian teaching, both theological and moral. Calvin intended it as instruction to the faithful in Christian living and as a response to the pastoral relationships that were forever adding to his work. Twenty-five more editions of *The Institutes* appeared before Calvin's death. The 1559 Latin edition, running to eighty chapters and 1,500 pages, is regarded as the definitive one.

Reading *The Institutes* is a daunting assignment, not because its thought is unclear — it can be unsettlingly, even brutally clear — but because of its relentless consistency and intellectual integrity. As a biblical theologian, Calvin felt called to explicate the Scriptures, supporting his positions with thousands of biblical citations. A single conviction pervades Calvin's reading of the Bible and everything he wrote; all else flows from it. That conviction is that God — glorious, honorable, exalted — reigns over all. The sovereignty of God is, as it were, a wall surrounding Calvin's inquiries. Sooner or later, regardless of the line of thought he is pursuing, he comes up against it and corrects his course accordingly.

Calvin states in the opening sentence of *The Institutes* that wisdom consists in the knowledge of God and of ourselves. God is by nature so far above us that we could never know God on our own, but God "accommodates" himself to us by communicating through a medium we can understand — human language. This happens through the written words of Scripture and preaching that expounds Scripture. Calvin is therefore much concerned with language and the text of Scripture, and his preaching is invariably biblical (though he is not a biblical literalist or a believer in verbal inerrancy). He sees preaching as the means God uses to instill faith in Christ, the divine Word. God implants faith in us when we identify with the obedience of Christ. It is a matter of the heart, not of the intellect. For Calvin, faith does not arise from a human decision (that would deny the sovereignty of God); it is a gift from God resulting in justification, forgiveness, and the confidence that we can stand without fear before the heavenly judgment seat. Good works are the confirmation of faith. And most important of all for Calvin, every bit of this is God's doing.

Prayer is also God's doing — Calvin calls it "a rare gift." In his section on prayer in *The Institutes,* Calvin deals only with petition. By prayer we reach those riches that God has laid up for us. God has promised good things to us, but he also bids us pray for what he has promised. In praying for our needs, we acknowledge our dependence and render to the sovereign God his due. Prayer fires up our hearts, directs our thoughts, makes us grateful, leads us to meditate on God's kindness, and confirms his power in our lives.

Calvin is known for three ideas that many experience as stumbling blocks. All three arise from his conviction of the absolute sovereignty of God. The first is his understanding of humanity's "total depravity." Human beings were created with the divine image implanted within, but that image is broken, defaced by sin. When Calvin speaks of "total depravity," he doesn't mean that no trace of divine goodness remains in us, but that no part of us is exempt from sin. And since God is righteous and will have no dealings with unrighteousness, we are — but for faith in Christ —

justly damned. Calvin could celebrate human achievement and was not interested in belittling humanity; his sole purpose in speaking this way was to glorify God.

The second idea that many find a stumbling block is divine providence. If God is sovereign over all, then everything that happens is attributable to God's plan, unknown to us. When we speak of God's omnipotence, we are not speaking of what God can do, but of what God is actually doing. There is no such thing as chance or good fortune — the will of God determines everything. What then becomes of free will? The first man, Adam, exercised his free will, but his disobedience means that everyone born since Adam suffers from a broken or warped will. Paradoxically, we sin by choice, but our warped wills make it impossible for us to choose otherwise.

Finally, we come to double predestination, the notion that the fate of every human soul has been determined from eternity in the mind of God. God has predestined some for eternal life (these are the "elect") and some for eternal damnation (the "reprobate"). The fate of the individual hangs not on human choices, behaviors, or beliefs, but solely on the free exercise of the divine will.

If these convictions have seemed dour and oppressive to some, even suggesting an arbitrary and tyrannical God, they did not seem so to Calvin. He refuses to fault God — we do not judge God or question why one person is among the elect and another among the reprobate. To speculate about the fate of specific persons or probe too curiously into the mystery of predestination can be confusing and dangerous. In any case, Calvin consistently emphasizes not judgment but grace, and his work shines with wonder at God's goodness. Calvin is at his most eloquent when writing of Christ's suffering on our behalf, thereby satisfying the requirements of divine justice that we could never hope to satisfy alone. Our place is not to question God, but to thank him for his gracious mercy. Since everyone deserves to be damned, God could have justly condemned the entire human race, but of his great goodness, he deigns to save some through faith in Jesus Christ. Calvin rejoiced and took comfort in the assurance that his salvation did not depend on his own merits and that there was no way he could undo it — it was due solely to the unfathomable goodness of God to an undeserving sinner.

IN HIS OWN WORDS

What is compatible with faith

What could be more compatible with faith than to acknowledge that we are naked of all virtue, so as to be clothed by God? Completely lacking in goodness, that we may be filled by him? Slaves to sin, that we may be freed by him? Blind, to be illumined by him? Lame, to be cured by him? Weak, to be supported by him? To strip away from ourselves any reason to glory, that he alone may shine in glory and we be glorified in him?

Institutes, Prefatory Address to the King of France

God's purity and man's impurity

So long as we do not look beyond the earth and content ourselves with our own righteousness, wisdom, and virtue, we sweetly flatter ourselves that we are nearly divine. But when we elevate our thought to God and ponder who he is, how utterly complete is his righteousness, wisdom, and power, we discover the straightedge to which we must be conformed. Then what had earlier masqueraded as righteousness, leading to a self-satisfied smugness, becomes filthy in its utter wickedness. What we adored as wisdom begins to stink of foolishness. What looked like power is seen as utter frailty. Anything that seems perfect or whole in us cannot correspond to the purity of God.

Institutes, 1.1.2

Scripture clarifies

Just as eyes dimmed by age, weakness, or some other defect see nothing clearly without spectacles, we are so weak that we are quickly confused unless scripture guides us in seeking God.

Institutes, 1.14.1

God's beneficence

Finally, whenever we call God the Creator of heaven and earth, let us at the same time remember that the ordering of everything he has made lies in his own hand and power and that we are truly his children, received and faithfully protected so as to be nourished and educated. . . . Every benefit that comes our way we are to acknowledge thankfully as a blessing from him. The great sweetness of his kindness and goodness invites us to study and love and serve him with all our heart.

Institutes, 1.14.22

God's secret plan governs all

Suppose someone falls among thieves or wild animals, is shipwrecked at sea by a sudden storm, or is killed by a falling house or tree. Suppose someone else wandering in the desert finds help, reaches safe harbor when tossed by the waves, is barely and miraculously spared his life. Earthly reasoning attributes all such things, good or bad, to fortune. But anyone taught by the lips of Christ that even the hairs of his head are numbered will look farther afield for the cause and will consider that God's secret plan governs all things.

Institutes, 1.16.2

Trust God in adversity

When thick clouds darken the sky, a raging storm arises, a dolorous fog blinds our eyes, thunder beats against our ears, and all our senses are numb with fear, and everything seems confused and snarled to us, a continual quiet and peacefulness prevail in heaven. We thus infer that though earthly disturbances deprive us of judgment, God, out of the pure light of his justice and wisdom, tempers these very things and guides them in the best-conceived order, to a right end.

Institutes, 1.17.1

The Spirit forms our ears to hear

There is no point in preaching [Christ] if the Spirit, our inner teacher, does not show our minds the way. No one comes to the Father but those who have heard him and been taught by him. What sort of hearing and learning would that be? It is where the Spirit, by a marvelous, unique power, forms our ears to hear and our minds to understand.

Institutes, 2.2.20

God works in us

God begins his good work in us by arousing our hearts to love and long for righteousness, or to say it better, by bending, forming, and directing our hearts to righteousness.

Institutes, 2.3.6

Faith is God's gift

The entire Bible teaches that faith is the free gift of God. Hence when we, whose whole heart is naturally inclined to evil, begin to will what is good, it is out of sheer grace that we do so.

Institutes, 2.3.8

The author of good works

The first part of a good work is the will to do it, the second a strong effort to do it. God is the author of both.

Institutes, 2.3.9

The suffering of Christ

If only Christ's body had died, it would have made no difference. No, it was expedient that at the same time he endured the severity of God's vengeance, appeasing his wrath and satisfying his just judgment. That is why he must also fight hand-to-hand with the hosts of hell and the dread of eternal death. . . . The point is . . . not only that Christ's body was given as

the price of our redemption, but that he paid an even greater and more excellent price by suffering in his soul the awful torments of a man condemned and abandoned.

Institutes, 2.16.10

Wonderful consolation

A wonderful consolation arises, namely, that we perceive judgment to be in
the hands of him who has already destined us to share with him the honor
of judging.

Institutes, 2.16.18

Faith is a matter of the heart

The Word of God is not received by faith if it flits around in the top of the
brain, but when it takes root deep in the heart and becomes an invincible
defense to withstand and drive away all the guiles of temptation. . . . It is
harder for the heart to be given assurance than for the mind to be given
thought.

Institutes, 3.2.36

Union with God

When we hear that we are united with God, let us remember that it must
be cemented by holiness. This is not because we commune with God on
account of our holiness, but because we first cling to him, and then, infused with his holiness, are able to follow wherever he calls us.

Institutes, 3.6.2

The great thing

The great thing is this: We are consecrated and dedicated to God that we
may thereafter think, speak, meditate, and do nothing but what glorifies
him.

Institutes, 3.7.1

We are not our own

We are not our own: therefore let neither our will nor our reason determine what we plan and do. We are not our own: therefore let us not seek what is pleasing to us in the flesh. We are not our own: therefore let us, as much as we can, forget ourselves and everything that is ours. On the contrary, we are God's: therefore let us live for him and die for him. We are God's: therefore let his wisdom and will rule all that we do. We are God's: therefore let everything in our life strive toward him, our only lawful goal. How very much it has profited the man who, taught that he is not his own, has shorn his reason of dominion and rule, yielding it to God! For as considering our self-interest is the pestilence that will surely destroy us, so the only refuge of salvation is to be wise in nothing and to will nothing regarding ourselves, but to follow the leading of the Lord alone.

Institutes, 3.7.1

Christ

For in Christ [the Lord] offers every happiness in place of our misery, all wealth in place of our neediness; in him he offers heavenly treasures to us, that our whole faith may contemplate his beloved Son, our whole expectation depend on him, and our whole hope cling to and rest in him.

Institutes, 3.20.1

The mystery of divine election

The covenant of life is not preached equally among everyone, and among those to whom it is preached, it does not gain the same acceptance, either in constancy or in degree. This diversity discloses the marvelous depths of God's judgment. . . . We shall never be entirely convinced, as we should be, that our salvation flows from the spring of God's free mercy until we come to know his eternal election, which illumines God's grace by this contrast: he does not indiscriminately adopt everyone into the hope of salvation but gives to some what he denies to others.

Institutes, 3.21.1

God's will

The highest standard of righteousness is God's will. That means that anything he wills must be considered righteous, simply because he wills it. If you ask why God has done something, the answer must be simply that he has willed it. If you go further and ask why he has willed it, you are asking for something greater and higher than God's will, which cannot be found. Let human rashness therefore be still and not look for what does not exist, lest perhaps it fail to find what does exist. . . . In the end, we must always return to the sole decision of God's will — and its cause is hidden in him.

Institutes, 3.23.2, 4

God's mercy to Calvin

[God] has pitied me, his poor creature, drawing me out of the abyss of idolatry which covered me, bringing me out into the light of his gospel and making me a participant in the doctrine of salvation, of which I was completely unworthy. . . . He has held me up among many sins and failings that should have caused him to reject me a thousand times. . . . He has so far extended his mercy to me as to use me and my work to convey and proclaim the truth of his gospel.

"Last Will and Testament"

FOR REFLECTION AND DISCUSSION

List the characteristics of God as Calvin understands God. How does it
    differ from a list describing God as you understand him?
What evidence is there for or against the "total depravity" of humankind?
Do you believe that things happen randomly or according to divine provi-
    dence? Is there some third position?
Explain why predestination was a great comfort and joy to Calvin. How
    do you feel about the doctrine of predestination?
What does it mean to say that God is sovereign?
How do you think the theology of Calvin would affect a believer's ethics
    and behavior?

Chapter 17

TERESA OF ÁVILA

1515-1582

The Spanish Mystics

L ATE SIXTEENTH-CENTURY SPAIN was an inhospitable place for innova-
tive Christian thinkers. During the previous century, the Renaissance,
the printing press, and the Protestant Reformation had released new ideas
into the European air, but most Spaniards feared that free thinking would
undermine the nation's new and still fragile unity. Moors and Jews who
would not convert to Christianity had been expelled from the country just
decades before, in 1492, and the newly established Catholic faith was seen
as a key safeguard of national unity. The Spanish Inquisitors, eager to protect the authority and purity of the church, held sway in ecclesiastical
councils, suspicious of any idea not originating in their offices. They particularly distrusted women, the families of converted Jews, persons claiming personal revelations from God, and Protestants. Teresa of Ávila was
suspect on all but the last count.

Teresa's paternal grandfather had converted from Judaism to Christianity, apparently for more than political reasons, for his sons and grand-
sons became devout Christians. But, as with Ignatius Loyola, Teresa's
Christian commitment took time to emerge, and as a young woman she
dreamt of chivalrous romance. Against her will, her father placed her in a
convent at the age of seventeen, from which she departed two years later
because she had become gravely ill. She was taken to her uncle's home
where, again like Ignatius, she read spiritual books available in the library.
Teresa then decided to become a nun, choosing a Carmelite convent distinguished, as she soon learned, for its lax discipline. She fell ill again (poor
health was to dog her throughout her life) and returned to her uncle's
home for another period of recovery, this one jeopardized by deplorable
medical treatments. But Teresa read more of her uncle's spiritual literature,
learning of the Franciscan practice of interior prayer and contemplation.

Teresa's real conversion occurred in 1554, at the age of thirty-nine. Following an extended time of spiritual desolation in which she had abandoned prayer altogether, she was struck by the love of Christ manifest in a
statue of his whipping by the Roman soldiers and by Augustine's conversion as recounted in his *Confessions*. Teresa realized she had not been trusting God to work in her soul, but had been seeking God through external
acts of piety.

This experience launched the freshly inspired Teresa on a new life as
monastic reformer, writer, and — most of all — woman of prayer. Teresa is
hardly a saccharine figure. Her writings teach the deepest levels of prayer,
but they also disclose an earthy, honest, hold-nothing-back woman. Teresa

is an engaging, attractive personality, conscious of her physical appearance (she is said to have been sexually appealing) and refusing to take her supposed sanctity seriously. It won't do for everyone to spend long hours in prayer, she says, because "there must be someone to cook the meals." Stories about her abound. When the donkey she was riding stumbled and threw her into a ditch, she blurted out, "If that's how you treat your friends, Lord, I don't wonder that you have so few of them!" It is said she liked to pray while seated in the latrine because no one would disturb her there. Teresa can be very funny, especially when writing words that appear submissive to the ecclesiastical authorities but also contain hints of another sort. She firmly and decisively stood by the authenticity of her prayer experiences when her often inept confessors and spiritual directors — and the ever watchful Inquisitors — tried to discredit her.

Much of Teresa's trouble with church authorities arose from her determination to be the kind of nun the founders of her order had envisioned. The Carmelite order had been established in the twelfth century, centered on extended periods of personal prayer. Over the years, however, the Carmelites had become more active in the world, and the original discipline had been relaxed. In some houses, like the one Teresa entered as a young woman, the sisters spent more time in gossip than in prayer. Teresa and her young contemporary, John of the Cross, sought to renew the Carmelite order along the lines intended by its founders. To that end, Teresa established seventeen new convents, and John established fifteen new monasteries for men. This meant that both traveled extensively, tended to administrative duties, and mediated disputes in the newly formed houses. Eventually these houses became a separate order. They are today called the "Discalced" (meaning "without shoes" — a feature of the original Carmelite discipline) Carmelites, while the continuing order is called the "Calced" Carmelites.

John of the Cross was also Teresa's close friend and, for a time, her spiritual director. He is usually named with Teresa as one of the two founders of the Spanish Carmelite school of spirituality, and their literary works support and complement each other. Both are writers of extraordinary power, though their literary styles are markedly different. John's poetry maps out the stages of spiritual growth systematically and is packed with allegorical symbols that allure and entice the reader but are hard to understand. John therefore wrote prose commentaries explaining what his poetry was meant to say. Teresa, on the other hand, rambles, forgets her place, and often comments in the text that she was interrupted in her writing some time ago and is only now sitting down to write again. She mentions topics she intends to write about and says she hopes she will remember to do so. Sometimes she doesn't. She did not edit what she wrote. Reading Teresa's work is like listening to conversation. Her images are picturesque, homespun, and readily understood. Of the two great Spanish Carmelites, Teresa is by far the more accessible and lively personality. After *Don Quixote,* her autobiography is the most widely read text in Spanish literature.

It may be a mistake to call Teresa's *Life* an autobiography. It contains little information about where she went, what she did, and whom she met — most of the "action" takes place within Teresa's soul. She wrote at the request of her spiritual director, probably as a means of proving her orthodoxy to the Inquisitors, to whom the manuscript of *Life* was sent and who kept it locked up until after her death. She says again and again in *Life* that she is no expert and that wiser authorities may need to correct her, insisting that she writes only of what she has experienced — and that experience was largely internal. Teresa is convinced, however, that everyone can receive such "divine favors," as she calls them, if they submit their wills to God. Inner experiences are, of course, beyond the control of external authorities and can pose a challenge to them. It was this feature of Teresa's spirituality that made her suspect to the Inquisition.

The best-known section of Teresa's *Life* comes in the middle of the work and makes no reference to the author at all. It is an extended metaphor about the stages in the life of prayer as Teresa has experienced them. The central image is that of a garden being watered. There are four stages in this watering, each a step further from what we do for God and closer to what God does for and in us. The land is barren at first. We begin to cultivate it by laboriously drawing water from a well and carrying it in a bucket to the garden. God is present with us in this stage of prayer — he has motivated us to desire a flourishing garden — but we do the work. Our will is meanwhile active and maturing. In stage two, we shift to a windlass, an irrigation scheme that we have constructed to work for us. Trees begin to blossom in the garden. Our reason backs off in this stage of prayer, responding to God rather than initiating; the will desires only what God wants to give. Our efforts are reduced still further in stage three, represented by a stream or spring from which water flows into the garden. Our faculties are asleep, though not lost, as we become more confident in God and begin to enjoy his delights. In the fourth stage, falling rain drenches the earth. The water and the earth are one. God is now fully present in the soul, and our place is to be still, completely passive, bathed in tears of joy.

Remember that Teresa is only writing about what she has experienced. She includes elsewhere in *Life* suggestions for beginners, including how to meditate quietly on Gospel stories to bring Christ into the soul. In this respect, her spirituality resembles that of Ignatius. Teresa may have learned from the Jesuits, to whom she turned for spiritual direction after dismissing her earlier directors.

Teresa's second major work is entitled *The Way of Perfection,* written to make available to the sisters in her convent what she had written in *Life,* locked away in the Inquisitors' files. It contains some unvarnished comments for her sisters that she had thought better of including in *Life.* The book opens with a discussion of the three things necessary to those who would walk the way of prayer: mutual love, detachment from worldly things, and humility. Humility, she says, is the most important of the three and includes the other two. Then follows a series of observations about contemplative prayer, which she wants to demystify and make accessible to all. Even so, she says, it is not for everyone, since people come to the Lord by different roads. Finally, the best-known section of the book is Teresa's powerful commentary on the Lord's Prayer, including her understanding of heaven as located within the human soul (where God dwells) and her insistence that to pray the Lord's Prayer authentically we must *already* have forgiven those who have sinned against us.

We come now to Teresa's most mature and carefully constructed work, *The Interior Castle.* It contains two suggestive images representing the human soul, the central image of a castle and that of a silkworm emerging from its cocoon. The reader is to imagine the soul as a castle and then to envision moving deeply into it. Spanish castles were typically less fortress-like than English castles, containing many buildings flowing one into another. In the center of the castle is the King, whose light illuminates its buildings, especially those near the center. There are seven "mansions" within the castle, each representing for Teresa a deeper level of prayer and union with God. Much of the content of the first four mansions can also be found in her earlier works, but in the fifth mansion Teresa breaks new ground. It is there that the silkworm image appears — it is like the soul enlivened and energized by the Holy Spirit. It spins its silk to build a house in which it will die and finally emerge again, transformed into a beautiful butterfly. Similarly, the soul, dead to the world, is recreated by its growing relationship to God. In the sixth mansion, Teresa writes of the soul's betrothal to God, which culminates in spiritual marriage in the seventh mansion. This union is like holding the ends of two wax candles together so that the flame is one.

Although Teresa writes of spectacular supernatural experiences in the depths of the soul, she always remains an outgoing, unaffected personality. Ever concerned for her sisters and other spiritual beginners, Teresa weaves into her accounts of raptures, visions, and voices her sage advice on the more practical and mundane aspects of the life of prayer, always drawn from her own experience.

IN HER OWN WORDS

Mental prayer

I see mental prayer as simply a friendly interchange and frequent solitary conversation with him who, we know, loves us.

Life, 8

Abandonment

I so long to see God that I forget everything, and this abandonment and loneliness seem better to me than all the company in the world.

Life, 20

Human effort or divine gift?

Do not believe people who are just beginning to taste of God and who think they advance more rapidly and receive greater consolations by aiding themselves. God can reveal himself quite well without our silly efforts when he wishes! Do as we will, God can move the spirit like a giant lifting a straw; all resistance is useless. It is a strange belief indeed that thinks if God wants a toad to fly, he will wait for it to do so by its own efforts!

Life, 22

Recognizing the devil's hand

I have had so much experience of the devil's doings by now that he knows I can recognize him and therefore torments me less in these ways than he once did. You can detect his part in an experience by the restlessness and discomfort at the beginning and the confusion he causes in the soul while the experience lasts, as well as by the darkness and affliction into which he plunges the soul and its subsequent aridity and lack of zeal for prayer or any other good thing. He seems to stifle the soul and squeeze the body, rendering both useless. True humility is quite different. The soul knows it is wretched . . . but there is no accompanying confusion or restlessness.

Life, 30

Taking God to task

How come, Lord, it is not enough for you to keep me in this miserable life, which I endure because I love you, in which I must live amid obstacles of all kinds that keep me from enjoying you? Why must I eat, sleep, transact business, and talk to everybody — all this, too, because I love you? You are quite aware that this is a great torture to me, Lord. Yet you hide from me, even in the few moments still remaining for you. How does this square with your compassion? How can your love for me allow such a thing? If I could hide from you the way you hide from me, you would not endure it, I think, because you love me so deeply. That is what I think and believe. Please consider the wrong you are doing to one who so deeply loves you!

Life, 37

Our rights

Would you be perfect? Then run as fast as you can from expressions such as: "I was right. . . . They were wrong to treat me like that. . . . The person who did that to me was not right." God deliver us from such a false understanding of right! Do you think it was right for our good Jesus to suffer so many insults? Were those who shouted insults at him right? Did they have a right to abuse him like that? If you think you should only bear the crosses you have a right to expect, then I can't imagine what you're doing in a convent. You should go back into the world, though of course such "rights" will not be honored there, either. Do you think you could ever endure so much that you ought not to have to bear anything more? What does "right" have to do with it, anyway? I don't know!

The Way of Perfection, 13

True humility

Consider that true humility is largely a readiness for what the Lord desires to do with you and happiness that he should do it, always regarding yourself as unworthy to be called his servant. If contemplation, mental and vocal prayer, tending the sick, serving in the house, and working at the lowliest task are all acts of service to the Guest who comes to stay with us and eat and take his rest with us, why should it concern us whether we do one of those things or another?

The Way of Perfection, 17

Perfect contemplation

The faculties rejoice not knowing how they rejoice; the soul is inflamed with love not understanding how it loves. It knows it rejoices in its beloved, but not how it rejoices in its beloved. It knows this joy cannot be achieved by the understanding but is embraced by the will, yet the will does not understand how. Insofar as it can understand anything at all, it perceives that even the merits of all the trials suffered on earth put together would not achieve this blessing. It is a gift from the Lord of earth and heaven, who gives it like the God he is. This, daughters, is perfect contemplation.

The Way of Perfection, 25

The Lord conforms to us

They say a wife must act this way if she is to be happy with her husband: she shows sadness when he is sad; she shows happiness (even if she doesn't feel happy) when he is happy. See what slavery you have been spared, sisters! Yet this, without any pretense, is really how we are treated by the Lord. He subjects himself to us and is pleased to let you be mistress and to conform to your will. If you are happy, look upon your risen Lord, and the thought of his rising from the sepulchre will gladden you. . . . If you suffer trials or are downcast, look upon him on his way to the garden.

The Way of Perfection, 26

God dwells within us

If I had understood then, as I do now, how this great King dwells within this tiny palace of my soul, I would not have left him alone so often, but would have remained with him, and I would never have allowed his residence to get so dirty! How marvelous it is that he whose immensity could fill thousands of worlds should confine himself within such small quarters! Being Lord, he is free to do anything, but because he loves us, he fashions himself to our measure.

The Way of Perfection, 28

Humility is truth

I once wondered why our Lord so loved the virtue of humility. Suddenly this reason came to me, though I had never thought of it before: it is because God is sovereign Truth, and to be humble is to walk in truth, for it is absolutely true that we have no good thing in ourselves, but only misery and vanity; and anyone who fails to understand this is walking in falsehood.

The Interior Castle, 6.8

Laying a firm foundation

Gaze upon the Crucified and nothing else will matter much to you. If his Majesty revealed his love to us by doing and suffering such astonishing things, how can you think to please him with mere words? Do you know what makes people really spiritual? It is when they become enslaved to God and are branded with his sign, the sign of the cross, signifying that they have handed over their freedom to him. Then he can sell them as slaves to the entire world, as he himself was sold. In doing this, he will be doing them no wrong, but a great favor. Unless you are determined to do this, don't expect to make much progress. The foundation of this whole edifice, as I said earlier, is humility, and if you lack true humility, the Lord will not want your edifice to rise very high. In fact, it will be best for you if it is not at all high. If it were, it would crash to the ground. Therefore, sisters, if you want to lay good foundations, you must seek to be the least of all and the slave of God. Try to please and serve all your companions. Do that and it will be more valuable to you than to them, and your foundation will be laid so firmly that your castle will not fall.

The Interior Castle, 7.4

FOR REFLECTION AND DISCUSSION

With which of Teresa's three images of the soul — garden, silkworm, and castle — do you most identify, and why?

Write a short prayer in which, as God's faithful servant, you take God to task.

Restate in your own words what Teresa means by the following statements:

- Consider that true humility is largely a readiness for what the Lord desires to do with you and happiness that he should do it.
- [The Lord] subjects himself to us and is pleased to let you be mistress and to conform to your will.
- This great King dwells within this tiny palace of my soul.
- To be humble is to walk in truth.
- Do you know what makes people really spiritual? It is when they become enslaved to God

What is the place of raptures, visions, and locutions in the life of prayer?

Chapter 18

GEORGE HERBERT

1593-1633

Anglican Spirituality

Anglican Spirituality

T HE ENGLISH REFORMATION WAS, at least initially, not about theology. It was about politics. Most of the English, including Henry VIII, were content with the church's worship and doctrine and saw no reason to alter them. But they resented the papacy and the pope's appointment to English bishoprics of Italians who lived grandly off revenues from their dioceses but never ventured across the English Channel. The last straw was the refusal of Pope Clement VII to grant an annulment of Henry's twenty-year marriage to Catherine of Aragon, who had not borne him a male heir to the throne. Henry, never one to acquiesce on a matter of any importance to him, persuaded Parliament in the 1530s to pass a series of acts abolishing papal authority in England but changing little else. Following Henry's death, the English church enacted further reforms, but even then, theology was usually addressed indirectly, within the context of prayer and worship. The theological underpinnings of the Church of England would be developed a couple of generations later.

To this day, some fault the Church of England, and the worldwide Anglican Communion that has sprung from it, for taking theology too casually. Anglicans reply that for them prayer and worship are primary — Anglicans pray first, then do theology. I was speaking a few years ago to a group of Lutherans about the difference between their church and the Episcopal (Anglican) Church. "If you ask a typical Lutheran about her church," I said, "she will probably tell you what Lutherans believe and perhaps show you the Augsburg Confession. She *may* say at the end something like, 'and we have a Book of Worship.' But if you ask an Episcopalian about her church, she will tell you of the Prayer Book, the songs she likes to sing, and the sacraments. She *may* add something about Episcopal beliefs." It is not surprising, therefore, that the Anglican soul has been shaped more by prayers, liturgies, poetry, sermons, hymns, and even novels and plays than by theological and spiritual treatises.

George Herbert is sometimes called the "poet laureate of Anglicanism." He was largely unknown in his own day. Born in a castle, the fourth son of a Welsh nobleman, Herbert was educated at Trinity College, Cambridge, where he studied classics and music. He pursued and, in 1620, attained the post of public orator at Cambridge. Herbert was also mulling over a career in the church at the time, but he expended most of his energy exploring more lucrative careers at court, managing to win the favor of James I through his effusive praise of the king. But when the king died in 1625, Herbert's prospects for a career at court dimmed. He continued to ruminate about whether to keep pursuing "the painted pleasures of a court life or betake himself to a study of divinity," in the words of biographer Izaak Walton. He retired to the house of a friend where he studied and prayed with such intensity that his health was affected. (Herbert was often in poor health.) He was torn between ambition and submission, pride and humility. Herbert fell in love and married (and his marriage was a very happy one), but lack of direction in life continued to torment him. Finally, in 1630, he was ordained priest and sent to Bemerton, a village one hour's walk from Salisbury Cathedral. In Bemerton, his indecision behind him, Herbert spent his remaining days happily serving his small flock. Those days were to be few, for Herbert died of tuberculosis three years later, one month shy of his fortieth birthday.

The popular picture of George Herbert is an idealized one, based somewhat on Walton's fawning biography, published in 1670 (Walton probably never met Herbert), but mainly on Herbert's own writings, published posthumously. His prose work *A Priest to the Temple; or, The Country Parson* describes the ministry of an Anglican priest serving a small rural parish, one much like Bemerton, which has led some to conclude that Herbert was describing himself. Perhaps he was, but he said in the work's opening paragraph that he had "resolved to set down the form and character of a true pastor, that I may have a mark to aim at, which also I will set as high as I can, since he shoots higher that threatens the moon than he that aims at a tree." Herbert was not trying to describe the parson he was, but the parson he aspired to be. Those who knew him, however, said he came close to hitting the mark.

The Country Parson is a charming work. It sometimes veers toward moralism, and a few of Herbert's recommendations may seem dated or presumptuous today, such as when traveling to call together the guests at an inn for evening prayers in the lobby. (I have tried and failed to envision myself doing this at a truck stop in, say, Tennessee.) But these occasional passages aside, *The Country Parson* offers a splendid picture of the conscientious, spiritually sensitive pastor. It's a practical book, a "how-to" manual for ministering in a small country parish, addressing subjects such as how to read the service ("with a grave liveliness, between fear and zeal"), sermons ("dangerous things"), the pastor's household ("a copy and model for his parish"), methods of religious instruction ("all the doctrine of the catechism, of the younger sort the very words, of the elder the substance"), and visits in parishioners' homes ("upon the afternoons in the weekdays").

The pastor is "the deputy of Christ," Herbert says, and his best sermon is a faithful life.

All this is for the purpose of nurturing a worshiping, praying community. It was in the church's public services of worship — daily, weekly, seasonally, faithfully following the pattern laid out in the Anglican *Book of Common Prayer* — that Herbert found God and where he expected others to find him. It is ironic that Herbert is chiefly remembered today as a poet, whereas he saw himself mainly as a pastor.

But Herbert's poetry is also about prayer and worship. Whereas *The Country Parson* discloses its author's inner life only indirectly and by inference, in Herbert's collection of poems, *The Temple,* he unmasks his soul for all to see. Herbert was part of a group of poets of the time, including John Donne, Andrew Marvell, and Henry Vaughan, whom Samuel Johnson later called "metaphysical poets." The term was not meant to be complimentary. Johnson found their poetry dense and pretentious. And it is certainly true that it bears careful reading — "light verse" it is not. To access the riches of *The Temple,* one must take the time to reflect upon it line by line, phrase by phrase. Subsequent generations of Christians (Johnson notwithstanding) have found Herbert's poetry richly rewarding. This has included believers of virtually all Christian denominations, perhaps because Herbert seems to have felt no sense of conflict with Rome or the Puritans, most unusual for his day.

Whatever else one may say of it, George Herbert's poetry is decidedly religious, even churchy. His poems bear titles like "Antiphon," "Evensong," "An Offering," and "Trinity Sunday." But if this suggests a saccharine, precious religiosity, the reader is in for a surprise. Herbert was not naive, simple-minded, or innocent, and his poems probe the deepest longings and questions of the human heart. He writes about traditional Christian teachings, worship services, and holy days as experiences within his own soul and invites others to experience them with him. This includes both the presence and the absence of Christ, times of affirmation and of desolation. Herbert's verses are challenging and intimate. Like the other metaphysical poets, he often produces unlikely, even inappropriate images. He leaves hanging and unresolved such opposites as faith and fear, intellect and emotion, ambition and submission, body and soul, intimacy and transcendence. The reader may wonder whether Herbert wrote his poems as teaching aids for his parish (he apparently did not share them widely during his lifetime) or out of his own need to express his spirituality in words.

Whatever his intent, Herbert bequeathed to future generations a subtle, powerful verbal picture of a soul in love with God.

A look at several of Herbert's poems will illustrate recurring themes in *The Temple*. He gives a kaleidoscopic picture of prayer in a poem entitled "Prayer (I)." Prayer is "the Church's banquet" (that is to say, not merely a treat for individuals), "angels' age" (that is, timeless), "God's breath" (enlivened by God, not by Christian believers themselves), "the soul in paraphrase" (an elaboration or enlarging of the soul), "the heart in pilgrimage" (growing, moving, changing). Herbert's imagery in describing prayer is bold — it is an "engine against th' Almighty," "reversed thunder," a "piercing spear." He links heaven to earth in a series of images — "the Milky Way, the bird of Paradise, Church-bells beyond the stars."

Herbert wrote five poems entitled "Affliction" in which he explores his feelings of being abandoned or ignored by the God he loves. In the first of these, he remembers his early joy as a Christian believer — "My days were straw'd with flow'rs and happiness;/There was no month but May" — but now he groans in sorrow and grief and wonders what God will do with him. He would rather be a tree than a human being. In his other poems of the same title, Herbert compares his own brokenness to the far more painful brokenness of Christ on the cross, perceives God present in his grief "To guide and govern it to my relief," describes his thoughts as "a case of knives,/Wounding my heart," and indicates his willingness to receive either joy or grief if it will bring him to God. In a similar vein, Herbert ponders the meaning of prayers that seem to miss their mark and go unheard in his poem "Denial." In "The Storm," he writes of his "throbbing conscience" assaulting and besieging the door of heaven and not ceasing until it gets an answer. Stormy days are best, he says, because they purge the air both outside and within the soul.

Herbert can also explore the joy and mirth of his faith. He is fond of musical imagery, and it is not hard to imagine him dancing as he recites his verses. Herbert often finds in the created order a hint of the loveliness of God. This is no sentimentalized nature worship, the religion of the pretty sunset and the mountain vista, but a gazing into the heart of all things earthly to see God within them:

Thou art in small things great, not small in any:
Thy even praise can neither rise, nor fall.

Thou art in all things one, in each thing many:
For thou art infinite in one and all. ("Providence")

Those of Herbert's poems that have become popular hymns often evoke this joy: "King of Glory, King of Peace, I Will Love Thee," "Come, My Way, My Truth, My Life," "Let All the World in Every Corner Sing," "The God of Love My Shepherd Is," "Teach Me, My God and King, in All Things Thee to See."

Perhaps no poem speaks of the intimacy of a Christian's relationship to God as powerfully as Herbert's poem "Love (III)." He envisions God, here called by the name of Love, inviting him to a feast. Herbert, knowing himself to be "guilty of dust and sin," draws back and declines, but Love persists, drawing nearer and asking if Herbert lacks anything. He replies that he lacks the worthiness to be in Love's presence, but Love asserts his authority by taking Herbert's hand and leading him to the banquet. Once in the banquet hall, Herbert insists that he must serve the meal, but Love responds that he has borne the blame. "I will serve. You must sit down . . . and taste my meat," says Love. "So I did sit and eat," the poem concludes.

IN HIS OWN WORDS

Note: All prose quotations are from *A Priest to the Temple; or, The Country Parson*

Good sermons

The country parson preacheth constantly, the pulpit is his joy and his throne. . . . The character of his sermon is holiness; he is not witty, or learned, or eloquent, but holy. . . .

Chapter 7

Limits of the congregation's endurance

The parson exceeds not an hour in preaching, because all ages have thought that a competency, and he that profits not in that time, will less afterwards, the same affection which made him not profit before, making him then weary, and so he grows from not relishing, to loathing.

Chapter 7

Scholars' temptation

Curiosity in prying into high speculative and unprofitable questions is another great stumbling block to the holiness of scholars.

Chapter 9

To whom the preacher preaches

For in preaching to others, he forgets not himself, but is first a sermon to himself, and then to others; growing with the growth of his parish.

Chapter 21

The priest at communion

Especially at communion times he is in a great confusion, as being not only to receive God, but to break, and administer him. Neither finds he any issue in this, but to throw himself down at the throne of grace, saying, "Lord, thou knowest what thou didst, when thou appointedst it to be done thus; therefore do thou fulfill what thou didst appoint; for thou art not only the feast, but the way to it."

Chapter 22

Old customs

The country parson is a lover of old customs, if they be good, and harmless; and the rather, because country people are much addicted to them, so that to favor them therein is to win their hearts, and to oppose them therein is to deject them. If there be any ill in the custom, that may be severed from the good, he pares the apple, and gives them the clean to feed on.

Chapter 35

"Sanctify and enable all my powers"

. . . Lord Jesu! Teach thou me, that I may teach them: Sanctify and enable all my powers; that in their full strength they may deliver thy message reverently, readily, faithfully, and fruitfully. O, make thy word a swift word, passing from the ear to the heart, from the heart to the life and conversation: that as the rain returns not empty, so neither may thy word, but accomplish that for which it is given. O Lord, hear, O Lord, forgive! O Lord, hearken, and do so for thy blessed Son's sake, in whose sweet and pleasing words, we say, Our Father, &c.

Redemption

Having been tenant long to a rich Lord,
   Not thriving, I resolved to be bold,
   And make a suit unto him, to afford
A new small-rented lease, and cancel the old.

In heaven at his manor I him sought:
   They told me there, that he was lately gone
   About some land, which he had dearly bought
Long since on earth, to take possession.

I straight returned, and knowing his great birth,
   Sought him accordingly in great resorts;
   In cities, theaters, gardens, parks, and courts:
At length I heard a ragged noise and mirth

   Of thieves and murderers: there I him espied,
   Who straight, "Your suit is granted," said, and died.

Easter (II)

I got me flowers to strew thy way;
I got me boughs off many a tree:
But thou wast up by break of day,
And brought'st thy sweets along with thee.

The Sun arising in the East,
Though he give light, and th' East perfume;
If they should offer to contest
With thy arising, they presume.

Can there be any day but this,
Though many suns to shine endeavor?
We count three hundred, but we miss:
There is but one, and the one ever.

Affliction (I)

When first thou didst entice to thee my heart,
    I thought the service brave:
So many joys I writ down for my part,
    Besides what I might have
Out of my stock of natural delights,
Augmented with thy gracious benefits.

I looked on thy furniture so fine,
    And made it fine to me:
Thy glorious household stuff did me entwine,
    And 'tice me unto thee.
Such stars I counted mine: both heav'n and earth
Paid me my wages in a world of mirth. . . .

At first thou gav'st me milk and sweetnesses;
    I had my wish and way:
My days were straw'd with flow'rs and happiness;
    There was no month but May.

But with my years sorrow did twist and grow,
And made a party unawares for woe. . . .

When I got health, thou took'st away my life,
   And more; for my friends die:
My mirth and edge was lost; a blunted knife
   Was of more use than I.
Thus thin and lean without a fence or friend,
I was blown through with ev'ry storm and wind. . . .

Now I am here, what thou wilt do with me
   None of my books will show:
I read, and sigh, and wish I were a tree;
   For sure then I should grow
To fruit or shade: at least some bird would trust
Her household to me, and I should be just.

Yet, though thou troublest me, I must be meek;
   In weakness must be stout.
Well, I will change the service, and go seek
   Some other master out.
Ah my dear God! though I am clean forgot,
Let me not love thee, if I love thee not.

Prayer (I)

Prayer the Church's banquet, Angels' age,
   God's breath in man returning to his birth,
   The soul in paraphrase, heart in pilgrimage,
The Christian plummet sounding heav'n and earth;

Engine against th'Almighty, sinners' tower,
   Reversed thunder, Christ-side-piercing spear,
   The six-days world transposing in an hour,
A kind of tune, which all things hear and fear;

Softness, and peace, and joy, and love, and bliss,
   Exalted manna, gladness of the best,

Heaven in ordinary, man well dressed,
The Milky Way, the bird of Paradise,

    Church-bells beyond the stars heard, the soul's blood,
    The land of spices; something understood.

The Flower

    . . . Who would have thought my shriveled heart
Could have recovered greenness? I was gone
    Quite underground; as flowers depart
To see their mother-root, when they have blown;
      Where they together
      All the hard weather,
Dead to the world, keep house unknown. . . .

    And now in age I bud again,
After so many deaths I live and write;
    I once more smell the dew and rain,
And relish versing: O my only light
      It cannot be
      That I am he
On whom thy tempests fell all night.

    These are thy wonders, Lord of love,
To make us see we are but flowers that glide;
    Which when we once can find and prove,
Thou hast a garden for us, where to bide.
      Who would be more,
      Swelling through store,
Forfeit their Paradise by their pride.

Love (III)

Love bade me welcome: yet my soul drew back,
    Guilty of dust and sin.

But quick-eyed Love, observing me grow slack
   From my first entrance in,
Drew nearer to me, sweetly questioning
   If I lacked anything.

"A guest," I answered, "worthy to be here."
   Love said, "You shall be he."
"I, the unkind, ungrateful? Ah, my dear,
   I cannot look on thee."
Love took my hand, and smiling did reply,
   "Who made the eyes but I?"

"Truth, Lord, but I have marred them; let my shame
   Go where it doth deserve."
"And know you not," says Love, "who bore the blame?"
   "My dear, then I will serve."
"You must sit down," says Love, "and taste my meat."
   So I did sit and eat.

FOR REFLECTION AND DISCUSSION

When did your life seem without direction? What did you learn from the
   experience? How did your resolution of it compare to Herbert's decision to be ordained and accept the call to Bemerton?

How would you describe Herbert's understanding of parish ministry?
   How does it compare to your understanding?

Write a kaleidoscopic poem or paragraph about prayer, piling together
   every image you think of that speaks of what prayer means to you.

As Herbert did in "Love (III)," write a short dialogue between you and
   God as you think it might be spoken when you come to communion
   or prepare to sit down at the heavenly banquet.

Look up the poems by George Herbert contained in the hymnal your
   church uses. What do these hymns say to you, and what about them
   do you think led the hymnal editors to include them?

Chapter 19

JOHN BUNYAN

1628-1688

The Non-Conformists

A MERICAN SCHOOLCHILDREN are not wrong to think of the New England Puritans as "founding fathers," but founding America as we know it was not what the Puritans set out to do. Their first goal had been to purify (hence their name) the British church and state along strict Calvinist lines. The Puritan agenda called for abolition of both the monarchy and the office of bishop. They prayed, worked, and fought toward this end for most of the seventeenth century, achieving their goal during Oliver Cromwell's Commonwealth in the middle of the century, when Puritan pastors occupied the pulpits of the Church of England. This was reversed when royalists and bishops regained power in 1660, after which Puritans were seen as insurrectionists. A variety of separatist groups, some also influenced by Calvin, vied for followers during this time as well. Bypassing the national church entirely to found independent Christian fellowships, they were known as Non-Conformists. Prominent among these were the Baptists (many of them Calvinists) and the Quakers (believers in an "inner light").

The hottest theological question among Calvinists of all stripes was predestination. The doctrine arises from Calvin's belief in the absolute sovereignty of God. Calvin had written of predestination in his *Institutes*, but he did not stress or dwell on it. Some of his later disciples, however, seemed to think of little else. The belief that God has exercised his sovereign will before the foundation of the world and predestined each human soul to eternal salvation or damnation can grip the mind. Not surprisingly, many English Protestants began to wonder on which roll their names had been written. How was one to know? An individual's behaviors and beliefs might not alter the eternal decree, but could they hint which fate had been decreed?

This concern for the fate of individual souls produced far-reaching ripples. In the early seventeenth century, groups of Puritans, discouraged at the prospects of winning the day at home, emigrated to America, where they founded a "New" (and presumably purer) England. The New England colonies stressed hard work and virtuous living as signs that one was among the saved (or "elect") At its worst, American Puritanism led to the Salem witch hunts; at its best, it produced confident and joyful Christians, including Jonathan Edwards, with his spirituality of love and other "holy affections" testifying to the presence of the divine Spirit. In both cases, the emphasis was on the individual soul. In later centuries, the saving of individual souls, with little or no reference to the historic Christian community or its creeds and sacraments, became a novel characteristic of American Protestantism.

The most influential British Calvinist, if book sales are any indication, was an uneducated Lincolnshire handyman named John Bunyan. Bunyan was born in 1628 to "the rank that is meanest and most despised of all families in the land," he wrote in his autobiography nearly forty years later (probably overstating his humble origin). He dropped out of primary school to assist his father in his work of repairing small household items, a trade he continued to practice as an adult. At the age of twenty, "I changed my condition into a married state," he wrote in the same autobiography, never naming his bride (and surely understating his romantic feelings for her).

His wife introduced Bunyan to the Christian faith by giving him two devotional books that had belonged to her father, apparently the only dowry she brought to the marriage. Bunyan read them and became a Christian, but a troubled one. He experienced frightful periods of depression over the fate of his soul. During this time, he overheard three or four poor women in the nearby town of Bedford talking about "the things of God . . . a new birth, the work of God on their hearts." Bunyan writes that he had already become "a brisk talker" on religious matters himself but had no inkling of what the women meant. This only intensified his despair, and he began worshiping at the Bedford Baptist church, where the women worshiped. For the next several years Bunyan wrestled with his fears and doubts, alternating between moments of desperation and moments of relative peace. As he grew to spiritual maturity, he began to testify and preach in Bedford, at the invitation of the small congregation, and was eventually asked to become their pastor. The congregation had been worshiping in the Bedford parish church, but after the monarchy and the episcopal government were restored, that was no longer possible. Preaching by non-episcopally ordained persons was forbidden by law. Bunyan continued to preach — although in private homes — and was arrested and imprisoned in 1660. This was the first of three imprisonments for Bunyan, all for unauthorized preaching. For these infractions he spent over thirteen years behind bars.

Jail did not dampen Bunyan's spirit (although he does write that parting from his wife and four children was "as the pulling of the flesh from my bones"). He found among his fellow inmates other prisoners of conscience and managed to have fellowship with them. He also discovered a stunning gift for writing. Bunyan wrote over sixty works, many of them while behind bars. Two are autobiographies of a sort. The first, *Grace Abounding to the Chief of Sinners,* written in 1666, is about Bunyan's life — but is hardly an autobiography in the modern sense, for like Teresa of Ávila's *Life,* it gives little information about outward events. The text concerns Bunyan's inner wrestling with the fate of his soul. His nameless wife appears only when her presence impacts the story of her husband's effort to determine whether he is among the elect. *Grace Abounding* is one of the first of what became a popular form of literary testimony among Puritans and other Calvinists (and among Quakers): the spiritual autobiography.

It is for his other autobiographical book, however, that Bunyan is chiefly remembered. For nearly three hundred years, *The Pilgrim's Progress* was the most-read devotional book among English-speaking Protestants the world over. It provided a lens through which they read their Bibles. *The Pilgrim's Progress* has been translated into dozens of languages. It is even less an autobiography in the usual sense than is *Grace Abounding.* It is the tale of a man named Christian — but his story bears an unmistakable resemblance to that of the author himself. We meet Christian as he flees from his place of residence, the City of Destruction, to begin a long journey to the Celestial City. Christian travels alone, not as part of a church or fellowship — the Puritan individualism — but links up now and then with fellow pilgrims with whom he compares travel notes. Christian's journey takes him to places undoubtedly familiar to Bunyan in his interior broodings, such as the Slough of Despond, Hill Difficulty, Doubting Castle, the Valley of the Shadow of Death, and Vanity Fair. Christian meets characters along the way whom Bunyan had no doubt known, such as Flatterer, Ignorance, Little-Faith, Faint-Heart, and Giant Despair. Christian is also aided by persons named Evangelist, Hopeful, and the Shining Ones. On one level, *The Pilgrim's Progress* is a good tale, one that has entertained millions of children and adults alike. On another level, it is the story of John Bunyan — and of every Christian — journeying through this life. He wrote a second part to *The Pilgrim's Progress* some years later, recounting the journey of Christian's wife, Christiana, to the Celestial City. Largely due to the counsel of a wise Baptist pastor, she faced fewer dangers and trials.

Several themes emerge from Bunyan's writing. One is his distrust of conventional wisdom. Early in *The Pilgrim's Progress,* Mr. Worldly-Wiseman seeks to dissuade Christian from continuing his journey on the grounds that he is meddling with things too high for him and falling into distractions. There is an easier way to peace of mind, he says, in a village named Morality, with a gentleman named Legality and his son Civility. Bunyan has no use for mere civic decency that passes for Christian faith (and in which he felt the established Church of England specialized). Such a religion asks no sacrifice, changes no lives, saves no souls.

A related theme is Bunyan's disgust at religion that is all talk or show and no action (another specialty of the Church of England, as he saw it). Three of the characters who seek to lead Christian astray are Formalist, Hypocrisy, and Talkative. The first two were born in the land of Vain-glory and are always seeking shortcuts to the Celestial City. Talkative looks better at a distance than close at hand. He actually speaks words that are true, but that's all he does; he sounds like an angel, but his talk is lifeless. "The soul of religion is the practical part," Christian observes. "Talking is not sufficient to prove that fruit is indeed in the heart and life; and let us assure ourselves that at the day of doom men shall be judged according to their fruits. It will not be said then, 'Did you believe?' but, 'Were you doers or talkers only?'" (James 1:22).

Bunyan scoffs at academic education (such as the Church of England expected of its clergy). Lacking a formal education himself, he quickly spotted those who tried to pass off intellectual attainment for genuine piety. His own education was of the self-taught kind, and his primary teacher was the Bible. Bunyan knew the Scriptures thoroughly, and part of the power of his writing is his ability not only to convey scriptural ideas, but to capture the nuances and rhythms of the King James Bible. What Bunyan writes *sounds* like the Bible.

It is also clear that for Bunyan, conversion is not a once-and-for-all event after which the believer is rewarded with a peaceful certainty about his relationship to God. Bunyan's conversion in *Grace Abounding* takes years, during which he grapples with some of his most frightful periods of doubt. Christian commits himself to the Lord *before* encountering the threats and seductions that await him, and he fears that he is drowning at the very moment he crosses into the Celestial City. Both Bunyan and the character he created mature in faith as they battle the devil in the depths of their souls. Mature faith, it would seem, is not possible apart from such battles.

So did John Bunyan ever receive the assurance of salvation he so desperately sought? Let Bunyan himself answer that question, in words found toward the end of *Grace Abounding:* "Now was I as one awakened out of some troublesome sleep and dream, and listening to this heavenly sentence, I was as if I heard it thus expounded to me: 'Sinner, thou thinkest that because of the sins and infirmities, I cannot save thy soul. But behold, my Son is by me, and upon him I look, and not on thee, and will deal with thee according as I am pleased with him.' At this I was greatly lightened in my mind and made to understand that God could justify a sinner at any time. It was but looking upon Christ and imputing of his benefits to us, and the work was forthwith done."

IN HIS OWN WORDS

Bunyan's burden

And now was I both a burden and a terror to myself, nor did I ever so know as now what it was to be weary of my life and yet afraid to die. O how gladly now would I have been anybody but myself, anything but a man, and in any condition but mine own. For there was nothing did pass more frequently over my mind than that it was impossible for me to be forgiven any transgressions and to be saved from the wrath to come.

> *Grace Abounding*, 149 (Note: Paragraph numbers in *Grace Abounding* refer to the 1680 edition.)

"My grace is sufficient for thee"

One day as I was in a meeting of God's people, full of sadness and terror, for my fears again were strong upon me, and as I was now thinking, my soul was never the better, but my case most sad and fearful, these words did with great power suddenly break in upon me: *My grace is sufficient for thee, my grace is sufficient for thee, my grace is sufficient for thee* [2 Cor. 12:9] — three times together, and O, methought that every word was a mighty word unto me; as *my* and *grace* and *for thee;* they were then and sometimes are still, far bigger than others be.

At which time my understanding was so enlightened that I was as though I had seen the Lord Jesus look down from heaven through the tiles upon me and direct these words unto me; this sent me mourning home, it broke my heart, and filled me full of joy, and laid me as low as the dust, only it stayed not long with me, I mean in this glory and refreshing comfort, yet it continued with me for several weeks, and did encourage me to hope. But so soon as that powerful operation of it was taken off my heart, that other about Esau returned upon me as before, so my soul did hang as in a pair of scales again, sometimes up, and sometimes down, now in peace, and anon again in terror.

Grace Abounding, 277

In the pulpit

Indeed I have been as one sent to them from the dead; I went myself in chains to preach to them in chains, and carried that fire in my own conscience that I persuaded them to beware of. I can truly say, and that without dissembling, that when I have been to preach, I have gone full of guilt and terror even to the pulpit door, and there it hath been taken off, and I have been at liberty in my mind until I have done my work, and then immediately, even before I could get down the pulpit stairs, have been as bad as I was before. Yet God carried me on, but surely with a strong hand: for neither guilt nor hell could take me off my work.

Grace Abounding, 284

In prison

I never knew what it was for God to stand by me at all turns and at every offer of Satan, etc., as I have found him since I came in hither [to prison]. For look now [when] fears have presented themselves, so have supports and encouragements. Yea, when I have started even as it were at nothing else but my shadow, yet God, as being very tender of me, hath not suffered me to be molested, but would with one scripture and another strengthen me against all.

Grace Abounding, 322

The darkness returns

I have wondered much at this one thing, that though God doth visit my soul with never so blessed a discovery of himself, yet I have found again that such hours have attended me afterwards, that I have been in my spirit so filled with darkness, that I could not so much as once conceive what that God and that comfort was with which I have been refreshed.

Grace Abounding, Conclusion

Christians together

Christians are like the several flowers in a garden, that have upon each of them the dew of heaven, which, being shaken with the wind, they let fall their dew at each other's roots, whereby they are jointly nourished, and become nourishers of each other.

Christian Behavior

Foolish fears

Now when [Christian] was got up to the top of the hill, there came two men running against him amain; the name of the one was Timorous, and of the other, Mistrust, to whom Christian said, "Sirs, what's the matter? You run the wrong way." Timorous answered that they were going to the City of Zion and had got up that difficult place, but "the further we go, the more danger we meet with. Wherefore we turned and are going back again."

"Yes," said Mistrust, "for just before us lie a couple of lions in the way, whether sleeping or waking we know not, and we could not think if we came within reach but they would presently pull us in pieces."

Then said Christian, "You make me afraid, but whither shall I fly to be safe? If I go back to mine own country that is prepared for fire and brimstone, I shall certainly perish there. If I can get to the Celestial City, I am sure to be in safety there. I must venture. To go back is nothing but death; to go forward is fear of death, and life everlasting beyond it."

. . . Then said Christian to himself again, "These beasts range in the night for their prey, and if they should meet with me in the dark, how should I shift them? How should I escape being by them torn in pieces?" Then he went on his way. But while he was thus bewailing his unhappy miscarriage, he lift up his eyes, and behold there was a very stately palace before him, the name of which was Beautiful, and it stood just by the high-way side. . . .

Now, thought he, I see the dangers that Mistrust and Timorous were driven back by. (The lions were chained, but he saw not the chains.) Then he was afraid and thought also himself to go back after them, for he thought nothing but death was before him. But the porter at the lodge, whose name is Watchful, perceiving that Christian made a halt as if he would go back, cried unto him, saying, "Is thy strength so small? Fear not the lions, for they are chained, and are placed there for trial of faith where it is, and for discovery of those that have none."

The Pilgrim's Progress

Vanity Fair

[Christian and his friend Faithful] presently saw a town before them, and the name of the town is Vanity, and at the town there is a fair kept, called Vanity Fair. It is kept all the year long; it beareth the name of Vanity Fair because the town where it is kept is lighter than vanity, and also because all that is there sold, or that cometh thither, is vanity. . . .

This fair is no new-erected business, but a thing of ancient standing; I will show you the original of it.

Almost five thousand years agone, there were pilgrims walking to the Celestial City, as these two honest persons are, and Beelzebub, Apollyon, and Legion, with their companions, perceiving by the path that the pilgrims made that their way to the city lay through this town of Vanity, they contrived here to set up a fair, a fair wherein should be sold all sorts of vanity, and that it should last all the year long. Therefore at this fair are all such merchandise sold, as houses, lands, trades, places, honors, preferments, titles, countries, kingdoms, lusts, pleasures, and delights of all sorts, as whores, bawds, wives, husbands, children, masters, servants, lives, blood, bodies, souls, silver, gold, pearls, precious stones, and what not.

And moreover, at this fair there are at all times to be seen jugglings, cheats, games, plays, fools, apes, knaves, and rogues, and that of every kind.

Here are to be seen too, and that for nothing, thefts, murders, adulteries, false swearers, and that of a blood-red color. . . .

Now, as I said, the way to the Celestial City lies just through this town where this lusty fair is kept, and he that will go to the city and yet not go through this town must needs go out of the world. The Prince of princes himself, when here, went through this town to his own country, and that upon a fair day, too. Yes, and as I think, it was Beelzebub, the chief lord of this fair, that invited him to buy of his vanities. Yes, would have made him lord of the fair, would he but have done him reverence as he went through the town. . . .

One chanced mockingly, beholding the carriage of the men, to say unto them, "What will ye buy?" But they, looking gravely upon him, answered, "We buy the truth." At that there was an occasion taken to despise the men the more, some mocking, some taunting, some speaking reproachfully, and some calling upon others to smite them.

The Pilgrim's Progress

FOR REFLECTION AND DISCUSSION

What does "salvation" mean to you, and can you be sure of it?
What would you say to someone frightened over the fate of his soul?
Is Christian faith mainly individual or mainly communal?
Recall a time when you were afraid because you didn't know the lions
    were chained.
Where is Vanity Fair?

Chapter 20

JEAN-PIERRE DE CAUSSADE

1675-1751

The Sacrament of the Present Moment

Y EARS AGO I felt trapped in a job I disliked and grew angry and despon- dent. Then I stumbled upon a slender volume entitled *Abandonment to Divine Providence* written 250 years earlier by a Jesuit priest I'd never heard of. The title called out to me — perhaps I could find peace if I turned everything over to "divine providence." As I began to read, I felt as if every word had been written expressly for me. It was the beginning of my emergence from the pit.

What is known of the author of that little book could be written on the back of a postcard. Jean-Pierre de Caussade was born on March 6, 1675, in Caussade, a village in the Quercy region of southern France. He became a Jesuit novice at eighteen and was ordained eleven years later, taking his final vows in 1708. He taught Greek, Latin, and philosophy at various schools in the area, including several years in the university town of Toulouse, and seems to have been recognized as a teacher, preacher, and confessor. Beyond the names of schools and the positions he held, nothing more is known of Caussade during these years. In 1729 he was appointed spiritual director of the Visitation Sisters in Nancy in northern France, where he led retreats and conferences. He was immediately acclaimed as a spiritual guide. Called back to Toulouse a year later, Caussade corresponded with many of the sisters whom he had directed at Nancy. He returned to Nancy in 1733 and re- mained there for six years. In his later years, he held several administrative posts, which (according to his letters) he disliked. Caussade became blind toward the end of his life, one of the few facts known about him. What he looked like and how he sounded when he spoke, no one knows.

Caussade published one book during his lifetime, an awkwardly con- structed catechetical text on prayer. It was little noted then and less noted later. A collection of his letters appeared after his death, but Caussade was largely forgotten until, in 1861, the French Jesuit Henri Ramière published a collection of notes and quotations from Caussade's conferences at Nancy, transcribed and preserved by the sisters there and circulated in private for over a hundred years. Ramière entitled this work *Abandonment to Divine Providence*. It has also appeared under the name *The Sacrament of the Pres- ent Moment*. The structure of the work as we have it is Ramière's, and he modified much of his material for his own theological reasons. Not until 1966 did a critical edition of *Abandonment* appear. It is for this work that Caussade is known today. His letters serve to supplement it, giving insights into his character and practical applications of the spiritual principles taught in *Abandonment*.

And what are those principles? The two titles by which the work is known encapsulate its main theme: Happiness is found in complete abandonment to the divine will as disclosed in the present moment. Caussade believed God speaks to us moment by moment through the events of our lives. God's word is sometimes obscure, however, and we often fail to recognize it, finding fault and trying to alter what God has ordained. But nothing, not even the falling of a leaf, happens apart from the will of God. The whole of history is but the story of what God is doing, with human beings contributing virtually nothing to it. Our place is to submit to God's will in whatever condition we find ourselves.

Seeing everything that happens as an expression of God's power and goodness is the way to supreme happiness, Caussade says. God's wishes are not only holy and to be adored, but infinitely beneficial to his humble and obedient creatures. What God does is always new and fresh, and he arranges everything for the best. God desires our happiness and is glorified in it.

How can Caussade say this in a world so full of cruelty and suffering? He does not go so far as to say that God is the author of such things — in fact, they often result from our getting our own way. But suffering is consistent with God's will in that God permits it and can turn it to good account when, by his grace, we respond in faith moment to moment. Trials can be the means through which God mediates his goodness to us, teaching us to be humble and to trust him completely. Caussade develops this thought most fully in his letters, where he addresses the particular sufferings of those who have written to him for counsel: "God is wise enough, good enough, powerful enough, and merciful enough to turn the seemingly most unpromising events to the advantage of those who know how to adore and humbly accept and cherish his glorious freedom. . . . Sometimes everything goes wrong, for which I still thank him and offer the troubles to him, and that done, God repairs everything, which is an agreeable surprise."

We must train ourselves to see each moment as a sacrament, approaching each task and each suffering with the same reverence with which we would approach Holy Communion. A sacrament has two parts: it is an outward sign of God's grace *and* the means by which that grace is received — it signifies something *and* it makes available what it signifies. This is precisely what Caussade means by his famous phrase "the sacrament of the present moment." Each moment points to God's grace *and* is the means by which we receive that grace. Jesus Christ is present in every fraction of a second and every atom of matter, whether or not we have eyes to see him. Some people try to return to past experiences or brood over past wrongs. Others obsess about the future. But God comes to us only in the present moment, and if we would know him, we must learn to see him there, Caussade says. Moreover, each moment is unique. What God called us to do yesterday is not what God calls us to do today. Abandon your desire to control and manipulate. Obey God right now and leave the past and the future in God's hands. Seize what each moment brings and then move on.

The idea of abandonment is easily misunderstood. In English the word can carry a negative connotation that is not true of the French *abandon*. Some have suggested it be translated as "resignation," "submission," "surrender," or "indifference" — but these English words carry negative connotations as well. Caussade suggests two analogies: that of the stone being shaped into a statue by a sculptor, and that of a bather on the beach running to the water and plunging herself into the waves. In the former analogy, the stone is inert and therefore entirely passive; in the latter, the bather acts freely. Robert Llewelyn suggests an analogy I find even more consistent with Caussade's thinking — that of floating in water. The swimmer "abandons" herself to the water, trusting and welcoming it, never allowing doubt, anxiety, or fear to cause her to struggle against it. And yet floating is not an entirely passive experience, for the swimmer makes almost imperceptible, perhaps even unconscious adjustments to correspond to the movement of the waves around her. These adjustments have their counterpart in the abandoned soul's acts of faith, hope, and love in response to divine providence.

The question of passivity versus activity is a subtle one in Caussade. Although some passages can seem to commend a passivity that borders on sloth, abandonment as Caussade uses the word is not a state of complete passivity. That would be Quietism, a popular movement in France at the time that sought inner calm by avoiding any activity at all. The church condemned Quietism, and some accused Caussade of being a Quietist. But in several places he expressly distances himself from Quietism. He speaks of an "active loyalty," which is obedience to God in all the duties imposed on us by our way of life, and a "passive loyalty," the acceptance of all God sends. At one moment, abandonment may call for engagement with the world and acts of charity, devotion, or study, while at another moment, it may require passive acceptance of realities beyond our control. Nor is Caussade's abandonment a repudiation or annulling of the human will. It is the aligning of the human will to the will of God, a total giving of the self to God and the desire to obey God at every moment, in all things. "The whole business of self-abandonment is only the business of loving, and love achieves everything," Caussade writes. He sums it up this way: "We must be active in all that the present moment demands of us, but in everything else remain passive and abandoned and do nothing but peacefully await the promptings of God."

Caussade's spirituality is a simple one, accessible to everyone. Compulsive praying and reading are not seeking God's will moment to moment, and grandiose acts of devotion can muddle the mind, he says. Although Caussade had mystical encounters and writes insightfully about them, referring in one of his letters to the darkness "that pleases me," "voluntary annihilation," and being "drowned in nothingness," he is suspicious of a spirituality based on ecstatic experiences. His is a practical, down-to-earth spirituality that makes no distinction between the sacred and the secular, since God comes to us in every circumstance. The life of faith is a process of growing in grace, he says, attained by countless small acts of obedient surrender to the will of God.

Caussade has his detractors. His approach has been faulted for neglecting social justice and the value of sound learning. Jesus sometimes seems peripheral to his spirituality, and he touches only briefly on the Incarnation, the Atonement, and the Trinity. But even those who feel Caussade occasionally goes too far acknowledge that his yearning for God and his uncompromising insistence on abandoning every moment to divine providence sound a note of sanity in a world where materialistic hedonism is trumpeted from every shop window and television set.

IN HIS OWN WORDS

True spirituality

God's activity runs through the universe. It wells up and around and through every created thing. Where they are, there it is also. It precedes them, accompanies them, follows them. They need merely to allow its waves to carry them on. If kings and their ministers, princes of the church and of the world, priests, soldiers, and ordinary people knew this, they could easily become very holy! They would need do nothing more than faithfully carry out the simple duties of Christianity and those called for by their station in life, cheerfully accept all the troubles that come their way, and submit to God's will in all they do and suffer (but of course without seeking any kind of trouble for themselves). . . . This is the true spirituality, valid everywhere and for everybody. . . . It is the ready acceptance of all that comes to us at each moment in our lives.

Abandonment, 1.3

The best and holiest thing

What God arranges for us to experience at each moment is the best and holiest thing that could happen to us.

Abandonment, 1.4

Are you wiser than God?

If you are unsatisfied with what God chooses for you, will anything please you? Does the food prepared for you by God himself disgust you? . . . What else do you want? Why do you look elsewhere? Are you wiser than God? Why do you seek anything but what he desires? Do you suppose that God, in his wisdom and goodness, can be wrong?

Abandonment, 1.7

"Follow the beloved"

Let us, as faithful souls, happy and tireless, follow the beloved as he grandly strides across the heavens. He sees everything. He walks above slender blades of grass and the cedar groves, and treads both the grains of sand and the mountain peaks. Anywhere we have walked, he has visited, and if we seek him continually we shall always find him, anywhere we go. No peace can exceed the peace we enjoy when faith discloses God to us in every created thing. Everything dark grows bright and what is bitter becomes sweet.

Abandonment, 2.2

Finding what is necessary

We can find all that is necessary in the present moment. We need never worry about whether to pray or remain silent, to withdraw into solitude or mix with people, to read or write, to meditate or clear our minds of every thought. Poverty and riches, sickness and health, life and death — none of this matters at all. What matters is what each moment brings, by the will of God. We must strip ourselves naked, renounce every desire for created things, and hold onto nothing of ourselves and for ourselves. That is the way to submit totally to God's will and thereby delight him. Our sole satisfaction must be to live in the present moment as if there were nothing to look for beyond it.

Abandonment, 2.10

Prayer of surrender

Your will is enough for me. I am happy to live and die as it ordains. I delight in it for itself alone, not because of what it does for me. It pervades everything and makes divine whatever it touches. Because of your will, it is as if I lived in heaven. Every moment is part of what you are doing, and whether living or dead, nothing makes me happier. No more shall I count the times and manner of your approach, my beloved: you are always welcome. I think, dear will of God, that you have revealed your majesty to me so that now nothing I do can fall outside its embrace, which is the same yesterday, tomorrow, and forever.

Abandonment, 2.11

Live in the dark

When God lives in us . . . we are abandoned and live in the dark. We are forgotten; death and nothingness are our portion. We know our needs and our wretchedness, but we do not know whether or from whence help will come. But we are not worried. We wait quietly for someone to come and help us, our thoughts ever fixed on heaven.

Abandonment, 3.1

Prayer of abandonment

You, Lord, are all I want or need. Use this little creature as you wish. Everything is yours, is from you and for you. I no longer have anything to tend to or do. Not a single moment is mine to control, for all is yours. I don't try to add anything to my standing or take anything away; I don't ask or even think about anything. It is all for you to deal with. Holiness, perfection, salvation, spiritual direction, repentance — all these are your concern, not mine. My place is to be content with you and do nothing that would attach me to anything. I leave all to your good pleasure.

Abandonment, 3.6

Holiness is for all

Not everyone can hope for the same special favors, but everyone can have the same love, the same abandonment, and the same God. Hence all can, without distinction, reach the heights of holiness.

Abandonment, 3.7

The faithful soul

The truly faithful soul, versed in the secrets of God, lives in peace. It is never frightened by things that happen to it, but comforted, for it knows beyond doubt that God guides it. It accepts everything as a manifestation of God's grace, paying no attention to itself but only to what God is doing. Love inspires it to perform its tasks faithfully and with care. Except for minor defects that grace can use for its purposes, the only thing a soul utterly abandoned to God sees with any clarity is what grace is doing.

Abandonment, 4.2

The darkness of faith

There is a kind of holiness in which all God's messages are bright and clear, but there is another kind, one of utterly quiet faith, in which everything God tells us is shrouded in an impenetrable darkness that obscures his throne. We feel confused, as if in the shadows. Like the prophet, at these times we are often afraid of running smack into a rock as we move through the dark. We should not be afraid, for we are on the right road, led by God. Nothing could be safer or less likely to lead us astray than the darkness of faith. Do we insist on knowing which way to go in this darkness? Go wherever you wish — it doesn't matter. No one can get lost when there is no road to be found.

Abandonment, 6.1

God's tapestry

What God does is like the front of a lovely tapestry. The worker creating the tapestry sees only the back as he stitches with his needle, but all those stitches are creating a splendid picture, the great beauty of which appears only when every stitch is done, and only from the other side.

Abandonment, 6.3

God in the ordinary

To know that God is working in every single event, at every moment, is the deepest knowledge of God's ways one can have in this life. It is a continuous revelation, an endlessly renewed converse with God. . . . When God gives himself this way, common things become extraordinary and nothing appears amiss. The very path we trod is itself so extraordinary that there is no need to ornament it with extraneous wonders. There may be nothing in it to dazzle the senses, but it is a miracle, a constant delight that turns every little thing into something rare and wonderful.

Abandonment, 6.11

Confound and punish me

O my God, if through ignorance or self-will I should ever desire anything but your will, may I be always confounded and punished, not because of your justice, but because of your pity and great mercy.

Letter 6

Suffering well

To suffer peacefully is to suffer well, and all the more so when we decline to make pretentious acts of acceptance.

Letter 19

Drowned in nothingness

You are convinced that you do nothing and deserve nothing — so there you are, drowned in nothingness. You are most fortunate since beyond any doubt, from the moment we are nothing, we are in God who is everything! What a precious state is nothingness! We must pass through it before we can be filled with God, because God cannot fill us with his Holy Spirit until we are totally empty. So you see, what troubles and worries you is the very thing that should calm you and fill you with holy joy in God.

Letter 20

Our spiritual weapons

Your main weapons must be divine love, infinite gratitude for God's mercy, simple trust in him, and a profound mistrust of yourself, but never with despair and always with peace.

Letter 26

Grace

You say that God often deprives you of the feeling of grace. Name one of his beloved friends to whom he has given this tangible assurance without interruption. . . . The saints themselves were never sure — and now you complain that you are not, either!

Letter 30

Doubt

If you doubt the truth of religion, don't worry about it. Doubt is not necessarily a bad sign. On the contrary, in some people, it signifies that God wants to lead them along the surer path of pure and simple faith, without the sensations and delights he gives as he may choose. To wait on God requires no effort (except against sin), but only peace and contentment. When you cannot manage to make an act of faith, say to yourself: "Oh, well. God sees everything that is done. He has seen my desire, so he will strengthen me to do it when he wishes. He is the Master. May his holy will and that only be my will as well, for I am only in this world to accomplish his will. It is my wealth and treasure. Let God give other people enlightenment, mercies, gifts, sweet spiritual awareness, as it may please him. For me, I want to be rich in such things only if that is his wish for me."

Letter 31

FOR REFLECTION AND DISCUSSION

How does one discern God's will in the present moment?

Which do you find more challenging — "active loyalty" to God or "passive loyalty" to God?

Is God's will something you are or something you do?

Do you find it easier to discern God's will for you or to live into it?

List the changes that would occur where you live if Caussade's spirituality became the norm.

How would you introduce Caussade's teaching to someone trapped in a dead-end job? To someone in prison? To someone confined to a wheelchair? To someone married to an abuser?

Chapter 21

JOHN WESLEY / CHARLES WESLEY
1703-1791 / 1707-1788

Methodism

WHEN SUSANNA WESLEY gave birth to her son Charles on December 18, 1707, it was her eighteenth child. She was to bear yet one more — a total of nineteen children in twenty-one years. Stunning though such fecundity may be to modern women, it probably seemed unremarkable to Susanna, since she herself was the twenty-fifth child of her father. Ten of the nineteen children born to Susanna and her husband, the Reverend Samuel Wesley, rector of Epworth in Lincolnshire, survived into adulthood: three sons and seven daughters. Two of the sons, John and Charles, made enormous contributions to Christian spirituality.

The perpetual presence — and frequent deaths — of children wasn't the only challenging feature of the Wesley household. Samuel was restless, high-minded, and uncompromising, and Susanna was at least his intellectual equal, a student of Greek, Latin, and French who knew the writings of the early church fathers. The Wesley children were curious and bright, fostering lively political and religious discussions over dinner. In 1701 Samuel moved out of the rectory and refused to have any dealings with his wife because she would not say "Amen" when he prayed for King William III. The marriage was saved, it seems, by the death of the king a year later, at which point Samuel moved back in, the conception of John following immediately upon his return.

A fire consumed the rectory in 1709, with young John narrowly escaping with his life. A new rectory was constructed, and for six months in 1717, evenings there were interrupted by strange voices, doors slamming, chains rattling, dishes breaking, and thumps on the floor, all emanating from the attic. This mysterious presence proved, however, to be a benign and courteous member of the household, lifting door latches when the Wesley daughters moved from room to room and refraining from making noises when Susanna appealed for quiet during her prayer time. The Wesley daughters happily named their cryptic guest "Old Jeffrey" and learned that they could bait him — and increase the noises — by making disparaging remarks about his intelligence. Accounts of Old Jeffrey's shenanigans survive from several family members, including John.

It is not for their expertise with poltergeists, however, that history reveres John and Charles Wesley. Although their names are primarily (and rightly) associated with the Methodist Church, the Wesley brothers' warm Christian devotion has impacted Anglicans and Protestants of virtually every stripe, especially in Britain and America. John enrolled at Christ Church College, Oxford, in 1725 and began reading Thomas à Kempis,

Jeremy Taylor, William Law (then just beginning his literary career), and other spiritual authors. "Instantly I resolved to dedicate all my life to God, all my thoughts and words and actions, being thoroughly convinced that there was no medium but that every part of my life (not some only) must be sacrificed to God or to myself: that is, in effect, to the devil," he wrote. Charles followed his older brother to Christ Church College and was initially more attracted to typical undergraduate diversions than to religion, commenting in response to John's urging him to a more faithful discipline, "What, you would have me to be a saint all at once?" But it was Charles, after he began weekly attendance at Holy Communion, who was first called a "methodist" (like "puritan," the term was originally one of derision). The two brothers soon joined with several other students to form an informal group named "the Holy Club," which was devoted to academic study, sacramental observance, prayer, and good works.

John was the more gifted leader. Structure and organization came naturally to him, both in his behavior and in his thinking. He was ordained in 1728, and for the next ten years (including an unhappy two-year stint as a missionary in Savannah, Georgia), he preached in his father's pulpit in Epworth and in churches and meetinghouses wherever he could gain an invitation.

What is usually (and not entirely correctly) called John Wesley's "conversion" came on May 24, 1738, at a meeting in a house on London's Aldersgate Street, where he "felt my heart strangely warmed" while listening to a reading of Martin Luther's preface to Romans. His preaching after Aldersgate began to appeal as much to the heart as to the mind. "Enthusiasm" was much feared in the staid British pulpits of the day, and as Wesley's preaching grew more heartfelt, invitations to preach became fewer. His friend George Whitefield suggested that if barred from the nation's pulpits, he could preach in the open air. This idea struck Wesley as "strange" and "vile," but on April 2, 1739, he accepted Whitefield's recommendation and preached his first open-air sermon. He delivered his last such sermon fifty years later, and between them came thousands of sermons — some in churches, some in fields, some on street corners. Wesley traversed Britain again and again, riding an estimated 250,000 miles on horseback, preaching wherever he could gather a crowd. And gather them he did — crowds of several hundred were commonplace. He eventually came to see the entire world as his parish, and he often began preaching at five o'clock in the morning.

The eighteenth century was a time of wrenching social change in England. It was largely the educated and secure who frequented services of the Church of England, but the masses who were leaving the countryside and thronging to the cities seeking jobs in the newly emerging factories had no relationship to the established church. It was often these people who responded to the impassioned preacher who sought them out and addressed them in the fields and streets.

What did John Wesley actually say when he preached? Wesley was a subtle and learned thinker, and his preaching was not mere emotionalism. He affirmed the central part played by the power and grace of God in the Christian life while also allowing room for individual freedom and decision. He began with the conviction that everyone is a sinner, estranged from God and therefore blocked from the benefits of God's love. Those who know this realize they are lost, a burden made only heavier by compulsive attempts to set things right through good works and religious observances. All the while, God is seeking to attract the sinner's attention, what might be called a divine "wooing." Wesley calls this "prevenient" or "preventing" (preceding) grace. Prevenient grace stirs the conscience and makes the sinner hunger for God. Then comes the breakthrough, such as the one that occurred to Wesley that evening in Aldersgate Street, when he finally trusted in Christ alone and felt an "assurance" that Christ had taken away his sins, "even mine." The sinner now becomes aware of God's "saving" or "justifying" grace and begins to experience the love of God in his heart. Finally, secure in the knowledge that God has acted on his behalf, the sinner receives "sanctifying" grace and begins to be transformed into the likeness of Christ. A key element in Wesleyan spirituality is that God acts not only *for* the believer, granting him a new status as justified sinner, but also *in* the believer, reshaping his thoughts, priorities, and relationships.

John Wesley was a gifted and far-sighted organizer. When converts came forward after hearing him preach, he organized them into small groups of a dozen or so persons and entrusted the leadership to local people who would still be there when Wesley himself moved on. This placed relationships at the heart of Wesleyan spirituality and kept it from slipping into an individualistic piety. Wesleyan chapels began springing up throughout the country where these small groups met for fellowship and worship. Both the Wesley brothers were in fact catholic churchmen in many ways. The historic church and its worship were integral to their faith, and they insisted that those drawn to their chapels partake regularly of the sacraments of the church. Hundreds of Charles's hymns were centered on the Eucharist. Methodist meetings were never to be scheduled at the same time the local parish church was holding services.

For seventeen years Charles was an itinerant preacher as well. His wife, Sarah, traveled with him and led the singing at evangelistic meetings for their first ten years together. Charles gave up itinerant preaching in 1756, however, in favor of a more settled life as a parish priest, first in Bristol and then in London. His marriage was a happy one that produced eight children, three of whom survived infancy. (John's marriage was childless and often strained.)

While the two brothers shared the same warm piety and both were captivating preachers, writing hymns was Charles's real passion. It seems he almost thought in verse. Perpetually absent-minded, he composed hymns in his head whenever the spirit moved him, often oblivious to the company of others around him. Charles Wesley wrote approximately nine thousand hymns, many of them running to twenty or more stanzas — an average of three hymns a week for sixty years. At first his hymns were sung only in Methodist chapels, but they soon gained a following in other Christian denominations as well. Four hundred of them are still sung today somewhere in the world.

In one respect, Charles's influence exceeds that of his more famous brother, for while few people can quote anything John Wesley said, Charles's hymns are beloved the world over, and millions of Christians can sing a few lines from one or more of them — "Come, Thou Long-expected Jesus," "Hark! the Herald Angels Sing," "O for a Thousand Tongues to Sing," "Jesus Christ Is Risen Today." It was through the singing of Charles Wesley's hymns, perhaps as much as through preaching, that Methodist spirituality was planted and nurtured.

Traditional Anglicans scorned these songs at first because of their warm, personal tone that appealed to the emotions as well as to the intellect and their liberal use of the first-person singular pronoun. Prior to 1700, only biblical and liturgical texts were sung in public worship in Britain, if anything was sung at all (and often it was not). Emotional songs that referred to the singer rather than to God were seen as vain, even blasphemous. But Wesley did not hesitate to season his songs with phrases like "*I* seek to touch *my* Lord," "keep *me* ever thine," and "thy blood shed for *me*." Such references bring the message of the hymn directly to the worshiper and invite her not only to learn about her Lord but to *experience* her Lord. Charles Wesley's hymns also serve to teach characteristic Wesleyan themes such as God's invitation to all persons to be reconciled to him (not just the elect, as the Calvinists taught), the centrality of the death and resurrection of Christ, the joy of an obedient life, growth in holiness following conversion, and the Eucharist as a means of grace in the believer's life.

John and Charles remained devoted to each other until the end, but one difference is worth noting. While both were loyal to the Church of England, John's frustration at the refusal of church authorities to provide ordained ministers — and thereby the sacraments — for the American colonies caused him, toward the end of his life and reluctantly, to authorize some of his lay preachers in America to baptize and celebrate the Holy Communion. Charles vigorously opposed this move as schismatic. A new Christian denomination, the Methodist Church, was the result, and it is hard to see how the Wesleyan witness could have continued in America without John Wesley's ordinations. From that witness later sprang the holiness and Pentecostal movements, to say nothing of the new vigor it brought to the Anglican and other older churches.

IN THEIR OWN WORDS

From John Wesley

Aldersgate

In the evening I went very unwillingly to a society in Aldersgate Street, where one was reading Luther's preface to the Epistle to the Romans. About a quarter before nine, while he was describing the change which God works in the heart through faith in Christ, I felt my heart strangely warmed. I felt I did trust in Christ, Christ alone, for salvation; and an assurance was given me that he had taken away my sins, even mine, and saved me from the law of sin and death.

Journal

Regeneration

Men are generally lost in the hurry of life, in the business or pleasures of it, and seem to think that their regeneration, their new nature, will spring and grow up within them, with as little care and thought of their own as their bodies were conceived and have attained their full strength and stature; whereas, there is nothing more certain than that the Holy Spirit will not purify our nature, unless we carefully attend to his motions. . . .

Sermon, "On Grieving the Holy Spirit"

Salvation

This then is the salvation which is through faith, even in the present world: a salvation from sin, and the consequences of sin, both often expressed in the word *justification;* which, taken in the largest sense, implies a deliverance from guilt and punishment, by the atonement of Christ actually applied to the soul of the sinner now believing on him, and a deliverance from the whole body of sin, through Christ formed in his heart. So that he who is thus justified, or saved by faith, is *indeed* born again.

Sermon, "Salvation by Faith"

The Lord's Supper

I showed at large (1) That the Lord's supper was ordained by God to be a means of conveying to men either preventing, or justifying, or sanctifying grace, according to their several necessities. (2) That the persons for whom it was ordained are all those who know and feel that they want the grace of God, either to restrain them from sin, or to show their sins forgiven, or to renew their souls in the image of God. (3) That inasmuch as we come to his table not to give him anything but to receive whatsoever he sees best for us, there is no previous preparation indispensably necessary but a desire to receive whatsoever he pleases to give. (4) That no fitness is required at the time of communicating but a sense of our state of utter sinfulness and helplessness.

Journal

The use of money

Gain all you can, without hurting either yourself or your neighbor, in soul or body, by applying hereto with unintermitted diligence and with all the understanding which God has given you. Save all you can, by cutting off every expense which serves only to indulge foolish desire; to gratify either the desire of the flesh, the desire of the eye, or the pride of life; waste nothing, living or dying, on sin or folly, whether for yourself or your children. And then give all you can, or in other words, give all you have to God. . . . Render to God not a tenth, not a third, not a half, but all that is God's, be it more or less, by employing all on yourself, your household, the household of faith, and all mankind, in such a manner that you may give a good account of your stewardship when you can be no longer stewards. . . .

Sermon, "On the Use of Money"

Real religion

Here then we see in the clearest, strongest light, what is real religion: A restoration of man by him that bruises the serpent's head to all that the old serpent deprived him of, a restoration not only to the favor but likewise to the image of God, implying not merely deliverance from sin, but being filled with the fulness of God. . . . nothing short of this is Christian religion. . . . Not *anything* else: Do not imagine an outward form, a round of duties, both in public and private is religion! Do not suppose that honesty, justice, and whatever is called *morality* (though excellent in its place) is religion! And least of all dream that orthodoxy, right opinion (vulgarly called *faith*) is religion. Of all religious dreams, this is the vainest, which takes hay and stubble for gold tried in the fire!

Sermon, "The End of Christ's Coming"

Sanctifying grace

There is likewise great variety in the manner and time of God's bestowing his sanctifying grace, whereby he enables his children to give him their whole heart, which we can in no wise account for. . . . God undoubtedly has reasons, but those reasons are generally hid from the children of men. Once more: Some of those who are enabled to love God with all their heart and with all their soul retain the same blessing, without any interruption, till they are carried to Abraham's bosom; others do not retain it, although they are not conscious of having grieved the Holy Spirit of God. This also we do not understand: We do not herein "know the mind of the Spirit."

Sermon, "The Imperfection of Human Knowledge"

Preventing grace

. . . No man living is entirely destitute of what is vulgarly called *natural conscience*. But it is not natural: It is more properly termed *preventing grace*. Every man has a greater or less measure of this, which waiteth not for the call of man. Everyone has, sooner or later, good desires, although the generality of men stifle them before they can strike deep root or produce any considerable fruit. Everyone has some measure of that light, some faint glimmering ray, which, sooner or later, more or less, enlightens every man that cometh into the world. . . . So that no man sins because he has not grace, but because he does not use the grace which he has.

Sermon, "On Working Out Our Own Salvation"

From Charles Wesley

Jesu, Lover of My Soul

Jesu, Lover of my soul,
    Let me to thy bosom fly,
While the nearer waters roll,
    While the tempest still is high:
Hide me, O my Savior, hide,
    Till the storm of life be past:

Safe into the haven guide;
    O receive my soul at last.

Other refuge have I none,
    Hangs my helpless soul on thee:
Leave, ah! Leave me not alone,
    Still support and comfort me.
All my trust on thee is stayed;
    All my help from thee I bring:
Cover my defenseless head
    With the shadow of thy wing.

Wilt thou not regard my call?
    Wilt thou not accept my prayer?
Lo! I sink, I faint, I fall,
    Lo! on thee I cast my care:
Reach me out thy gracious hand!
    While I of thy strength receive,
Hoping against hope I stand,
    Dying, and behold I live!

Thou, O Christ, art all I want,
    More than all in thee I find:
Raise the fallen, cheer the faint,
    Heal the sick, and lead the blind.
Just and holy is thy name,
    I am all unrighteousness,
False and full of sin I am,
    Thou art full of truth and grace.

Plenteous grace with thee is found,
    Grace to cover all my sin:
Let the healing streams abound,
    Make and keep me pure within:
Thou of life the fountain art:
    Freely let me take of thee,
Spring thou up within my heart,
    Rise to all eternity!

Redemption Hymn No. 9 (1747)

Love divine, all loves excelling,
  Joy of heaven, to earth come down,
Fix in us thy humble dwelling,
  All thy faithful mercies crown:
Jesu, thou art all compassion,
  Pure, unbounded love thou art,
Visit us with thy salvation,
  Enter every trembling heart.

Breathe, O breathe thy loving Spirit,
  Into every troubled breast,
Let us all in thee inherit,
  Let us find that second rest:
Take away our power of sinning,
  Alpha and Omega be,
End of faith as its beginning,
  Set our hearts at liberty.

Come, almighty, to deliver,
  Let us all thy life receive;
Suddenly return, and never,
  Nevermore thy temples leave.
Thee we would be always blessing,
  Serve thee as thy hosts above,
Pray, and praise thee without ceasing,
  Glory in thy perfect love

Finish then thy new creation,
  Pure and spotless let us be,
Let us see thy great salvation,
  Perfectly restored in thee:
Changed from glory into glory,
  Till in heaven we take our place,
Till we cast our crowns before thee,
  Lost in wonder, love, and praise!

FOR REFLECTION AND DISCUSSION

Have you had an experience like John Wesley's at Aldersgate? If so, how is your life different because of it?

Can "enthusiasm" be dangerous?

How are John Wesley's three kinds of grace related, and how have you experienced them in your life?

The three verbs *earn, save,* and *give* are central in Wesley's sermon "On the Use of Money." What do you think accounts for his omission of the verbs *spend* and *borrow*?

Jot down some elements in Wesley's theology that have entered American popular religion. Then jot down some that have not.

Look in the index of your hymnal for hymns by Charles Wesley. Read them, then choose one and write a few sentences about what it means to you.

What dangers or excesses are possible from singing hymns written in the first-person singular? Can you think of particular texts that seem to encourage such dangers and excesses?

Chapter 22

SØREN KIERKEGAARD

1813-1855

The Spirituality of Paradox

Y OU WILL FIND at least four Søren Kierkegaards rumbling through the pages of academic studies of his work. First noticed was Kierkegaard the literary prankster. He was a meticulous Danish stylist (much of which is lost in translation), but his early works were convoluted in structure and often spoke through several voices ascribed to pseudonymous authors with strange names. It seemed he was daring his readers to try to decipher his meaning. Then came Kierkegaard the bipolar neurotic. For several decades after his death, most commentators saw his work as an effort to come to terms with two troubled relationships, one with his wealthy, imaginative, and guilt-ridden father, the other with Regine Olsen, a young woman he adored but whom he convinced to terminate their engagement for reasons never disclosed. Then, in the mid-twentieth century, when existentialism was the rage in the sophisticated salons of continental Europe, its proponents discovered a Kierkegaard who had stood isolated and defiant before the advancing tide of nihilism and was therefore the first of their number, the founder of their philosophical school.

Something can be found in Kierkegaard's varied and voluminous writings to support each of these three readings of his work, and I do not discount them. But I shall here deal mainly with a fourth Søren Kierkegaard, with Kierkegaard as he saw himself. He commented toward the end of his life that all his published work, including his perplexing early philosophical treatises, had been meant to explore the question of "how to become a Christian" and to "re-introduce Christianity to Christendom." And though his reputation rests largely on those philosophical works, he published at the same time several volumes entitled *Edifying Discourses*, which he might have called sermons had he been ordained. His last book of philosophy appeared in 1846, and thereafter he produced nothing but overtly religious works until his death in 1855.

Kierkegaard is known as a brooding, morose figure, a reputation only partially deserved. His father had left him a small fortune so that he never had to work for a living and could devote himself entirely to his literary pursuits. Following his mysteriously aborted relationship with Regine Olsen, she married someone else, and Kierkegaard never had another serious relationship. He was often the butt of cruel jokes, first as a bookish schoolboy and later as an awkward-looking literary dilettante around Copenhagen, a town of a hundred thousand people in his day. His dour reputation arises from those early psychological studies of his life and from his having been embraced by later existentialists who gloried in gloom and claimed him as one of their own. Moreover, some of Kierkegaard's best-known works bear names like *Fear and Trembling, The Concept of Anxiety,* and *The Sickness unto Death,* hardly suggesting that their author was a cheery soul. Finally, his health began to fail in his late thirties, and he died at the age of forty-two. A closer reading of all Kierkegaard's literary output, however, discloses a man with a splendid (if sometimes caustic) sense of humor who, while no stranger to inner suffering and doubt, was motivated by an orthodox Christian faith expressed in rich passages on divine love and hope. There was far more to Søren Kierkegaard than gloom and doom.

The two kinds of writing that come from Kierkegaard's pen are related, and it would be a mistake to ignore either of them. His early philosophical works are very challenging. They debunk Hegelian idealism, the reigning philosophy of the day, which claimed to have created a synthesis of all previous thought and to have superceded Christianity.

In his *Philosophical Fragments* Kierkegaard explores faith as paradoxical, a favorite theme, and contrasts Christ to Socrates. Socrates was a teacher only in the sense that he asked probing questions that enabled the thinking student to pull the truth from within himself. Since the truth lay within the student all along, the real teacher, the real discloser or discoverer of the truth, was the student, not Socrates. The teacher was important only as the facilitator of the student's self-discovery and was, at least in theory, unnecessary and dispensable. The moment of discovery could, again in theory, be any moment at all. Kierkegaard contrasted this understanding with the Christian view of human beings as essentially without the truth (or sinful) and therefore standing desperately in need of a revelation (or redemption). Christianity sees the teacher (Christ) as absolutely essential because the truth is made known only on the initiative of the teacher, and at a specific moment in time chosen by the teacher. The important thing now ceases to be the content of the teaching and becomes the teacher himself, the redeemer, and faith ceases to be a form of knowledge or understanding and becomes a response or relationship to a person. We are left in the end with the ultimate paradox: the eternal enters the world and discloses itself by means of a specific historical person/event.

The oddly titled and constructed *Concluding Unscientific Postscript* is the most daunting of Kierkegaard's works, five times longer than *Philosophical Fragments,* to which it is ostensibly an addendum. Here Kierkegaard virtually creates a new philosophical vocabulary, redefining "existence" as a quality unique to human beings, to be explored and developed by each human person. You are human, unique, and confined in time and space, Kierkegaard says. Therefore, be faithful to your own existence. Religious questions are properly explored not in the arid confines of the academic study, with its useless abstractions and objective formulae, but by every living soul, and with subjective passion, because we have an "infinite interest" in how religious questions are answered. Don't just *be* a Christian, Kierkegaard says, but *become* one — become *subjective*. This does not mean to affirm subjectivity as an idea, but to recognize that truth *is* subjective. Christianity for Kierkegaard is not a set of teachings to be accepted, perhaps glibly and with little thought — that would be to re-introduce objective truth and remove it from the self. It is rather an ardent groping toward a truth that is ever-present but cannot be nailed down — that is part of the paradox of faith.

We turn now to Kierkegaard's religious writings, some written at the same time as his philosophical works and some later. Those who know Kierkegaard only from his philosophical works are sometimes surprised to discover here a Christian of solidly orthodox, Incarnation-centered theology. Yet such theological views are entirely consistent with his philosophical treatises. In these other writings Kierkegaard reflects on biblical passages, writes prayers, and seeks to guide his reader to make the right choices so as to become a real "self" (or an "I"), a person of authentic faith.

What does this faith look like? Kierkegaard says it is a passion, a leap to *exist* in the fullest sense. It is a decision to obey and follow Christ as Pattern — Christ who served and was as nothing to the world. Because faith is interior, subjective, and often hidden, its authenticity cannot depend on outward forms or religious authorities. It issues in ethical behaviors but is not defined by behaviors. It endures, persists, is patient. It is less concerned with defining God than with how it relates to God. The "knight of faith" appears quite ordinary and moves about in the world much like anyone else. He accepts and does not flee from uncertainties and ambiguities, but is at ease with himself, having relinquished the false certainties of the world and then received the world back again. If this seems absurd, that is in keeping with the nature of faith.

When Kierkegaard looked at the nineteenth-century Lutheran Church in Denmark, that is not what he saw. What he did see appalled him — it wasn't Christianity but Christendom, a nation officially but blandly committed to a lifeless Christianity consisting of doctrinal statements and little more. All Danes considered themselves Christian and could say something about Christian teachings — but there were no knights of faith in Denmark, no one willing to suffer with Christ, no one willing to embrace the absurd. A church at peace with the world cannot produce knights of faith, Kierkegaard said. Christendom is the greatest enemy of genuine Christianity. He saw himself as a spy, even a martyr for truth, and therefore set out to skewer the national church. He rails at the Danish church as an institution that has abandoned the Christian gospel, sold out to the false security of objective truths, and lost its soul.

Several features of this picture were among the reasons that later existentialists embraced Kierkegaard. The existentialist movement took its name from the subtitle of one section of *Postscript*, "An Existential Contribution." We see Kierkegaard reveling in subjectivity and denying the validity of objective truth. We see him challenging his reader (and himself) to become a real, autonomous self. We see him seemingly alone and disconnected from others. We see him glorying (some would say wallowing) in paradox and the absurd. We hear him speak of faith as a "leap." And we watch as he pierces the superficial, complacent pieties that surrounded him. All this he had in common with the later existentialists.

Kierkegaard is widely seen today as a prophetic figure, anticipating before anyone else the advent of the secular age, when the old certainties would come under siege and the tide of the sea of faith would recede. He saw this prefigured in the Danish church of his day, which, despite its outward prestige, was a mere shell of faith, soon to be abandoned, in fact, by most of the populace. Much of the gloom with which Kierkegaard's name is associated in the popular mind arose from his sense of this impending loss. Yet he did not lose faith or hope. He is perhaps a patron saint for the modern age.

IN HIS OWN WORDS

A prayer

Lord Jesus Christ, you entered the world not to be served or admired or worshiped in that way. You were the way and the truth and it was not you but your followers who demanded things. Arouse us, then, if we have dozed off in this delusion. Save us from the error of wanting to admire you rather than willingly to follow you and bear your likeness.

Training in Christianity

A prayer

Lord Jesus Christ, so permeate my thoughts that it is obvious I am think-ing of you. How would it be obvious? In my glancing up to the heavens? That could mean I was looking at the stars or at visions or at chimeras. No, but if your example so convicted me that I proclaimed what you teach even though scorned and ridiculed, then people could see in me — not in my glance, but in my daily living — that I was thinking of you.

And you celestial powers, you who support what is good, you heavenly host, help me raise my voice that the whole world may hear it. I have only one word to say, but if the power were given me to utter it, that single phrase, so that it would be fixed and unforgettable, then my choice is al-ready made and I know what I would say: "Our Lord Jesus Christ was nothing; O Christendom, remember this!"

Papers

The king and the maiden

Suppose a king loved a lowly maiden. . . . Then a concern arose within him: . . . Would she be happy living at his side? Would she ever grow confident enough to forget what the king wanted to forget — that he was king and she had been a lowly maiden? For if that happened, where would be the glory of their love? . . . In that case, she would have been happier remaining in obscurity, loved by someone her equal, contented in her humble hut but certain in her love and cheerful all the time. . . . [Or] the king could appear before the lowly maiden in all his splendor, let the sun of his glory rise over her hut, shine on the spot where he appeared, and let her lose herself in adoring admiration. That might satisfy the girl, but it would hardly satisfy the king, for it was the girl's glorification that he sought, not his own, and he would grieve because she did not really understand him; but if he de-ceived her, it would grieve him all the more. . . . So the union could never be achieved by ascent — it must be achieved by descent. . . . the god must become . . . the equal of the lowliest person, take the form of a servant. . . . But this servant form is not something put on like a garment and easily removed. On the contrary, the god must suffer everything, endure everything, experience everything. He must hunger in the desert, thirst in agony, and be forsaken at the time of his death, like the absolute humblest.

Philosophical Fragments, 2

Ancient and modern times

. . . to tell in one sentence the difference between ancient times and our own, we would have to say: "In ancient times only a few people knew the truth, but now everyone knows it; but the conviction with which it is held is inversely proportional to the number of people holding it."

Concluding Unscientific Postscript

How is as important as what

How the truth is accepted is as important as the truth itself, even more so. It does no good to convince millions of the truth if the way they accept it turns it into falsehood.

Concluding Unscientific Postscript

The tasks of faith

Most believers are more afraid of something that is probable than of anything else because they realize that when they hang onto probabilities, they are starting to lose their faith. Faith has two tasks: first to discover in every moment what is improbable, paradoxical; and then to hold firmly to it with an inner passion. . . . Where the understanding despairs, there is faith, making the despair properly decisive, so that the movement of faith does not become a mere exchange where the understanding strikes up bargains.

241

To believe against the understanding is martyrdom; to begin to move the understanding a bit in one's favor is temptation and retrogression.

Concluding Unscientific Postscript

"Objective uncertainty"

Being a Christian is not a matter of *what*, but of *how*. The *how* corresponds to just one thing, the absolute paradox. There can be no mushy talk about "just accept, just accept, just accept," as if that's what being a Christian means. . . . But *to believe* is specifically different from any other inward appropriation. Faith is the objective uncertainty caused by the inner passion's repulsion of the absurd, in this case intensified to the highest degree. This formula applies to believers only, to no one else, not to a lover, an enthusiast, or a thinker, but simply and solely to the believer who is relating to the absolute paradox.

Concluding Unscientific Postscript

Loving God

Let us say someone insists in the most solemn and emphatic terms that he loves God and only God. Moreover, let us say that when asked why he loves God, he says, "Because God is the highest, holiest, and most perfect Being," and then, when asked whether he has ever loved God for a different reason, he says he has not. That man could reasonably be considered a fanatic. . . . The simple and humble thing is to love God because we need him. . . . You may think it noble to love God for his perfection and selfish to love him because we need him, but actually, the latter way is the only way we can love God. Pity the poor person who boldly tries to love God without needing him!

Christian Discourses, 3.3

Either-Or

There is an either-or. It is either God or — the rest does not matter. Choose what you will, if you choose anything but God, you lose out; both you and your choice are lost. The only thing that counts about your other choice is that it is not God. The emphasis is emphatically on God. It is God, as object of our choice, who makes deciding such a tense matter, truly an either-or. If someone, out of frivolity or melancholy, should think there are more than two choices where God is concerned, he is lost — or rather, he has lost God. . . . What does God demand in this either-or? He demands obedience, unconditional obedience. If you do not obey in everything, without conditions, you do not love God. And if you do not love God, you hate him.

The Lilies of the Field and the Birds of the Air, 2

Faith

[Faith] can only be had if it is continually acquired, and can only be acquired if it is continually developed.

Edifying Discourses

Impatience

Impatience assumes many forms. At first it is scarcely recognizable because it is so gentle, flexible, attractive, and energizing, so sad and sympathetic. But when it has exhausted all its art, it finally becomes vociferous and defiant, insisting it can explain everything though it has understood nothing.

Edifying Discourses

Faith, hope, and love

If you continue to aspire to the eternal in faith, you will never be so satisfied that you stop hungering. If you foresee a benign future in hope, you will never be paralyzed by the past, for you will have turned your back on it. If you love God and your fellow-man, you will always have something to do, even in times of greatest need and deepest despair.

Edifying Discourses

Becoming a Christian

Being a Christian poses two dangers. The first comes from the inner suffering of abandoning reason and being crucified to a paradox. . . . Then the Christian encounters the danger of trying to make clear that he is a Christian while living among worldly people. . . . Finally, after all this, the question bursts upon him with great force: how does it ever occur to someone to subject himself to this? Why must I be a Christian when it is so hard? Someone might answer: "Shut up! Christianity is the Absolute, a Must." But someone else could answer: "You must be a Christian because your consciousness of your sin gives you no peace and its pain strengthens you to bear anything, if by so doing you can find redemption." (1848)

The real conflict between Christianity and humanity is that Christianity is *absolute*. It teaches that there is something absolute and that this absolute something demands of the Christian that his life manifest its existence. That is why I say I have never known a Christian — because I have never met anyone whose life manifested *that*. (1848)

It is a mistake to argue with people about what Christianity is, because nearly always what they are really trying to do is defend themselves from any understanding of Christianity. That is because they suspect it is not difficult to understand Christianity — and that if they did understand it, it would interfere with their lives. (1850)

You can see how far Christianity is from being a living reality by looking at me, for despite my knowledge of it, I am no Christian. . . . My position is quite difficult enough. I am not a heathen, to whom an apostle expounds Christianity briefly and pointedly, but a man who must, as it were, discover Christianity on his own, dig down deep to unearth it from the perverted state it has sunk to. (1854)

Diary entries

FOR REFLECTION AND DISCUSSION

When you speak of faith, do you mean something of which you are certain or something of which you are uncertain?
What does it mean to love God?
Is Christian faith paradoxical and absurd, or does it make sense to you?

Is *how* one becomes a Christian more or less important than *what* a Christian believes?

Do you approach life on "either/or" terms, on "both/and" terms, or on "a range of possibilities" terms?

How does the church today resemble and differ from the church Kierkegaard knew?

Write a few sentences outlining what you would say if you could spend an hour with Kierkegaard.

Chapter 23

R. A. TORREY
1856-1928

Fundamentalism

246

T HE FUNDAMENTALIST MOVEMENT takes its name from a series of books published in the United States between 1910 and 1915 called *The Fundamentals: A Testimony to the Truth.* Written by Protestant scholars as "a new statement of the fundamentals of Christianity," the project was a response to the acceptance within mainline Protestant denominations of new scientific theories such as evolution and the new biblical scholarship that questioned the authorship and traditional interpretations of the Bible. The books were sent at no charge (through the generosity of two wealthy laymen) to every pastor, evangelist, theological professor, and theological student in the English-speaking world.

Although some Fundamentalist ideas are less than two centuries old, by seeking to preserve traditional Christian teachings, Fundamentalism provides a spiritual anchor and compass in a world where social and religious change threaten beliefs once assumed to afford stability. It is a resilient spiritual movement more vibrant now than a century ago, repeatedly surprising those who would dismiss it as a passing fad. Fundamentalist churches are growing today around the world.

Fundamentalism is diverse and adaptable, blending elements derived from several streams. These elements are related and often support each other, although not every Fundamentalist thinker embraces them all. Among them are the following:

- *Enlightenment rationalism.* Beginning in the seventeenth century, the Western world began to distrust mystical and intuitive insights, long a staple of Christian spirituality, in favor of observable, demonstrable facts. Scholars call this new understanding the Enlightenment. Many Christians began to view religious truth, including the Bible, the same way. Earlier understandings of a multidimensional Bible, with allegorical, metaphorical, and moral layers of meaning, were discounted, and the Bible came to be seen as a book of facts — historical, scientific, theological. Fundamentalism embraces this new understanding.
- *Biblical inerrancy.* Princeton scholars Charles Hodge (1797-1878) and Benjamin Warfield (1851-1921) developed an intellectually subtle and tightly reasoned defense of the Bible as verbally inspired. They held that God had overseen the biblical writers so that they produced "an errorless record of the matters he designed them to communicate." Hodge and Warfield were Calvinists, however, for whom belief in the verbal inspiration of the Scriptures was not a fundamental tenet of

faith. Their faith centered on the glory of God, which they felt could accommodate various understandings of biblical inspiration. For some later Fundamentalists, however, belief in an inerrant Bible became an essential article of faith.

- *Dispensationalism.* John Nelson Darby (1800-1882), a linguist, scholar, and clergyman from Plymouth, England, devised a theology based on the belief that apocalyptic passages in the Bible contain details of future events, especially of the end times. He divided history into seven epochs or "dispensations," and taught that the seventh, a one-thousand-year period called the millennium, was about to begin. Today "premillennial dispensationalists" hold that Christ will return before the millennium, while "postmillennial dispensationalists" believe he will return after the millennium. Influential dispensationalists have included Cyrus Y. Scofield (1843-1921), editor of the *Scofield Reference Bible;* Hal Lindsey (1929-), author of *The Late, Great Planet Earth;* Jerry Falwell (1933-2007), founder of the Moral Majority; and Tim LaHaye (1926-) and Jerry B. Jenkins (1949-), authors of the popular "Left Behind" novels.
- *The holiness movement.* Beginning in the 1870s and centering on an annual conference at Keswick in the English Lake Country, the holiness movement sought to work out the practical implications of Christian faith. It was ecumenical and emphasized evangelism and instantaneous conversion over gradual spiritual growth, followed by amendment of life. Baptist F. B. Meyer (1847-1929) was the leading early holiness thinker. In addition to influencing Fundamentalism, holiness spirituality has greatly impacted the charismatic and Pentecostal movements.
- *Revivalism.* The eighteenth-century "Great Awakening" in which Puritan theologian Jonathan Edwards (1703-1758) played a leading role was but the first of several periods of renewal in the history of American Protestantism. The nineteenth century saw organized revivals, often featuring itinerant evangelists who gathered large crowds and preached for conversion and an open confession of Christ as Lord and Savior. Such meetings began in the tents of frontier camps but soon spread to urban areas as well. Modern evangelists circle the globe and utilize mass media. Prominent American revivalists have included Charles G. Finney (1792-1875), Dwight L. Moody (1837-1899), Billy Sunday (1862-1935), and Billy Graham (1918-).

• *Bible colleges.* Often shut out of mainline theological schools for lack of formal academic credentials, dispensationalists, holiness preachers, and revivalists founded Bible colleges of their own. These schools turned out energetic, highly committed pastors willing to serve in small, out-of-the-way places shunned by better-educated pastors. They have become vital centers of Fundamentalist life. Among the more important are the Moody Bible Institute in Chicago, William Bell Riley's Northwestern College in Minneapolis, Jerry Falwell's Liberty University in Virginia, and Bob Jones University in South Carolina.

If anyone exemplifies all of these elements of Fundamentalist spirituality, it is surely Reuben Archer Torrey — pastor, educator, author, Bible scholar, mass evangelist, and man of prayer. Torrey did not fit the stereotype of the typical "hot gospeler." Cool, unemotional, controlled, meticulously dressed, and almost mathematical in his approach, he was not one to weep, wail, or wave his Bible to woo a crowd — but woo the crowds he did. Part of Torrey's appeal lay in his unswerving conviction of the truth of the biblical message and his equally unswerving devotion to proclaiming that message. He stayed focused and would not be sidetracked; doubt and ambiguity were unknown to him. Torrey lived what he believed and refused to compromise or water down his message to make it palatable. Absolutely devoted to his Lord, he demanded the same devotion of others — and got it.

The son of a New York City corporate lawyer and banker, Torrey entered Yale University at the age of fifteen. Religion was not on his mind as he enjoyed student life. But Torrey became depressed and began to think of suicide. At the age of eighteen, in a desperate moment, he knelt at his bed and prayed, "O God, deliver me from this burden — I'll even preach!" Three years later, while listening to Dwight L. Moody preach in New Haven, Torrey decided to spend his life winning souls for Christ. He was ordained a Congregationalist minister in 1878 and served a pastorate in Ohio for five years, where he also married. The Torreys eventually had five children.

In 1882 Torrey went to Germany to study the new higher criticism, where he became — briefly, as it turned out — a theological liberal. Upon his return to America, he accepted the pastorate of a small church in Minneapolis. It grew quickly. In 1889 Dwight L. Moody named Torrey the first superintendent of his Chicago Evangelization Society (later, Moody Bible

Institute), a position Torrey held until 1908. He became a renowned Bible teacher and also pastored a Chicago church where he regularly preached to congregations of two thousand or more.

It was in 1902 that Torrey began his globe-trotting evangelism, with a month-long series of preaching missions in Australia during which twenty thousand Australians came forward to commit their lives to Christ. In the months that followed, Torrey preached in New Zealand, India, and England, with similar results. For the next two decades, Torrey traveled the world, with vocalist Charles M. Alexander, preaching to tens of thousands at a time. He also conducted training seminars and Bible conferences and continued to lecture at the Moody Bible Institute. He published forty books, many of them transcriptions of his sermons and evangelistic addresses. Torrey wrote three of the essays in *The Fundamentals*.

R. A. Torrey's spirituality was Christ-centered, based on the view that Christ had died in place of sinners, bearing on our behalf the punishment we deserve. It is by faith, accepting Jesus Christ, believing the promises found in the Bible, that we appropriate that saving act to ourselves, he said. Those who do not accept Christ will suffer eternal punishment. In all this, Torrey did not diverge from orthodox Protestant understandings, but his preaching was distinguished by his distinctive use of Scripture, his appeal for instantaneous conversion, and his emphases on the new birth, the baptism with the Holy Spirit, and the return of Jesus in the flesh.

Torrey's method was the same in virtually every sermon: his preaching was systematic, orderly, planned. He began with a proposition, then supported it with several biblical citations, and then illustrated it with a striking incident, often from his personal experience — his certainty arose from his having tested his beliefs in practice. He typically ended his addresses with an appeal for the listener to make a public confession of Jesus Christ.

The heart of R. A. Torrey's preaching was his use of the Scriptures. Since he was convinced that the words of the Bible had come directly from God, Torrey had no interest in the historical context or human authorship of biblical texts and was skeptical of those who, looking for symbolic and metaphorical meanings, found things in the Bible contrary to its plain sense. The Bible contained facts disclosed by God, he said, not the opinions of human authors, and the words meant precisely what they appeared to mean. Moreover, Torrey believed the whole of the Bible was about Jesus Christ, and texts from various parts of the Bible could therefore be placed next to each other, applied to Christ, and treated as if they were from the same author — which Torrey believed they were. Benjamin Warfield, among others, found this use of the Bible disconcerting, faulting Torrey for trying "to formulate doctrine on the basis of a general impression derived from a cursory survey of the scriptural material or on the basis of the specific study of a few outstanding texts isolated from their contexts and then to seek support for it in more or less detached passages."

Controversial as it may have been, Torrey's method of preaching brought great results, and he was loath to depart from it. When a friend suggested that he preach a series of sermons on a topic in the news of the day, Torrey responded, "What is wrong with the message I have given all these years? Isn't my theme true to the teaching of the Bible? When God ceases to bless the message I am giving, I will change it."

Torrey spoke and wrote eloquently of the power of prayer. Prayer for him was largely petition, asking a supernatural God to guide, protect, and bless human endeavors. How do we know God answers prayer? In typical fashion, Torrey says we know it first because the Bible says so, but he also knew it because God had answered his own prayers. "Time and time again throughout the years I have asked God for things which he alone could give, for things that there was no probability whatever of my getting, and I have told no one else of my need, and God has given me the very things I asked." God promises to answer the prayers of the faithful, Torrey said, and if not all prayers are answered, it is because we are "not right with God and in a position where God can wisely answer prayer." The trouble with many so-called revivals, Torrey wrote, is that they are man-made and not God-sent, worked up and not prayed down: "Prayer is the key that unlocks all the storehouses of God's infinite grace and power. All that God is, and all that God has, is at the disposal of prayer. But we must use the key. Prayer can do anything that God can do, and as God can do anything, prayer is omnipotent."

IN HIS OWN WORDS

Biblical inspiration

If we can make it clear that the writers of the various books of the Bible were inspired of God, that they were so gifted and taught and led and governed by the Holy Spirit in their utterances as recorded in the Bible, that they taught the truth and nothing but the truth, that their teachings were absolutely without error — then we have in the Bible a court of final appeal and of infallible wisdom to which we can go to settle every question of doctrine or duty. But if the writers of the Bible were "inspired" only in the vague and uncertain sense that Shakespeare, Browning, and many other men of genius were inspired, only inspired to the extent that their minds were made more keen to see the truth than ordinary men, but still only in such a way that they made mistakes . . . then we are all at sea, in hopeless confusion, so that each generation must settle for itself what the Holy Spirit meant to say through blundering reporters; and it is absolutely certain that no generation can determine with anything approximating accuracy what the Spirit meant. . . .

The Fundamental Doctrines of the Christian Faith

Inerrant Word of God

When we read the words that Jeremiah wrote and Isaiah wrote and Paul wrote and John wrote and James wrote and Jude wrote and the other Bible writers wrote, we are reading what God says. We are not listening to the voice of man, but we are listening to the voice of God. "The Word of God" which we have in the Old and New Testaments, as originally given, is absolutely inerrant down to the smallest word and smallest letter or part of a letter.

Fundamental Doctrines

God in history

The God of the Bible is a God who is personally and actively present in the affairs of the universe today. He sustains, governs, cares for the world he has created; he shapes the whole present history of the world. He has a present personal interest and an active hand in the affairs of men and he it is that is back of all the events that are occurring today. He reigns and makes even the wrath of men to praise him, and the remainder of wrath doth he restrain. The Kaiser may rage, armies may clash, force and violence and outrage may seem triumphant for the passing hour, but God stands back of all; and through all the confusion and the discord and the turmoil and the agony and the ruin, through all the outrageous atrocities that are making men's *hearts* stand still with horror, he is carrying out his own purposes of love and making all things work together for good to those who love him.

Fundamental Doctrines

Born again

Have you been born again? I put this question to every man and woman here. I do not ask you whether you are a church member. I do not ask if you have been baptized. I do not ask, have you gone regularly to the communion. I do not ask, have you turned over a new leaf. I do not ask, are you an amiable, cultured, intelligent, moral, socially delightful gentleman or lady. I *ask you, have you been born again?* If not, you are outside the Kingdom of God and you are bound for an everlasting hell unless you are born again. But if you are not already born again, you may be born again today, you may be born again before you leave this building, you may be born again right now. . . . It is up to you to say whether or not you will do it.

Fundamental Doctrines

Impossible to believe

The Bible is simply God's love story, the story of the love of a holy God to a sinful world. That is the most amazing thing in the Bible. People tell us the Bible is full of things that it is impossible to believe. I know of nothing else so impossible to believe as that a holy God should love a sinful world, and should love such individuals as you and me, as the Bible says he does. But impossible as it is to believe, it is true.

Revival Addresses

Believing on the Lord Jesus

What does it mean to believe on the Lord Jesus? I have given a very careful and thorough study to this subject; I have gone all through my Bible looking up the word "believe," and all words related to it, and I have found out what I suspected to be the fact when I began, viz., that "believe" means in the Bible just exactly what it means in modern speech. What is it to believe on a man? To believe on a man means to put confidence in him as what he claims to be. To believe on a physician means to put confidence in him as a physician, resulting in your placing your case in his hands. To believe in a teacher is to put your confidence in him as a teacher and accept what he teaches; to believe in a banker means to put your confidence in him as a banker and to put your money in his bank. And to believe on the Lord Jesus means to put your confidence in him as what he claims to be.

Revival Addresses

No easier way

I am not looking for an easier way. I abominate these easy ways. I believe in getting people converted. I could pass around cards and get them to sign their names, saying that they hoped to go to heaven; but a month after I had gone the effect would be nothing, or worse than nothing. I do not take any stock in any faith that does not lead to an open confession of Christ before the world, and I do not take any stock in the Christianity of your professed Christians unless it leads you to go out into the world and witness for the One who saved you.

Revival Addresses

The power of the Word

If we will not take time to study the Bible we cannot have power, any more than we can have physical power if we will not take time to eat nutritious food.

How to Obtain Fulness of Power

Bible as testimony to Christ

In fact, that is exactly what the whole Bible is, the Holy Spirit's testimony to Jesus Christ. The whole testimony of the book centers in Jesus Christ.

The Holy Spirit

Absolute surrender

The attitude that you must take toward God in order that the Holy Spirit may bear his testimony to Jesus Christ directly to your heart is the attitude of absolute surrender to the will of God.

The Holy Spirit

Prayer

We do not live in a praying age. A very considerable proportion of the membership of our evangelical churches today do not believe even theoretically in prayer, that is, they do not believe in prayer as bringing anything to pass that would not have come to pass if they had not prayed. They believe in prayer as having a beneficial "reflex influence," that is, as benefitting the person who prays, a sort of lifting yourself up by your spiritual boot-straps, but as for prayer bringing anything to pass that would not have come to pass if we had not prayed, they do not believe in it and many of them frankly say so, and even some of our "modern ministers" say so.

The Power of Prayer

Church history

When you read many of the church histories that have been written, the impression you naturally get is that the history of the church of Jesus Christ here on earth has been very largely a history of misunderstandings, disputes, doctrinal differences, and bitter conflicts; but if you will study the history of the living church, you will find it has been very largely a history of revivals.

The Power of Prayer

Praying in the name of Jesus

To pray, then, in the name of Jesus Christ means simply this: That we recognize that we have no claims whatever on God. That we have no merit whatsoever in his sight, and to recognize, furthermore, that Jesus Christ has immeasurable claims on God, and has given us the right to draw near to God not on the ground of our claims, but on the ground of his claims. And when we thus draw near to God in prayer, God will give us what we ask.

The Power of Prayer

FOR REFLECTION AND DISCUSSION

What lack or need in the modern church does Fundamentalism seek to fill?

Do you agree that God "shapes the whole present history of the world"? On what do you base your answer?

Where do people today seek to transform the biblical message into "an easier way"?

What does Torrey mean when he says that the whole Bible is "the Holy Spirit's testimony to Jesus Christ"? Do you agree?

What does it mean to say that the Bible is "the Word of God"?

How do Torrey's assumptions about God and reality compare with yours?

Do you find anything missing in Fundamentalist spirituality?

Chapter 24

AMY CARMICHAEL

1867-1951

The Spirituality of Missions

D AVID AND CATHERINE CARMICHAEL were settling into a pleasant life in the village of Millisle in County Down when their daughter Amy was born in 1867. Six more children would follow. For years David Carmichael made a good living milling flour, but when he died in 1885, the family fell on hard times and relocated to Belfast. Later that year, on a rainy Sunday, Catherine and the children, devout Presbyterians, were walking home from church when they encountered "a poor, pathetic old woman who was carrying a heavy bundle." The Carmichael children had never seen such a person, and the sight troubled eighteen-year-old Amy. She and two younger brothers assisted the woman. "It was a horrid moment," Amy wrote later. "We were only two boys and a girl, and not at all exalted Christians. We hated doing it." But Amy Carmichael would never be the same. The experience had, as she later said, "changed life's values."

Amy Carmichael launched a series of classes for the downtrodden of Belfast, including a Sunday school for young women working in factories who could not afford clothing suitable for church. Hundreds of them turned out for her Sunday instructions at Rosemary Street Presbyterian Church until their presence began to irritate other churchgoers. They were no doubt relieved when the group's numbers required that a hall accommodating five hundred be rented and the young women no longer frequented the church. Carmichael later moved across the Irish Sea to Manchester, where she undertook similar work in that city's slums, sharing living quarters with cockroaches and bedbugs. It would be good training for what was to come.

Amy Carmichael had long wanted to become an overseas missionary. When she attended the Keswick Convention in 1888, that thought crystalized. The Keswick emphasis on personal holiness and commitment to Christ was for Carmichael a call to respond to "the cry of the heathen." In 1892 she became the first overseas missionary sponsored by the Keswick Convention, even though she said, looking back fifty years later, that she was "no more fit to be a Keswick missionary than a Skye terrier puppy."

But where was Carmichael to go and what was she to do there? She sailed to Shanghai, stayed there briefly, then headed to Japan. As in Belfast and Manchester, Carmichael began work among the factory girls, meeting in dark rooms, courtyards, and the streets. Never of robust health, she grew weaker from the strain. Colleagues urged her to take more rest, but Carmichael said that she didn't wonder "that apostolic miracles have died — apostolic living certainly has." She carried on. "Satan is so much more in earnest than we are — he buys up the opportunity while we are wondering how much it will cost," she commented later.

After fifteen months in Japan, however, failing health forced Carmichael to return to England — briefly. As soon as she regained strength, she was off again, this time to India, arriving in 1895. She would not leave that country again. For several years Carmichael worked and taught in South India, but her life's calling began in 1901 when Pearl-eyes, a girl of seven, fled in terror from a Hindu temple where she was about to be wed to the god Parumal — and a life of temple prostitution. A kindly native woman found Pearl-eyes in the street and took her home, eventually entrusting her to Carmichael. Pearl-eyes told of "things that darkened the sunlight."

Other girls followed. There was Pappamal, a sixteen-year-old who sought to become a Christian and had to be taken away to the hills for protection. There was Preena, a child of seven who fled to Carmichael from a temple where her family had sold her to be forcibly wed to a priest. Her hands had been branded with a hot iron. There was five-year-old Kohila, whom Carmichael rescued from forced prostitution by arranging her "disappearance," an act for which Carmichael was nearly imprisoned. There were hundreds of others.

Child prostitution was sanctioned by India's caste system. It was anathema to Carmichael. Sometimes infant girls, offered by their parents to Hindu temples, learned the trade as they matured; others became prostitutes as adolescents when they were sold to the temples. Once taken into a temple, they were guarded closely. Escape was rare. The caste system also permitted mistreatment of children in other ways. Carmichael never forgot one scene from early in her time in India. A small boy of three or four lay in a bag hung from a roof, crying pitifully. Two months later, he was still there, crying more weakly. His face was drawn and his hands pressed over his burning eyes. Night and day he cried. The child was suffering from ophthalmia, a disease of the eye that ended in either blindness or death. The boy's parents said he had not slept for months. Carmichael begged the mother to allow her to take the boy to the hospital for treatment, but the mother refused because it was against their caste. "He doesn't make much noise now," she said. Carmichael pleaded. The mother responded, "What can we do? Can we destroy our caste?" The last thing Carmichael heard the mother say to the boy was, "Cry softly, or we'll put more medicine in!"

The caste system was entwined with the religion, history, and social fabric of the land. Carmichael compared it to a banyan tree: "In India we have a tree with a double system of roots. The banyan tree drops roots from its boughs. These bough roots in time run as deep underground as the original root. The tap root and its runners, and the branch roots and theirs, get knotted and knit into each other, till the whole forms one solid mass of roots, thousands of yards of a tangle of roots, sinuous and strong." The caste system was like the banyan tree, Carmichael said — nearly impossible to uproot.

For fifty-six years, Amy Carmichael would labor, against entrenched opposition, to defeat the caste system and afford endangered Indian children a refuge of safety, discipline, and love. The place chosen was Dohnavur ("vur" rhymes with "poor"), "a sunburnt spot out on the plains under the mountains to the west, a huddle of huts and small houses" at the southern tip of the Indian subcontinent. Carmichael gathered children through many means, some of them illegal. Within a dozen years, she was caring for over 130 children. Together with volunteers from England, India, and elsewhere, she built first a nursery, then several more, then a home, a school, a hospital, a retreat house, a farm, and gardens — first for girls, and later for boys as well. She rode a large tricycle from place to place to supervise the construction. Eventually, over a thousand youngsters entered Dohnavur and became Amy Carmichael's children.

Carmichael was a combination of principal, spiritual guide, mentor, and most of all, mother. She was universally called "Amma," a term of endearment meaning "mother." Even today, it is often said that Dohnavur is not an orphanage, but a family. Carmichael liked the story of a mother bear and her cub. The cub said to the mother, "Shall I move my right paw first or my left, or my two front paws together, or the two hind ones, or all four at once, or how?" The mother grunted, "Leave off thinking, and walk!" Carmichael sought to run Dohnavur that way: "We tried to let the children grow as the green things about them grew, not too closely regarded, not pulled up at frequent intervals to see how they were getting on. And there was always the hope that they would be part of the crown of flowers that our Lord would wear one day."

Carmichael never asked for money, and often said it wasn't needed when it was. Sometimes she returned money sent to her. But whenever Dohnavur had spent its last farthing, a check would arrive from somewhere. The ministry was financed through gifts inspired almost entirely by Carmichael's many writings. Beginning in 1895, she published nearly forty books about Dohnavur, its children, and Christian missions, often including devotional poems and photographs. Her books pioneered the use of illustrative photography. Unlike many other books by missionaries, Carmichael's did not play up the (often few) success stories, but spelled out in graphic detail the deprivation, isolation, opposition, oppressive climate, and frequent failure of missionary endeavors. One of her best-known books, published in 1903, is *Things As They Are,* a title perhaps meant to suggest that certain other missionary books described "Things As They Aren't." It is a gripping account of Hindu temple prostitution and the usually futile efforts of Carmichael and other Christians to root it out. No one could accuse Amy Carmichael of false advertising. She told would-be missionaries not to expect to be welcomed and to come only if "the cross is an attraction." Missionary work is "not glamorous," but "desperately hard," she said — iron would snap under the strain of it. "We do not find, as a rule, when we go to the houses . . . that anyone inside has been praying we might come. I read a missionary story 'founded on fact' the other day, and the things that happened in that story on these lines were most remarkable. They do not happen here."

None of this caused Carmichael to doubt the validity of her call from Christ. "If one is truly called of God, all the difficulties and discouragements only intensify the call," she wrote in *Things As They Are.* "If things were easier there would be less need. The greater the need, the clearer the call rings through one, the deeper the conviction grows: *it is God's call.* And as one obeys it, there is the joy of obedience, quite apart from the joy of success. There is joy in being with Jesus in a place where his friends are few."

Obedience was always foremost in Amy Carmichael's mind. "Our Master has never promised us success," she wrote. "He demands obedience. He expects faithfulness. Results are his concern, not ours." Some faulted Carmichael for forcing her religion on those who did not want it. She answered that Christ had said to "Go ye into all the world and preach the gospel to every creature" (Matt. 28:19) and that she was simply obeying him. "All the world" meant everywhere, and "every creature" meant everyone in it. Carmichael saw no ambiguity there. Moreover, no one was forced to accept Christ; it was always a choice, and one that often entailed courageous sacrifice. Others criticized Carmichael for breaking up families by insisting on baptism as a sign of discipleship. Again, her answer was simply that she was obeying Christ, who had commanded that his servants be baptized, and that Christ had anticipated the break-up of families. And it wasn't the newly baptized who sought to leave their families, Carmichael pointed out, but their families who rejected them unless they returned to the caste system. Others questioned why missionaries go to those who are not Christian when there is so much work to be done among nominal, marginal Christians at home. Carmichael's answer, again, was that her Master had told her to do so and that others were holding tent revivals to reach nominal Christians elsewhere.

On October 24, 1931, Carmichael fell into a pit, breaking her leg and twisting her spine. A full recovery was expected, but it was not to be. The leg was not set properly, and infection set in. For the remaining twenty years of her life, Carmichael was largely confined to her bed. She would never again be well, as maladies that had long dogged her became more severe — insomnia, neuralgia, heart trouble, hypertension, tic douloureux, and iritis. She gave these ailments biblical names like Jezebel, Sennacherib, and Apollyon. The greater her weakness, the greater the opportunity to demonstrate the strength of Christ, she thought. Children and Indian Christian volunteers continued to visit Carmichael in her room, called the Room of Peace, for counsel and guidance.

Amy Carmichael died on January 18, 1951, having lived long enough to witness a newly independent India abolish the caste system. She is buried at Dohnavur, with no grave marker, as was her request. Her devoted children placed a birdbath over the spot where she lies.

IN HER OWN WORDS

For our children

Father, hear us, we are praying,
Hear the words our hearts are saying,
We are praying for our children.

Keep them from the powers of evil,
From the secret, hidden peril,
From the whirlpool that would suck them,
From the treacherous quicksand, pluck them.

From the worldling's hollow gladness,
From the sting of faithless sadness,
Holy Father, save our children.

Through life's troubled waters steer them,
Through life's bitter battle cheer them,
Father, Father, be thou near them.
Read the language of our longing,
Read the wordless pleadings thronging,
Holy Father, for our children.

    And wherever they may bide,
    Lead them Home at eventide.

No scar?

Hast thou no scar?
No hidden scar on foot, or side, or hand?
I hear thee sung as mighty in the land,
I hear them hail thy bright ascendant star,
Hast thou no scar?

Hast thou no wound?
Yet I was wounded by the archers, spent,
Leaned me against a tree to die; and rent
By ravening beasts that compassed me, I swooned:
Hast *thou* no wound?

No wound? No scar?
Yet, as the Master shall the servant be,
And piercèd are the feet that follow me;
But thine are whole: can he have followed far
Who has nor wound nor scar?

Tune thou my harp

Tune thou my harp;
There is not, Lord, could never be,
The skill in me.

Tune thou my harp;
That it may play thy melody,
Thy harmony.

Tune thou my harp;
O Spirit, breathe thy thought through me,
As pleaseth thee.

God will not hear our prayers

God will not hear our prayers for the heathen if he means us to be out among them instead of at home praying for them, or if he means us to give up some son or daughter, and we prefer to pray.

Things As They Are

Just point

You cannot pull people uphill who do not want to go; you can only point up.

Ponnammal: Her Story

Down

He that is down cannot get between God and his glory.

Gold Cord

Missionaries

Is it not a mercy that missionaries can laugh?

Gold Cord

True Valor

True valor lies, not in what the world calls success, but in the dogged going on when everything in the man says Stop.

Rose from Brier

God answers in the deeps

Sometimes we do not see how the thing granted is at all what we desire. And yet it is. For, after all, what the deepest in us wanted was not our own natural will, but the will of our Father. So what is given *is* our heart's desire. He hath not withholden the request of our lips. *But God always answers us in the deeps, never in the shallows of our soul;* in hours of confusion, to remember this can help.

Ploughed Under

Meditation

There is a way into the greenwood which is not much used in these days of feverish rush. Its name in the scriptures is meditation. ("Let my meditation be sweet unto him" [Ps. 104:34].) We should plough a deeper furrow if we knew more of that way. We should be quieter then, and there is nothing creative in noise. "Friend, when does thou *think?*" asked the old Quaker after listening to a modern timetable; we cannot think by machinery. We cannot consider the lilies without giving time to the lilies. Often our flash of haste means little. To read a book in an hour (if the book has taken half a lifetime to write) means nothing at all. To pray in a hurry of spirit means nothing. To live in a hurry means to do much but effect little. We build more quickly in wood, hay, and stubble than in gold, silver, precious stones; but the one abides, the other does not.

Gold by Moonlight

Acceptance

To accept the will of God never leads to the miserable feeling that it is useless to strive any more. God does not ask for the dull, weak, sleepy acquiescence of indolence. He asks for something vivid and strong. He asks us to cooperate with him, actively willing what he wills, our only aim his glory. To accept in this sense is to come with all the desire of the mind unto the place which the Lord shall choose, and to minister in the name of the Lord our God *there* — not otherwise. *Where the things of God are concerned, acceptance always means the happy choice of mind and heart of that which he appoints, because (for the present) it is his good and acceptable and perfect will.*

Gold by Moonlight

Unspiritual work

If by doing some work which the undiscerning consider "not spiritual work" I can best help others, and I inwardly rebel, thinking it is the spiritual for which I crave, when in truth it is the interesting and exciting, then I know nothing of Calvary love.

If

The peace of God

If we open the shutters in the morning the light will pour in. We do not need to beseech it to pour in. It will pour in if we will let it. If we open the sluice in flood-time the water will flow through. We do not plead with it to flow. It will flow if we will let it. It is so with the peace of God. It will rule in our hearts if only we will let it. If a heart that is disturbed about anything will "let the peace of God rule" (instead of its own desires), that heart may this very day prove this truth.

Edges of His Ways

The devil's voice

The devil kept on whispering, "It's all right now, but what about afterwards?"

Candles in the Dark

Wilt love me? Trust me? Praise me?

O thou beloved child of my desire,
Whether I lead thee through green valleys,
   By still waters,

266

Or through fire,
Or lay thee down in silence under snow,
through any weather, and whatever
   Cloud may gather,
   Wind may blow —
Wilt love me? Trust me? Praise me?

No gallant bird, O dearest Lord, am I,
That anywhere, in any weather,
   Rising singeth;
   Low I lie.
And yet I cannot fear, for I shall soar,
Thy love shall wing me, blessed Savior;
   So I answer,
   I adore,
I love thee, trust thee, praise thee.

The question

I hear thee in the silence of the mountains,
The thunder of the falls,
The wind-song of the grasses, melody
Of bird upon the tree;
And all things high or lowly
Discourse of thee to me.
What profit is it if thou be not holy?

I see thee in the light upon the river,
The shadows of the wood;
The wild-flowers on the mountainside profess
The colors of thy dress;
As though for my joy solely
All things do thee confess.
What profit is it if thou be not holy?

I know thee in the seeping of the tempest,
The smothering of a mist;

In delicate glories of the earth and air,
In changes fierce or fair,
Proceeding swift or slowly,
I am of thee aware.
What profit is it if thou be not holy?

Prayer

Prayer is the core of our day. Take prayer out, and the day would collapse, would be pithless, a straw blown in the wind. But how can you pray — really pray, I mean — with one against whom you have a grudge or whom you have been discussing critically with another? Try it. You will find it cannot be done.

Roots

Make me thy fuel

From prayer that asks that I may be
Sheltered from winds that beat on thee,
From fearing when I should aspire,
From faltering when I should climb higher,
From silken self, O Captain, free
Thy soldier who would follow thee.

From subtle love of softening things,
From easy choices, weakenings,
Not thus are spirits fortified,
Not this way went the Crucified,
From all that dims thy Calvary,
O Lamb of God, deliver me.

Give me the love that leads the way,
The faith that nothing can dismay,
The hope no disappointments tire,
The passion that will burn like fire,
Let me not sink to be a clod:
Make me thy fuel, Flame of God.

FOR REFLECTION AND DISCUSSION

How does one distinguish a call from God from a desire to do something for other reasons?

How would you respond to the objections raised against Carmichael's missionary work?

Can one follow Christ with no scar? Why so, or why not?

Is it possible to know God and yet be not holy?

Is it wrong to pray to be sheltered from the wind and from faltering?

Chapter 25

THÉRÈSE OF LISIEUX

1873-1897

Spiritual Childhood

SOME THINGS ABOUT Thérèse of Lisieux give one pause. Her writings display a sentimental, saccharine piety that, while popular in her day, is not widely appreciated today. They also disclose a self-reflective, even a self-absorbed young woman. And finally, Thérèse set out to become a great saint, thought she was one, and said so. Can such a person seriously be held up as a spiritual giant?

Thérèse Martin was born to a devout bourgeois family in Alençon, in northern France, the youngest of five daughters. Her early childhood was radiantly happy. Both parents were devoted and attentive, and relationships among the sisters were tender. "My first memories are of smiles and loving caresses," Thérèse later wrote. But Thérèse's mother died six months before Thérèse's fifth birthday, beginning a "most unhappy" decade for the young girl. "I had been lively and cheerful, but I became timid and quiet and a bundle of nerves," she said. Thérèse adored her father, Louis Martin, a watchmaker and a man of vibrant faith sometimes called "Monsieur Saint Martin." He taught his daughters obedience, compassion, and self-sacrifice, by both precept and example. "I cannot put into words how much I loved Daddy," Thérèse said. "I admired everything about him."

To their father's great joy, all five girls became nuns. Amazingly, that had been Thérèse's intention since before her third birthday. She never abandoned the thought and tried to enter the Carmelite monastery in nearby Lisieux at the age of nine. The prioress informed her that sixteen was the minimum age. Finally, when Thérèse was fifteen, her father agreed to let her enter Carmel, but when the bishop said no, Thérèse, her sister Céline, and their father traveled to Rome to appeal to Pope Leo XIII. A line of pilgrims had been instructed to kneel, kiss the pope's foot, and move quickly on, but Thérèse paused and addressed Leo. "Most Holy Father, to mark your jubilee, allow me to enter Carmel at fifteen," she said. The vicar-general, shocked and annoyed at this brazen behavior, sought to whisk her away, but Thérèse persisted until the pope said, "You will enter if God wills." Thérèse entered the Carmelite monastery in Lisieux the following year, on April 9, 1888, receiving the veil two years later.

Thérèse would spend less than a decade at Carmel before, after an illness of eighteen months, tuberculosis took her life on September 30, 1897, when she was twenty-four. For a time, Thérèse had served as novice master at Carmel (a post not usually given to one so young), but her behavior and demeanor had been so reserved that she attracted little attention. So unnoted had been her presence that the nun assigned to write Thérèse's obituary for the Carmelite order said she could think of nothing to say. Again one wonders how this young woman came to be seen as a spiritual giant.

It is largely on her slender autobiography *The Story of a Soul,* supplemented by letters and poems from her hand, that Thérèse's reputation rests. Hardly a literary masterpiece (a modern editor would take a sharp red pencil to Thérèse's rampant italics and exclamation points), *The Story of a Soul* is nonetheless one of the most popular devotional texts of the last century. The prioress at Lisieux (Thérèse's biological sister Pauline) instructed her to write the story of her early life, an assignment that Thérèse obediently undertook in 1895 during the few moments of privacy between her other duties at Lisieux. She sat in her chilly cell in the evenings with a stubby pencil, jotting down her recollections in two-cent notebooks. After her tuberculosis had weakened her, Thérèse was asked to bring the work up to date, which she did in the summer of 1897, writing chapters nine and ten of the standard version. She wrote a final chapter for her sister Marie, also a nun at Lisieux, who had asked Thérèse to leave her a "souvenir" relating the secrets Jesus had disclosed to her.

The Story of a Soul is not a book to analyze and dissect; Thérèse was not a systematic thinker. The book does, however, bear careful reading, for while its teachings are not original, they are presented with rare simplicity and transparent honesty. Thérèse's writings disclose a soul totally in love with Jesus and blissfully at home in his embrace. On Christmas Day, 1886, "Jesus the Child, then only an hour old, flooded the darkness of my soul with torrents of light," she wrote. "By becoming weak and frail for me, he gave me strength and courage." Thérèse called that moment her "complete conversion." It ended her decade of disorientation following her mother's death. The Child Jesus also afforded Thérèse a new name. Upon entering Carmel, she became known as Thérèse of the Child Jesus, assuming from that moment the role of a child with Jesus, both as a playmate for the boy Jesus and as an infant held in the arms of a strong and loving Savior.

Perhaps the most obvious characteristic of a child is its small size, and littleness became a defining theme of Thérèse's spirituality. She calls her teaching the "little way," a way open to everyone, even people of no great stature whose works and presence will never be noted. "To remain little is to recognize one's nothingness, expecting everything from the good God, *as a little child expects everything from his father,*" she writes. To progress spiritually, "remain little always. That is what I have done." Thérèse saw herself as "a very small soul which can offer only very small things to the good Lord." Small things have great value, she says, because it is not the size of the action that matters to God, but the love with which it is undertaken. She fancied herself a grain of sand, "obscure, hidden from all eyes, that Jesus alone can see it. Let it become smaller and smaller, reduced to *nothing*." Thérèse loved her littleness because it enabled her to find a place within the loving arms of Jesus.

Closely linked with Thérèse's understanding of littleness is humility. Her humility is not the sort that grovels and bemoans its awfulness, but an honest and happy acceptance of one's weakness and a confidence in the goodness of the Father. "Humility is truth," she says, and it is important to see ourselves as we truly are. Thérèse had no use for pretense and grandiosity. It is the nature of divine love to stoop down, she says, and we are therefore closest to God when we do the same.

Thérèse rarely used terms like "sin" and "repentance," preferring words like "weaknesses" and "imperfections." Just two months after her entry into Carmel, she said she had "never been guilty of a single grievous sin." She went to confession regularly, not to recite her wrongdoings, but to confirm her "little way." Children do not stew about their wickedness, Thérèse says, but readily resume playing after punishment because they are confident of the love of their families. Four months before her death, she wrote to Pauline, "I am happier for having been imperfect than if, upheld by grace, I had been a model of sweetness. It does me so much good to see that Jesus is always so sweet, so loving to me!" Her faults were blessings to her that, through her struggling against them, brought her closer to God.

Thérèse experienced God's love much as she had experienced love in her childhood home. Her confidence in the love of God was unwavering. God is more loving than people think, she says, and the way to Jesus is "through his heart." Jesus loves to forgive and to welcome the recalcitrant child home again. Powerful though our Lord is, she says, he has "one great weakness" — when it comes to sins, he cannot add.

Thérèse saw her mission as twofold: to love Jesus in return for his love, and to lead others to love him. This included loving other people as Jesus loved them. After she entered Carmel, Thérèse set out to love in particular those within the monastery whom it was hardest to love. On one occasion, she vowed to express her love for a crotchety and disagreeable sister whom other nuns shunned. Whenever they passed, Thérèse smiled and greeted this sister warmly. One day the sister asked, "What is it about me that you like so much?" Thérèse replied, "I'm just happy to see you."

Detachment from worldly things and spiritual poverty are also part of Thérèse's "little way." Children own little or nothing; they depend entirely on the good will, wisdom, and strength of others. When they are confident that they are loved and will be cared for, such detachment is easy. The "little way" is not meant to be demanding. This confidence is never based on our merits or accomplishments, but solely on the nature of God. Even if she had committed every sin, Thérèse says, she would throw herself into the arms of God with confidence.

Thérèse's writings contain several images that describe her relationship with Jesus. She compared herself to a grain of sand (already mentioned). She referred to herself (and is often referred to today) as the "Little Flower." In a letter to Pauline she pictures herself as a baby lamb bounding upwards toward the way opened by the Lamb. Elsewhere she sees herself as "a little reed gently waving." A favorite image is that of a toy ball with which the Child Jesus plays and which delights him. Four months before her death, Thérèse wrote to a missionary for whom she had been praying that by herself she was a zero, but "what encourages me is the thought that by your side I can be of *some* use; after all zero, by itself, has no value, but put alongside *one* it becomes potent."

Thérèse's short life was not without suffering. During her final years, she experienced long periods of spiritual dryness when she felt only the absence of Christ. Her confidence did not waver during these times, which she assumed were designed by God to teach her to trust him more deeply. "Jesus will tire sooner of making me wait than I shall tire of waiting for him," she said. She was also in severe physical pain during her final months, but suffering did not detract from Thérèse's joy. She embraced it as a blessing that would draw her closer to Christ. During the latter years of her life, finding meditating on the Passion of Christ helpful, Thérèse added the words "of the Holy Face" to her name "of the Child Jesus." The face was that of the crucified Christ.

From childhood, Thérèse had always hoped to die at a young age so as to attain complete union with Christ. Her final words, moments before her last breath, were "Oh! I love him, my God. . . . I . . . love . . . you!"

IN HER OWN WORDS

Act of offering

Thank you, my God! For all the graces granted me, and especially for having made me pass through the crucible of suffering. I shall look with joy on you at the Last Day, bearing the scepter of the cross, and since you have deigned to give me that most precious *cross* as my portion, I hope I shall be like you in heaven and see the sacred stigmata of your Passion shining in my body. After my earthly exile, I hope to enjoy you in the Homeland, but I want not to accumulate merits for heaven, but to work *solely for the love* of you, with no other aim but to please you. . . . *You yourself* are the only *throne* or *crown* I want, O my *Beloved!*

"Act of Offering to the Merciful Love of the Good God," 1895

Seek the last place

Never seek what seems great to the eyes of creatures. Solomon, the wisest king ever on earth, considered every kind of work that people do under the sun — painting, sculpture, the arts — and realized that *all* these *things* were *subject to envy* and proclaimed that they were nothing but "vanity and affliction of spirit" [Eccles. 1:14]. The one thing people do not *envy* is the last place; the *last place* is the only thing that is not vanity and affliction of spirit. . . . It is enough to humble ourselves and patiently bear our imperfections — that is real holiness. Let us take each other's hand . . . and run to the last place. No one will dispute us for it.

Letter, 1897

Saints

You cannot be half a saint. You must be a whole saint or no saint at all.

Letter, 1897

Anticipating her death

Not only does the thought of heavenly bliss not bring me joy, but I wonder whether I *could* be happy without suffering. Jesus, of course, will change my nature [in heaven], for otherwise I would look back and long to suffer in the valley of tears. I have not asked God to let me die young; that would have seemed cowardly to me. But from my childhood he has deigned to give me the intimate conviction that my life here below will be a short one. The one cause of all my joy is the thought of doing the Lord's will.

Letter, 1897

A parable

Imagine a father with two mischievous and disobedient sons. When the father starts to punish them, he sees one trembling and terrified, trying to get away from him but admitting deep down that he deserves to be punished. Meanwhile, his brother does the opposite, throwing himself into his father's arms and expressing his sorrow for having caused him pain, assuring his father that he loves him and that he will prove it by behaving in the future. Then, if this child asks his father *to punish him* with a *kiss,* I don't think the heart of the delighted father could resist such filial confidence, for he would know his son loved him sincerely. He would also know, of course, that his son would fall into the same faults again, not once but often, but he would be ready to pardon him time and again if his son *takes him* by *the heart.* I will say nothing of the first boy . . . you will know whether the father can love him as deeply or treat him with the forgiveness he gave to the other.

Letter, 1897

The garden of Jesus

[Jesus] opened for me the book of nature and I saw that all the flowers he had created are lovely. The rose's splendor and the lily's whiteness do not rob the little violet of its scent nor the daisy of its simple charm. I realized that if every little flower aspired to be a rose, then spring would lose its loveliness and there would be no wild flowers to brighten the meadows. It is the same with the world of souls, which is the garden of Jesus. He has created the great saints to be like lilies and roses, but he has also created many lesser saints, and they must be content to be the daisies or the violets which gladden his eyes when he glances down. Perfection is doing his will, being what he wants us to be.

The Story of a Soul

To be a saint

I was made to understand that the glory I would win would never be seen during my lifetime. My glory was to become a great saint! This desire may seem presumptuous, since I was and still am weak and imperfect, even after eight years as a nun, but I always feel a fearless certainty that I shall become a great saint. I don't rely on my own merits, since I have none, but I hope in him who is goodness and holiness itself. Satisfied with my feeble efforts, he alone will raise me to him, clothe me with his own merits, and make me a saint. I did not realize then how much a saint must suffer, but God soon showed me. . . .

The Story of a Soul

The loving Father

Imagine that the son of a gifted physician stumbles in the road and breaks his leg. His father rushes to him and lovingly uses all his skill to heal the son. His son, now healed and grateful, quite properly loves such a father. But now imagine that the father learns that a dangerous stone lies in the road, goes there before his son, and, unseen by anyone, removes the stone. Now the boy, knowing nothing of what his father has spared him by his loving foresight, will show him no particular gratitude and will love him less than if his father had healed him. But if the boy knew the danger he had escaped, would he not love his father all the more? I am that child, protected by the foreseeing love of a Father who sent his Son "to call sinners, not the righteous" [Mark 2:17]. He wants me to love him because he has forgiven me not much, but everything. He did not wait for me to love him with a great love like that of St. Magdalene, but made me to understand that he loved me first with a complete, all-seeing love, so that now I adore him even foolishly. I have heard it said that a pure soul does not love with the passion of one that has sinned but repented. What a lie that is!

The Story of a Soul

Spiritual chatter

I thought it better to speak to God than about him. There's often so much self-love in chatter about spiritual things!

The Story of a Soul

God comes

[God] does not come down from heaven every day to lie in a golden ciborium. Rather, he comes to find another heaven which is infinitely dearer to him, the heaven of our souls, created in his image, the living temples of the adorable Trinity!

The Story of a Soul

That the will of God be accomplished

Today my only guide is self-abandonment. That is my only compass. I no longer even know how to beg for anything except that the will of God be perfectly accomplished in my soul.

The Story of a Soul

The justice of God

I know that souls are different. There must be different kinds of souls so that each of God's perfections can be specially honored. He has revealed his infinite mercy to me and I see all his other attributes in the light of that — they all seem to glow with love. Perhaps more than any other attribute, God's justice seems clothed with love, for it is a very sweet joy to think of God as just, that he makes allowances for our weaknesses and understands the frailty of our human nature. So what have I to fear? If the perfectly just

God shows mercy like that in forgiving the prodigal son, will he not also be *just* to me, "who am always with him" [Luke 15:31]?

The Story of a Soul

A time of darkness

I get no joy from singing of the bliss of heaven and the eternal possession of God, for I sing only of *what I want to believe*. I admit that occasionally a tiny ray of sunshine pierces the darkness, and then, for just a second, my suffering stops. But instead of comforting me, the memory of this makes the darkness even blacker. Never before have I felt so strongly how gentle and merciful God is, for he sent me this cross at precisely the time I was strong enough to bear it. At any other time, it would have disheartened me, but now it merely removes all natural satisfaction from my longing for heaven.

The Story of a Soul

Prayer

Prayer for me is an upward leap of the heart, an untroubled glance toward heaven, a grateful and loving cry from the deepest depth of sorrow as well as from the height of joy. Its supernatural grandeur enlarges the soul and unites the soul with God.

The Story of a Soul

FOR REFLECTION AND DISCUSSION

How would a spirituality of littleness find expression in your life?
What can the church and the world learn from Thérèse?
Take a few moments to imagine yourself as Jesus' playmate. Imagine yourself as Jesus' toy. How does that feel to you?
What role does Thérèse ascribe to suffering in living faithfully?
Why does Thérèse suggest that we "run to the last place"? How would one do this?

Chapter 26

MARIA SKOBTSOVA

1891-1945

Martyrdom

T HE MARTYRS OF Roman times are well known, but the real age of
Christian martyrdom was the twentieth century. Historians estimate
that beginning with the apostles, 70 million Christians have died for their
faith, with 45.4 million of them — nearly two-thirds — killed in the twentieth century. The toll was particularly grim for Russian Christians. It is often unclear whether victims were killed because of their religion, political
views, ethnic background, or a combination of factors, but one estimate is
that 20 million Russian Christians, mostly Orthodox but also including
many Roman Catholics, died in prison camps under Josef Stalin, nearly
three million of them as a direct result of professing their faith. Another
million Christians died in Nazi prison camps, many of them Russians as
well.

Among the twentieth century's Russian martyrs was Maria Skobtsova.
Born in Riga, Latvia, the young Elizaveta (as she was then named) grew up
in Anapa, on the semi-tropical shore of the Black Sea, where her father
owned an estate of vineyards. The Skobtsovas were devout Orthodox
Christians, and Elizaveta shared their devotion. At the age of seven, she
asked her mother whether she was old enough to become a nun. When
Elizaveta's father died in 1906, her mother moved the family to St. Peters-
burg, where Elizaveta took up with the city's literary and cultural left. She
married a young Bolshevik in 1910, a marriage that ended in 1916.

When civil war broke out in 1917, Skobtsova returned to Anapa, where
she was briefly mayor. But as the Bolsheviks began to prevail, Skobtsova
and her family — including her mother, new husband, daughter, and an
unborn son in her womb — fled in the putrid hold of a steamer across the
Black Sea, first to Tbilisi, then to Istanbul and through Yugoslavia, finally
arriving in Paris in 1923. They were part of a multitude of Russians to arrive in the West fleeing the Bolsheviks.

Skobtsova joined the Russian Student Christian Movement in Paris
and began traveling throughout France, visiting émigrés, giving talks on
Russian history, and providing spiritual counsel to individuals, often into
the early morning hours. Nor had she forgotten her childhood desire to
become a nun. When her second marriage ended, Skobtsova approached
the émigré Russian Metropolitan Evlogii Georgievskii about becoming a
nun and was professed in 1932. She was given the name Maria.

Evlogii expected his new nun to help develop a monastic system similar to the one left behind in imperial Russia. But Skobtsova's vision of monastic life did not call for recreating the past. She wanted "to share the life

of paupers and tramps." Skobtsova visited the still-functioning Orthodox monasteries in Latvia and Estonia (those in Russia were being closed by the government) but was unimpressed. Those monasteries preserved the past, she said, but were unaware that "the world is on fire." She saw the 1930s as an "apocalyptic" time, demanding radical new responses. "Open your gates to homeless thieves, let the outside world sweep in to demolish your magnificent liturgical system, abase yourself, empty yourself, make yourself of no account," she wrote. Skobtsova saw the entire world as her convent.

The French government offered benefits to Russian émigrés, but a permanent address was required, and many émigrés were homeless. Skobtsova therefore leased a house where homeless émigrés could sleep. She had no financial backing, saying she would be required "to walk on water" to pay the rent. She was apparently able to do so, for she not only paid the rent but managed to acquire other properties as well, eventually overseeing a ministry called Orthodox Action, which ran homeless shelters throughout Paris. When the home where Skobtsova herself resided grew crowded, she gave her bed to others and slept in a corner in the boiler room.

"Mother Maria," as she was called, was a controversial figure around Paris, seen on the street in her nun's habit, often soiled from manual labor, smoking cigarettes and occasionally swilling beer. Not only did she foreswear the security of the convent, but she was often absent from worship services held at the shelters she ran. Traditionalists questioned her calling as a nun. Mother Maria explained that she felt it more important to buy vegetables, cook food, and feed the hungry than to spend time in chapel. "Piety, Piety! But where is the love that moves mountains?" she wrote in her journal. "The liturgy must be translated into life," she said. Was this a foolish way to run a ministry? Mother Maria embraced the notion of being a "fool for Christ" and identified with a long list of saints who had done the same. "To an outsider I might seem reckless. I don't care. Rather than make calculations, I submit," she said.

In 1939 she wrote, "At the Last Judgment, I shall not be asked whether I was successful in my ascetic exercises, how many bows and prostrations I made. I shall be asked: 'Did I feed the hungry, clothe the naked, visit the sick and the prisoners?' That is all I shall be asked. About every poor, hungry, and imprisoned person the Savior says 'I': 'I was hungry and thirsty, I was sick and in prison.' To think that he puts an equal sign between himself and anyone in need!"

Mother Maria did not merely wait for the needy to appear at her door (though they appeared by the hundreds), but sought them out. At one point she toured French insane asylums, discovering Russian émigrés who had been diagnosed as insane and confined in deplorable quarters for decades when the problem was merely that they could not converse in French. She gained their release.

One of Mother Maria's favorite stories was a tale of two fourth-century saints. Nicholas of Myra and John Cassian had returned to earth. A peasant whose cart had slipped into a ditch asked their assistance. Cassian replied that he was due back in heaven soon and could not risk soiling his white robe. Nicholas, already knee-deep in mud working to return the cart to the road, said nothing. When God learned why Cassian appeared before him in immaculate garb while Nicholas's robe was caked in mud, he called for a revision of the church calendar, designating two days to commemorate St. Nicholas (May 9 and December 6) while assigning Cassian's feast to February 29, to be observed once every four years.

Monastic reform was dear to Mother Maria's heart. Unlike most Russian émigrés, she looked upon the dispersion as an opportunity rather than a burden. Monasticism — and the church generally — had ceased to embody genuine Christian ideals in Russia, she felt, but reform would have been unlikely under either the czar or the communists. But now, on foreign soil and unencumbered by social and political demands unrelated to the Christian gospel, she felt renewal was possible.

Mother Maria rethought the traditional monastic vows of chastity, obedience, and poverty, moving them from the cloister into the world. She said that the vow of chastity, as it was traditionally understood, called for abandoning only one aspect of family life while offering all the other amenities afforded by familial relationships. Obedience was a genuine virtue, but to whom? And poverty had been observed only in the technical sense, she said — monks and nuns owned nothing in their own names, but monasteries themselves often owned vast estates off which the cloister lived luxuriously. This would not do. The only thing that mattered to Mother Maria was that people become more Christ-like, which meant feeding the hungry, clothing the naked, and sheltering the homeless.

The most direct statement of Mother Maria's views was lost, then recovered in 1996. In an essay entitled "Types of Religious Life," she ruthlessly debunks four kinds of religion. First is the church as a reflection of national identity and civility. Second is the church defined by ritual. Then comes the aesthetic church centered on beauty and good taste. Finally, there is the ascetic church, urging self-denial that can degenerate into spiritual pride. None of these churches, all well-known to Russian Christians, lives the gospel of love, Mother Maria says. She urges instead a return to the "evangelical" type of church (not to be confused with what that word has come to mean in the West), which seeks to "Christify" all of life. Christification (as distinguished from merely belonging to a church) means "it is no longer I who live, but Christ who lives in me" (Gal. 2:20). Christ gave two commandments — love God and love our neighbor — and it is impossible to obey one without also obeying the other, Skobtsova says.

Mother Maria would soon be given the opportunity to show how deeply she believed this. After Paris fell to the Nazis on June 14, 1940, she and her chaplain began providing certificates of baptism to Parisian Jews facing deportation. When the authorities intercepted a letter requesting such a certificate and demanded to see a list of all "recent" baptisms, Mother Maria declined to provide it. The occupation posted notices at her hostels urging the unemployed to volunteer as workers in German factories. Mother Maria ripped them down. Her hostels became links in an underground railroad that helped Jews leave the country. When the Nazis required all Jews to wear a Star of David in public, Mother Maria was told that this was not a "Christian problem" and that she should not involve herself with it. "Don't you understand?" she replied. "There is no such thing as a 'Christian problem.' Christianity is under siege. If we were true Christians we would all wear the Star. The age of confessors has arrived."

On February 10, 1943, Mother Maria was arrested. Two months later, she saw her son Iura (who, along with her mother, worked with her) for the last time. He told her that he prayed constantly "Lord Jesus Christ, Son of God, have mercy on me, a sinner" and that this prayer made him feel close to her. Later that day, Mother Maria was transported to Germany. On December 16, Iura was arrested and sent to the concentration camp in Buchenwald, where he died within a few months. Mother Maria lived two more years at the Ravensbrück concentration camp. People slept three to a bunk and "lice devoured us," according to one survivor. Mother Maria was a constant source of joy to her fellow prisoners, who often brought her extra rations of food, which she shared with those in greatest need. She was skilled in embroidery. During her final months, as her health failed, other inmates brought her thread and a needle stolen from the camp's tailoring workshop. Mother Maria completed two embroideries while incarcerated: an icon of the Blessed Virgin holding the infant Jesus and a depiction of the Allied landing on Normandy Beach. "In the conflict with doubt, cast your thought wider and deeper. Do not let your thought be debased; let it transcend the conditions and the limitations of this earth," one survivor recalls her saying.

Mother Maria died in the gas chamber on Saturday, March 31, 1945, as the sounds of gunfire from the advancing Soviet army were heard in the distance. It was Easter Eve.

IN HER OWN WORDS

The true disciple

Anyone who loves the world, lays down his life for others, and is ready, even at the cost of being separated from Christ, to win salvation for his brothers — that person is a disciple and follower of Christ. And inversely, anyone who remains in the temptation to seek his own salvation alone, refuses to assume the responsibility of the pain and sin of the world, and follows the way of "egoism," even "holy" egoism, simply does not hear what Christ is saying and does not see the purpose of Christ's sacrifice on Golgotha.

"The Second Gospel Commandment"

The basis of brotherly love

Our relationship to other people should not be a sort of extra burden added to our own crosses, not some pious exercise or duty or act of virtue. There is just one law here. Only this determines our relationship: seeing the image of God in the other, and then adopting him as a son. This is where duty, virtue, and pious exercise all fade away.

"On the Imitation of the Mother of God"

Into the world but not of the world

The more we go out into the world and give ourselves to the world, the less we are of the world, because what is of the world does not give itself to the world.

"The Mysticism of Human Communion"

The immense and the insignificant

The Lord's truth wipes out the difference between the immense and the insignificant. Let us try to build our small, insignificant lives the same way the Great Architect builds the planetary system of the immense universe.

"The Mysticism of Human Communion"

Christ is freedom

Christ is freedom: the face of Christ is the affirmation in every person of his own free and God-like face. The church is a free and organic union of the faithful with Christ and with Christ's freedom. Christ calls those who labor and are heavy laden to take up his burden, which is light because it is taken up freely. Thus Christ and coercion are incompatible.

"The Cross and the Hammer-and-Sickle"

Two ways to live

There are two ways to live: You can walk on dry land with utter legitimacy and respectability, measuring, weighing, and planning ahead. Or you can walk on the waters, and then it becomes impossible to measure or plan ahead because the only thing necessary is to believe at every moment. An instant of doubt, and you start to sink.

Notebook manuscript

Egocentrism or spiritual poverty?

Egocentrism is defined less by material miserliness and greed than by their spiritual manifestations. The egocentric is greedy for and accumulates spiritual riches. He staunchly opposes the world, which becomes a kind of background for his development, a favorable or unfavorable milieu with no meaning or importance of its own. But of course this is not some abstract idea of a world, but the concrete, actual world that surrounds him. The lexicon of the egocentric is saturated with the words "I" and "mine." "His" friend is someone he needs and wants to use. "His" family consists of material assets which are to afford him comfort and deliver him from solitude without asking anything of him. His science, his art, his country — these things are indeed dear and necessary to him, but only for what they contribute to his spiritual and material soundness and weightiness. He is the center; all creation exists for him. . . . Poverty of spirit is not the renunciation of any intellectual interests, nor some sort of spiritual idiocy. It is the renunciation of one's spiritual exclusiveness, the giving of one's spirit to God's work on earth, and it is the only path for common life in the one united organism of the church.

"Toward a New Monasticism II"

The nonpossessing person

Nonpossession is generally opposed to two vices between which we rarely make any distinction, miserliness and greed. A miserly person may not be greedy, whereas a greedy person may be a spendthrift. One can picture these two vices in this way: A miserly person says, "What is mine is mine," but does not always add, "What's yours is also mine." A greedy person says, "What's yours is mine," but may not add, "What's mine is also mine." The greedy person may obsess about getting hold of what is not his but be unconcerned about holding onto it once he has it. There is, of course, a level at which miserliness and greed combine, where one says, "What's mine is mine, and what's yours is also mine." A nonpossessing person will be free of both miserliness and greed. He will say, "What's mine is yours and what's yours is also yours." And it would be naive to think that this concerns only material goods.

"The Poor in Spirit"

Holiness and martyrdom

Every era of church history contains examples of real holiness. Denial of freedom in no case diminishes the possibility of holiness. It may be precisely during times of maximum privation of freedom that the most obvious and unquestionable holiness blossoms. So it is in times of persecution, which are also times of martyrdom.

"Under the Sign of Our Time"

Fools for Christ

It would be a great lie to say to a searching soul, "Go to church because there you will find peace." The opposite is true. The church says to those who are already sleeping peacefully, "Go to church because there you will become frightened over your sins, your perdition, and the world's sins and perdition. There you will feel an insatiable hunger for Christ's truth. There your lukewarmness will be inflamed, your peacefulness alarmed, and the wisdom of this world be switched out for the foolishness of Christ." . . . We will become fools for Christ because we know not only the difficulty of this path, but also the immense joy of feeling God's hand on what we do.

"Under the Sign of Our Time"

No gospel chronology

In a way, every human soul depicted in the gospel is reflected in the course of human history. The fallen woman still washes the Savior's feet with her tears in the same way. The herd of swine throws itself into the deeps in the same way. The publican is converted in the same way. And in the same way the disciples leave their nets to follow Christ. Peter eternally denies Christ and, through faith, eternally walks on water. Christ is eternally opposed by doctors of the law, scribes, and Pharisees, who ask him devious questions and betray him. And the crowd continually shouts, "Crucify him! Crucify him!" In the macrocosm of the universe and world history, we recognize entire periods that stand beneath one or another sign of the gospel story. There is, then, no gospel chronology because, within God's providence, our temporary earthly sequence is accidental. Perhaps the whole stream of gospel events exists all the time, the Nativity simultaneously with Golgotha, and Golgotha with the Resurrection. . . . And there is something more: besides this external macrocosmic incarnation of the gospel in the world, there is a microcosm of the gospel story, which is every individual human soul.

"A Justification of Pharisaism"

War and pacifism

Do we accept it? Do we reject it? Is war heroic? Is it organized crime? Is a soldier a martyr, a "passion bearer"? Were soldiers in ancient times denied communion? Are some wars just, almost righteous? There are so many questions. They show how very contradictory war is. On the one hand, war is sin, misfortune, catastrophe. But on the other hand, there is something egoistically vegetarian in consistent pacifism which makes one sick at heart.

"Insight in Wartime"

The two great commandments

Christ gave us two commandments, to love God and to love our neighbor. Everything else, even the commandments in the Beatitudes, merely adds detail to these two commandments. They contain in themselves the entire "good news" of Christ. Moreover, Christ's life on earth is nothing more than the revelation of the mystery of the love of God and the love of neighbor. These two commandments are not only the summary, but the true and only measure of everything. It is remarkable that their truth is found only in their conjunction. Loving only humanity leads to the dead end of anti-Christian humanism, from which the only exit is often to refuse to love individual persons, to reject them in the name of "humanity." Love of God without love of neighbor, however, is also condemned: "You hypocrite, how can you love God whom you have not seen, if you hate your brother whom you have seen?" [1 John 4:20]. The conjunction of these two is not just a conjunction of two great truths taken from two spiritual realms. It is the conjunction of two parts of a single whole.

"Types of Religious Life"

FOR REFLECTION AND DISCUSSION

What would it mean to live the vows of chastity, poverty, and obedience outside the monastery?

What do you think Skobtsova meant by saying she lived in an apocalyptic time? How does faithful living differ in apocalyptic times from faithful living in other times?

Where have you experienced the "types of religious life" of which Skobtsova writes? How would you evaluate them?

"The liturgy must be translated into life," Skobtsova said. How do you do this in your life?

What is "the temptation to seek [our] own salvation alone," and where do we see it today?

If "Christ is freedom," how does this differ from "Do whatever you want"?

Chapter 27

DONALD GEE

1891-1966

Pentecostal Spirituality

"HOLY ROLLERS" we called them when I was a boy. I never knew a Holy Roller. They met on the second floor of a downtown bank building, from which wailing could be heard through open windows on warm Sunday evenings. When I thought of the Holy Rollers, I imagined something emotional, disreputable, and embarrassing. Usually, I didn't think of them at all.

That was in the 1950s. Having grown into a vibrant Christian fellowship spanning the globe, the Pentecostals cannot be so summarily dismissed today. Though earlier incidents foreshadowed it, the Pentecostal movement first gained prominence with the Azusa Street revival in 1906, centered in a black holiness church in downtown Los Angeles. That revival featured three worship services a day, seven days a week, for nearly four years. Thousands received something called the "baptism in the Holy Spirit" and spoke in unknown tongues. As the young movement began to grow, existing denominations rejected the Pentecostals (using derogatory terms like "Holy Roller"), and they formed fellowships separate from the historic churches.

Donald Gee was one of those early Pentecostals. He "definitely and personally accepted the Lord Jesus Christ as my Savior" in 1905 at a Congregational Church in North London. Seven years later, Gee's widowed mother met a missionary on furlough from India. "We felt a little nervous when first introduced to her, as we were warned she might be a little strange," Gee later wrote. Some attributed her strangeness to sunstroke. But she seemed sane enough to Donald and his mother as she spoke of a joyful Christian experience unknown to them. Even so, young Donald was leery, banging out loud tunes on the piano to make conversation difficult when the missionary came to call. He soon attended his first Pentecostal meeting — but remained skeptical.

The breakthrough came several years later, in January of 1913, when Gee took part in a night of prayer. "I had never heard such praying," he wrote. "They prayed as though God was intensely real, and as though his presence was actually in the room, which indeed was true." In March, Gee prayed to receive the baptism in the Holy Spirit. "I had no immediate manifestation, but went home supremely happy," he wrote, and two weeks later, while praying alone at his bedside, "I found myself beginning to utter words in a new tongue. I was in a condition of spiritual ecstasy, and taken up wholly with the Lord."

The next few years were not easy for Donald Gee and his new wife,

Ruth. He worked for a time as a sign painter. When World War I broke out, Gee, like most Pentecostals, was a conscientious objector. That meant he would be imprisoned unless he found alternative service deemed supportive of the war effort. He went to work on a farm, also leading a small nearby Pentecostal fellowship. Following the war, Gee was named pastor of a struggling Pentecostal chapel near Edinburgh called Bonnington Toll. He remained there throughout the 1920s and saw the fellowship grow and prosper. Lacking a formal education, Gee educated himself in Edinburgh by reading widely. For the rest of his life, Gee would look upon his years at Bonnington Toll as a time of great happiness. He never lost touch with the people there.

But Gee's future was not to be limited to a single congregation. He made contact with other Pentecostal leaders at the International Pentecostal Conference in Amsterdam in 1921, published the *Redemption Tidings Hymn Book* in 1924 (he was a talented musician), and began writing for religious journals. In 1928 Gee accepted an invitation to teach the Bible in Australia and New Zealand (extended by a former parishioner at Bonnington Toll who had emigrated to Australia) and wrote his first book, *Concerning Spiritual Gifts,* while on board ship. This sojourn lasted seven months, after which Gee taught in Stockholm and the United States.

By the time he resigned his pastorate at Bonnington Toll in 1930, Donald Gee was an international figure. He would make his mark in the years to come as Pentecostalism's "apostle of balance," giving speeches, writing books, and editing two periodicals in which he explained and commended the Pentecostal experience to those on the outside, while urging sound scholarship, moderation, and humility to those on the inside. Gee disliked cheap, sugary piety and was aware that the spiritually gifted are often tempted by pride. He had a lively sense of humor and easily laughed at himself. Gee's writings display a calmness and an openness to other views that was unusual among the early Pentecostals. He attended meetings of the World Council of Churches and cooperated with evangelist Billy Graham, for which other Pentecostals criticized him. Shortly before his death, at the suggestion of his son, Gee undertook a study of theologian Paul Tillich.

Although in conversation with the more traditional churches, Donald Gee never wavered from the understanding of the Christian life that came to him in 1913. At the heart of it — and at the heart of Pentecostalism today — was an outpouring of supernatural power called baptism in the Holy

Spirit. Like most Pentecostals, Gee was a Fundamentalist theologically but emphasized personal experience more than doctrinal correctness. Baptism in the Holy Spirit is not belief in a supernatural power, but a direct personal experience of it, like that which occurred on the Day of Pentecost, described in Acts 2. It comes at some point after one's initial Christian commitment and regeneration and is a specific, recognizable, and memorable event, usually accompanied by prayer and the laying on of hands. To receive the Holy Spirit, one must repent, trust Jesus, and invite Jesus to bestow the baptism. The result is a new sense of joy and power, accompanied by outward signs, or "spiritual gifts." Spiritual gifts bring power for service and witnessing beyond a believer's natural abilities, Gee says. They are supernatural manifestations.

These spiritual gifts, listed in 1 Corinthians 12:8-10, are the word of wisdom, the word of knowledge, faith, healing, miracle-working, prophecy, discernment of spirits, speaking in tongues, and interpretation of tongues. The older denominations have typically downplayed spiritual gifts, claiming that some were meant for apostolic times only and identifying others with natural abilities, thereby eliminating the supernatural element. But Pentecostals say the age of miracles has not ended (thereby parting company not only with some theological liberals but also with other Fundamentalists). In a column in *Redemption Tidings* magazine, Gee writes that Pentecostalism insists "the supernatural is still a rightful part of normal Christian experience today. The Pentecostal movement therefore believes that the sick can be healed, and that demons can be cast out, in the name of the Lord Jesus as in apostolic days. It claims that all the miraculous gifts of the Spirit which were manifested in the early church . . . should be operating today, and that the reason for their absence in the experience of the church as a whole is not that God withdrew these gifts, but that the church lost them through her unbelief and lukewarmness."

Speaking in tongues, or ecstatic speech, is the most controversial and perplexing of the gifts to outsiders. Gee regards tongue-speaking as the initial evidence of Spirit baptism and "a quite logical outcome from an intense fullness of emotion." Its chief purpose is communion with God in prayer and praise, but it can also seize an unbeliever's attention. An excessive use of this gift, however, can disrupt an assembly of worshipers when no one is present to interpret or translate what is said, so Gee recommends that tongue-speaking be regulated in public worship.

Toward the end of Donald Gee's life, Anglicans, Roman Catholics, and others began to receive the baptism in the Holy Spirit, usually calling it the "charismatic" movement. Older or "first wave" Pentecostals, remembering how these churches had ostracized them, kept their distance, but Gee welcomed these "second wave" Pentecostals as brothers and sisters, urging others to do the same.

In the century since its humble beginnings at the Azusa Street revival, Pentecostalism has grown into a worldwide fellowship embracing hundreds of millions of Christians, in both explicitly Pentecostal churches and traditional denominations. The movement's growth continues to this day and is especially vigorous in Africa, Latin America, and China. Future historians may count the rise of Christian Pentecostalism as the twentieth century's foremost religious event.

IN HIS OWN WORDS

Christian ministry today

Having established the principle that all true Christian ministry springs from a divine equipment, it is well to pause for a moment to measure how far we have wandered from this principle today when men are accepted for the work of ministry who do not even have any real witness to the New Birth, let alone the baptism in the Holy Ghost, which is the first great essential for effective service. And added to this, the average training given is simply a packing in of purely natural knowledge and the improvement of purely natural endowments with practically no regard for spiritual gifts.

Concerning Spiritual Gifts

Prophecy and teaching

Prophetic and emotional types of ministry tend to preponderate in times of revival but quickly degenerate into fanatical error unless balanced by teaching and logical ministry. Teaching tends to assume the ascendancy as a wave of revival recedes until once again the old prophetic fire asserts itself, and the church becomes rightly stirred by profound emotion. . . . Prophecy appeals mostly to the emotions; teaching, to the intellect. Prophecy sets on fire that which teaching enlightens. . . . They are, moreover, mutually corrective. If teaching is needed to correct the danger of fanaticism as a result of too much prophesying, yet truly inspired prophecy is also needed to correct the equal dangers of a purely intellectual and rational line of ministry.

Concerning Spiritual Gifts

The supernatural

. . . the early church *was,* and the church in every age *should* be, enjoying constant experience of the supernatural in its meetings for worship and also in the daily life of its members.

Concerning Spiritual Gifts

Speaking in tongues

Probably one reason there has apparently been an excessive manifestation and exercise of the gift of tongues during recent years is the *abnormal* spiritual condition of a church that has drifted tremendously from New Testament standards, and in nothing more than in its denial of the supernatural. Tongues have been needed again as a "sign," even in the church; and in addition to this, there has been the inevitable emphasis always placed upon a neglected truth or experience when it is first restored.

Concerning Spiritual Gifts

Gift or Giver?

Nothing more surely defeats the purpose of any love gift than for the recipient of it to put the gift before the giver. Yet such a danger is decidedly real where spiritual gifts are concerned. There can easily arise a morbid "gift-consciousness" that dwells upon either the real or the fancied possession of some spiritual gift far more than upon the life of fellowship with the Giver. There have been believers who have become so taken up with gifts and offices that the whole subject has become nauseous. Only the divine Giver can satisfy the soul — never just his gifts.

Concerning Spiritual Gifts

Baptism in the Holy Spirit

The New Testament appears to record as an unmistakable historical fact that there can be, and should be, a separate personal reception by the believer of the Holy Spirit in [the Spirit's] own distinctive and proper personality, subsequent to that first incoming at regeneration. This experience is called the "baptism in the Holy Spirit," and its purpose is not to impart life, but power. Its distinguishing manifestations are not fruit, but gifts.

The Fruit of the Spirit

The reality of the supernatural

. . . *the* great principle to stand for concerning the ministry is that it must be based upon spiritual gifts. This involves a recognition of the reality of the supernatural in Christian experience today: it will lead us to see afresh the lordship of Christ in giving such gifts and their resultant ministries (Ephesians 4:11) as he will. . . . *We must not confuse imitation with inspiration. . . . We must not let ourselves be misled by mere labels of office.* True ministry gifts consist not in name but in power. The gift will make the office: and until divine grace has bestowed the spiritual gift we can only wait and pray.

The Ministry Gifts of Christ

Expect the unexpected

A Pentecostal meeting where you always know what is going to happen next is backslidden.

Pentecost

"No room for individualists"

Some people think they are the ones God speaks to, and the rest are so backslidden that they cannot hear his voice. If you could read their minds you would see something like this, "As to the General Council, pooh! It is far too carnal to ever know the mind of the Lord! And as to the Executive Presbytery, it is all carnal!" There are some people who are so individualistic, so loose and rebellious, that they cannot submit to their brethren for five minutes. Those folk always make a mess of things, and they always will; they may succeed for awhile, but they will some time crash, for God has no room for individualists. The church of Christ is a *body* and we are members one of another.

Pentecost

Don't be too spiritual

I was attending a street meeting one time and listening to a fine young woman giving her testimony. She was full of the Holy Ghost, on fire for God, and had a real desire to win souls. She was talking to a bunch of coal miners and drunkards, and saying to them, "Dear ones," this. . . . "Dear ones," that. . . . "Dear ones," etc. They were not dear ones by a long way, and they did not like being called dear ones! You see, she had lived in the sugary sweet atmosphere of Pentecostal prayer meetings and had lost contact with the world. Prayer meetings are fine, God help us to attend more of them, but we must also keep our contact with mankind. If we live in an atmosphere of camp meetings, and shut ourselves in a glass house, and want to get sent to heaven labeled "Wrapped up with care," we lose that human touch which appeals to men and women, and we cease to be interpreters between God and man.

Pentecost

Let ecstatic feelings go

Let not those in the first flush of a new adventure in God rashly criticize those who for years have been, and still are, pressing on the upward way.

And let not those who commenced long ago look wistfully at the innocent enthusiasm of the neophyte as though it were something *they* should desire. To each his own joy. Ultimately our joy must come to rest simply in God himself.

After Pentecost

Tongue-speaking and holiness

Do not think that speaking in tongues will ever take the place of walking with God. The source of holiness is Christ, and the source of fruit is Christ enthroned in the heart and life.

After Pentecost

"Not a labor-saving device"

So many people have a mistaken idea that the baptism in the Holy Ghost does away with all need of hard work. I love to impress this upon our students at our Bible Schools: the baptism in the Holy Ghost is not a labor-saving device. You say, "I suppose I won't need to study; I won't need to think; I won't need to pray." That is the very reason so many people who have had the baptism in the Spirit have no ministry. They have had gifts but have never been diligent. Oh, the childish bubbling in tongues that we hear in some places!

After Pentecost

Don't avoid the cross

Many who have had a glorious baptism have absolutely lost out because they haven't taken up their cross and followed it after Pentecost. The outflow of the Spirit depends upon death to self. You may say, "Oh, I want an easy time; I want lots of friends, popularity, money, and plenty of leisure." ... The people who have a real fragrant ministry for God and souls do not have their cross on display, but it is in their lives; they know what it is to die daily.

After Pentecost

Unity

Unity is an essential thing, the keynote of growth. The unity here was unity of heart. Some of our brethren are fighting for unity of doctrine. The older I get the more tolerant I become, and the more I see that there are very few absolute essentials. Lots of things that we make issues of we shall blush about when we come before the judgment seat of Christ. God make us bigger.

After Pentecost

A new era

A new era appears to be dawning for that revival of the manifestations of the Holy Spirit that for the last fifty years has been associated almost exclusively with the Pentecostal movement. Can we rise by the grace of God to the challenge and responsibility of a new situation? We must shed our complexes, bred by the ostracism of half a century, and boldly take our place alongside our brethren in Christ in the older denominations who may now surprise us by their openness to new movings of God's Spirit. To share in such a new springtime of Pentecostal grace and power will be thrilling.

Address to British Assemblies of God Conference (1960)

Strife and division

[This is a time] for deep searchings of heart, and perhaps for reassessment of some things we have cherished in easier days, when we could afford the luxury of denominational strife and division. We are making ourselves liable to become companions of John and excommunicate those who have not signed on our dotted lines. We want all men to be "with us" rather than "for" the Son of God. Heresy-hunting is often a mark, for the discerning, of a receding fullness of the Spirit. We persecute, and we are persecuted, for things that are only relatively important. Yet we pride ourselves [that] we are fighting the battle of the Lord.

Pentecost column (1961)

The lure of the spectacular

Our constant danger, human nature being what it is, is to admire and emulate the spectacular rather than things of solid worth. This holds good in many spheres. We must face the fact that it applies to the Pentecostal order of things. We like miracles; we like inspiring oratory; we like to, in some sense or other, "move mountains." We are not so prone to inquire as to the ultimate results from the miracles or the inspired oratory in the spiritual and moral realm; neither do we always ask ourselves just *why* the "mountains" should be removed, or what lasting benefit their removal would bestow.

Fruitful or Barren?

Ostracism

To ostracize young fanatics and fanatical movements is almost to compel them to form new and strange sects outside the main body of the churches and even outside more worthy streams of revival. A double evil is the result. The zealots are deprived of the compensating qualities and ministries found in the whole Body of Christ, and lose themselves in a quagmire of spiritual pride, reckless extravagance, and endless subdivisions as they mistake their partial revelations for the whole. On the other hand, the main body robs itself of revivifying influences that, wisely harnessed, could yield lasting good.

All with One Accord

FOR REFLECTION AND DISCUSSION

Do miracles occur today? Have you observed one? What is a miracle?
Do you agree that "all true Christian ministry springs from a divine equipment"? How does one distinguish between "divine equipment" and "natural endowments"?
Where do you see evidence of the "constant experience of the supernatural" in your church?

Do you agree that today's church is in an "*abnormal* spiritual condition"
and "has drifted tremendously from New Testament standards"?
How so?

If "unity of heart" is more important than "unity of doctrine," of what use
is doctrine?

How does the church "confuse imitation with inspiration"?

Chapter 28

DOROTHY DAY

1897-1980

The Catholic Worker Movement

D OROTHY DAY GAVE BIRTH to a baby girl in March of 1926 and decided to have her baptized in the Roman Catholic Church. It was a wrenching decision. For years Day had worked as a journalist for radical newspapers in New York and traveled with socialists, communists, and anarchists who scorned the church for opposing everything noble and true. She was also much in love with Forster Batterham, her common-law husband and the father of her daughter, an atheist who fell into stony silence when Day mentioned religion. But she was drawn to the Catholic Church because of its sense of the transcendent and because the poor seemed to find solace there. Day also wanted to spare her daughter the rootless wandering she herself had known. But to present a child for baptism in the Catholic Church, "you must be a Catholic yourself," said a nun who had befriended Day. How could she sign on with an institution that seemed the very definition of hypocrisy, worldliness, and entrenched power? Day felt a "struggle for my own soul" and kept putting off a decision. "It got to the point where it was the simple question of whether I chose God or man," she said. Day wanted a family and feared that becoming a Catholic would sever relationships and condemn her to a life alone. But she was also lonely for God — in fact, she entitled her later autobiography *The Long Loneliness* — and that loneliness would not abate. Dorothy Day's daughter, Tamar, was baptized in June of 1926. When Day herself was baptized later that year, most of her friendships ended, as did her marriage to Batterham, though she continued occasionally to see him and talk with him over the telephone. She never stopped wanting Batterham and said of him, years later, "You can't be held responsible for sinning in your dreams."

One thing that did not change was Day's commitment to the poor. That commitment was one reason she had put off converting to Roman Catholicism. As a political radical, she had viewed the masses of immigrants swelling the streets of New York as both the victims and the heroes of history. How could so many of them find a spiritual home in an organization whose leaders seemed oblivious to their existence? Day became convinced that to choose God meant also to choose compassion, justice, and peace. But how was that to be made clear and put into practice?

For several years Dorothy Day struggled with this conundrum while eking out a living as a freelance writer. In December of 1932 she found herself in Washington, D.C., to write about a hunger march organized by her old communist friends. Moved by the plight of the marchers, she went to the National Shrine of the Immaculate Conception and prayed "with tears and anguish that some way would open up for me to use what talents I possessed for my fellow workers, for the poor." When she returned to her apartment in New York, Peter Maurin was awaiting her.

Maurin had received Day's name from a mutual friend. He was a disheveled Frenchman in his mid-fifties who had wandered around North America for twenty years, bouncing from one laboring job to another. Like Francis of Assisi, he had taken "holy poverty" as his bride, taking what little he earned and spending it on books or giving it away. His mind always seemed to be in another world. But Maurin had a vision and evangelical passion. He became Day's teacher. First he taught her about the papal encyclicals that urged charity and justice for the poor. Then he opened her eyes to envision a different world. Maurin sought to unite economics and politics with the Christian gospel, to re-organize society not around production and profits, but around helping people become all God had placed it in them to become. And he saw the church as the key to this. Maurin's vision was not one of government programs, but of the conversion of human souls.

Maurin and Day decided to found a newspaper. The first edition of *The Catholic Worker*, which appeared on the streets of New York in May of 1933, was an eight-page tabloid selling for a penny. The initial press run was 2,500 copies; by the end of the year, 100,000 copies were being printed each month, and many parish churches began ordering copies in bulk. *The Catholic Worker* contained commentary on the Christian life and how to create a world where, in Day's words, "it is easier to do good." Dorothy Day would edit the paper for forty-seven years, until her death. She traveled the world to give voice to the poor, writing firsthand accounts of events and conditions overlooked in the mainstream press. Her column, entitled "On Pilgrimage," was a potpourri of reporting, devotion, travelogue, editorial, personal journal, and quotations from other sources. The column was fresh and spontaneous — Day said time spent refining her prose could better be spent serving the poor. She gave to religious concepts a specific time, place, and face. Day's words could — and still can — rivet a reader's attention and shake his soul.

But Dorothy Day was more than a journalist, and her convictions were more than ideas — she lived what she wrote. "We do not feel that we can talk in the paper about something we are not practicing," she wrote in 1936. Day not only visited and reported on the poor; she lived with the poor — by choice.

During the first year that *The Catholic Worker* was being published, destitute people began showing up at the paper's offices in the Bowery. What was to be done with them? It did not take Day long to answer that question. She kept a pot of hot coffee on the stove, cooked and served meals, and gave away what clothing she could beg. And beg she did — her columns typically included unapologetic appeals for clothing, money, and labor. The paper's readers responded not only by volunteering at *The Catholic Worker* offices but by founding and running other "houses of hospitality" all over the world. Visiting these houses and encouraging the volunteers and the poor they served became a regular part of Day's life. Her columns often carried bylines far from home. Hundreds of these houses continue to serve the poorest of the poor today.

Poverty resulting from unjust social conditions is horrible and demeaning, Day says, but poverty voluntarily embraced is a glorious thing, ennobling the soul. "Precariousness" is an essential element of true spiritual poverty, she says — one need not know where the next meal will come from, and to store up funds for tomorrow is a faithless denial of one's dependence on God. Voluntary poverty, manual labor, detachment from material things, and the primacy of the spiritual are the hallmarks of Dorothy Day's spirituality. On one occasion, when an eager young volunteer had come to write for *The Catholic Worker* and asked how one got on the editorial board, Day responded, "Your work begins at the kitchen sink."

The Catholic Worker community had no membership standards; it consisted of whoever showed up. Day noted the dignity and courage of people insufficiently clad and fed and deprived of worldly goods, and called them a "bright spot" in her life. Perhaps the most famous story about Day is of the morning a wealthy patron approached her and said, "Miss Day, I have a little something for you." It was a diamond ring. Day accepted the ring and then gave it to a dirty and irascible woman known as "the Weasel" who lived in a nearby tenement and cared for her mentally retarded adult son. Asked why she had not sold the ring and used the money to pay the Weasel's rent, Day replied, "She has her dignity. If she wants to sell the ring, she is free to do so and pay her rent. If she wants to take a cruise to Bermuda, she can do that, too. Or she can wear the ring, just like the woman who gave it to us. Do you suppose God made diamonds just for the rich?"

The drunkenness, laziness, and dissoluteness of many whom she served was not lost on Dorothy Day, but she refused to favor the "deserving" or even to ask who was deserving and who was not. "Always room, always enough for one more — everyone just takes a little less," she said. Her love did not discriminate. She never pretended it was easy to love a sick and destitute old woman with lice in her hair and open sores on her body, but in everyone who came to her, she looked for the face of Christ. Whether they had any religious belief didn't matter — unlike most other religious missions to the poor, Day's Catholic Worker House made no effort to convert people. There were no sermons or lectures, only an unremarked crucifix on the wall.

How long were people permitted to stay at the Catholic Worker House? "We let them stay forever," Day once said. "They live with us, they die with us, and we give them a Christian burial. We pray for them after they are dead. Once they are taken in, they become members of the family. Or rather, they always were members of the family. They are our brothers and sisters in Christ."

Her conviction that Christian love embraces everyone without reservation led Day to pacifism. For her, the enemy fell within the embrace of Christ, and she therefore opposed killing — of anyone, always, everywhere, for any reason. When most Catholics around the world were supporting Francisco Franco against the communists and republicans in the Spanish Civil War in the 1930s, Day took neither side. That would probably not have gotten her into trouble had she not held to that position after the Japanese attacked Pearl Harbor in 1941. During World War II, her uncompromising stance angered many who had previously supported *The Catholic Worker*. Day was urged to stick to feeding the poor, but she insisted that works of mercy could not be separated from works of peace. Subscriptions to the paper were cancelled by the thousands, yet Day held firm. Circulation did not reach its pre-war level again until twenty years later, when, during the Vietnam war, Day's position — unchanged — found wider support.

Day's relationship with the Roman Catholic hierarchy was tenuous. That she was a woman and a layperson probably kept her out of some trouble. She also attended mass daily, prayed at length every morning, and was known for her orthodox theological views. But in private, Day often referred to the church as "the cross upon which Christ is crucified." One observer said the chancery office regarded her as "a kind of time bomb" that could explode and create trouble at any moment. Angry Catholics often wrote to New York's Cardinal Francis Spellman asking him to "talk to that woman." Once she was summoned to the chancery office, asked to be seated, and told, "We got some complaints in our office about what you're doing. But we know what you're doing. We don't need to be instructed by other people. We told them we would talk to you. Now we have seen you and we have done that. That is enough. Thank you for coming."

Dorothy Day died on November 29, 1980, with her daughter, Tamar, at her side. At her funeral, along with cardinals, bishops, monsignors, and hundreds of homeless people, Forster Batterham was seen to make his communion.

IN HER OWN WORDS

On her life

I feel that I have done nothing well. But I have done what I could.

The Long Loneliness

The scandal of the church

I loved the church for Christ made visible. Not for itself, because it was so often a scandal to me. Romano Guardini said the church is the cross on which Christ was crucified; one could not separate Christ from his cross, and one must live in a state of permanent dissatisfaction with the church. The scandal of businesslike priests, of collective wealth, the lack of a sense of responsibility for the poor, the worker, the Negro, the Mexican, the Filipino, and even the oppression of these, and the consenting to the oppression of them by our industrialist-capitalist order — these made me feel often that priests were more like Cain than Abel. "Am I my brother's keeper?" they seemed to say in respect to the social order. There was plenty of charity but too little justice. And yet the priests were the dispensers of the sacraments, bringing Christ to men, all enabling us to put on Christ and to achieve more nearly in the world a sense of peace and unity. "The worst enemies would be those of our own household" [Matt. 10:36], Christ has warned us.

The Long Loneliness

Live with the poor

Going around and seeing such sights is not enough. To help the organizers, to give what you have for relief, to pledge yourself to voluntary poverty for life so that you can share with your brothers is not enough. One must live with them, share with them their suffering too. Give up one's privacy, and mental and spiritual comforts as well as physical.

The Long Loneliness

Because I want to

I believe because I want to believe, I hope because I want to hope, I love because I want to love.

Loaves and Fishes

Humility

One must be humble only from a divine motive; otherwise humility is a debasing and repulsive attitude. To be humble and meek for love of God — that is beautiful. But to be humble and meek because your bread and butter depends on it is awful. It is to lose one's sense of human dignity.

House of Hospitality

Prayer

But more and more I see that prayer is the answer, it is the clasp of the hand, the joy and keen delight in the consciousness of that Other. Indeed, it is like falling in love.

The Third Hour

Thanks for your response

The editors wish to thank all the good friends who responded so immediately to the letter of appeal sent out a few weeks ago. God is with us, the saints protect us. Each time we have asked for aid, the money was immediately forthcoming to pay each and every bill. True, this leaves nothing for the next printing bill, which will be due as you read this paper. But God seems to intend us to depend solely on him. We must live this lesson of dependence on him that we preach in these pages. Economic security, something every reader and we ourselves would like to have, is not for us. We must live by faith, from day to day. . . .

"On Pilgrimage," February 1934

What right have we?

What right has any one of us to security when God's poor are suffering? What right have I to sleep in a comfortable bed when so many are sleeping in the shadows of buildings here in this neighborhood of the *Catholic Worker* office? What right have we to food when many are hungry, or to liberty when the Scottsboro boys and so many labor organizers are in jail?

"On Pilgrimage," July-August, 1935

Day's vision

The vision is this. We are working for "a new heaven and a new *earth*, wherein justice dwelleth" [Isa. 65:17; Rev. 21:1]. We are trying to say with action, "Thy will be done on *earth* as it is in heaven." We are working for a Christian social order.

"On Pilgrimage," February 1940

Joy amid suffering

There is poverty and hunger and war in the world. And we prepare for more war. There is desperate suffering with no prospect of relief. But we would be contributing to the misery and desperation of the world if we failed to rejoice in the sun, the moon, and the stars, in the rivers which surround this island on which we live, in the cool breezes of the bay, in what food we have and in the benefactors God sends.

"On Pilgrimage," July-August 1940

Sentimentality?

Another Catholic newspaper says it sympathizes with our sentimentality. This is a charge always leveled against pacifists. We are supposed to be afraid of the suffering, of the hardships of war. But let those who talk of softness, of sentimentality, come to live with us in cold, unheated houses in the slums. Let them come to live with the criminal, the unbalanced, the drunken, the perverted. (It is not the decent poor, it is not the decent sinner who was the recipient of Christ's love.) Let them live with rats, with vermin, bedbugs, roaches, lice (I could describe the several kinds of body lice). . . . Then when they have lived with these comrades, with these sights and sounds, let our critics talk of sentimentality. As we have often quoted Dostoevsky's Father Zossima, "Love in practice is a harsh and dreadful thing compared to love in dreams."

"On Pilgrimage," February 1942

The joy of doing one's duty

For a total Christian, the goad of duty is not needed — always prodding one to perform this or that good deed. It is not a duty to help Christ; it is a privilege.

"On Pilgrimage," December 1945

To love others

When you love people, you see all the good in them, all the Christ in them. God sees Christ, his Son, in us. And so we should see Christ in others, *and nothing else*, and love them. . . . And this is not easy. Everyone will try to kill that love in you, even your nearest and dearest; at least, they will try to prune it. "Don't you know this, that, and the other thing about this person? He or she did this. If you don't want to hear it, you must hear. It is for your good to hear it. It is my duty to tell you, and it is your duty to take recognition of it. You must stop loving, modify your loving, show your disapproval. You cannot possibly love — if you pretend you do, you are a hypocrite and the truth is not in you. You are contributing to the delinquency of that person by your sentimental blindness. It is such people as you who

311

add to the sum total of confusion and wickedness and soft appeasement and compromise and the policy of expediency in the world. You are to blame for Communism, for industrial capitalism, and finally for hell on earth!" The antagonism often rises to a crescendo of vituperation, an intensification of opposition on all sides. You are quite borne down by it. And the only Christian answer is *love*, to the very end, to the laying down of your life.

"On Pilgrimage," April 1948

To see Christ in others

To love with understanding, and without understanding. To love blindly, and to folly. To see only what is lovable. To think only of these things. To see the best in everyone around, their virtues, rather than their faults. To see Christ in them!

"On Pilgrimage," December 1948

Martyrdom

Martyrdom is not gallantly standing before a firing squad. Usually it is the losing of a job because of not taking a loyalty oath, or buying a war bond, or paying a tax. Martyrdom is small, hidden, misunderstood. Or if it is a bloody martyrdom, it is the cry in the dark, the terror, the shame, the loneliness, nobody to hear, nobody to suffer with, let alone to save. Oh, the loneliness of all of us in these days, in all the great moments of our lives, this dying which we do, by little and by little, over a short space of time or over the years. One day is as a thousand in these crises. A week in jail is as a year.

"On Pilgrimage," January 1951

Let go

The main thing is not to hold on to anything. But the tragedy is that we do, we all do hold on — to our books, our tools, such as typewriters, our clothes; and instead of rejoicing when they are taken from us we lament.

We protest when people take our time or privacy. We are holding on to these "goods" too.

"On Pilgrimage," May 1952

Saint Dorothy?

Don't call me a saint. I don't want to be dismissed that easily.

Day's frequent response to doting admirers

FOR REFLECTION AND DISCUSSION

Has there ever been a time of which you would say, "It got to the point where it was the simple question of whether I chose God or man"? How did you choose? Would you make the same choice again? What distinguishes the one choice from the other?

If it is possible to believe, hope, and love because you want to, why do so many people struggle with believing, hoping, and loving?

How would you answer the questions Day poses in the quotation entitled "What right have we?"

Is there such a thing as a "Christian social order"? If so, what does it look like? If not, what kind of social order should we strive for?

Must love be "a harsh and dreadful thing"?

How is it possible to "see Christ in others, *and nothing else*"?

Chapter 29

THOMAS MERTON

1915-1968

Solitude

T HE NAME OF Thomas Merton burst upon the American literary scene in 1948 with the publication of his autobiography, *The Seven Storey Mountain.* The hardback edition sold 600,000 copies almost immediately, and paperback editions soon followed. The book's success stunned its author and everyone else, for a volume more at odds with the prevailing culture could hardly have been imagined. Most Americans returning from World War II were eager to get an education and a job and then settle down to raise their families in the comfortable new suburbs. *The Seven Storey Mountain* confronted them with a man who had tasted that dream, then abandoned it for a life most would have considered quaint, bizarre, and irrelevant: Merton became a Trappist monk.

Why did he do this? *The Seven Storey Mountain* tells the tale, often passionately and in colorful detail. Merton wandered rootlessly in his early life. His mother, from Ohio, and his father, from New Zealand, had met in France, where Merton was born in 1915. His mother died when the boy was five years old. Thereafter, his father, an itinerant musician and painter, cared for his son when he could, often aided by Merton's maternal grandparents. The young Merton spent time in Bermuda, Maryland, Long Island, France, and England. He earned a degree in English from Columbia University and then taught at St. Bonaventure. He embraced communism for a time, as was fashionable among young intellectuals in the 1930s, and slogged through his young adult years with a mix of intellectual hubris, cynicism, and sensuality.

But Merton knew something was amiss in his life. He refers to "the devils that hung like vampires in my soul." He began reading Augustine, Thomas à Kempis, William Blake, and Jacques Maritain, and was baptized into the Roman Catholic Church. He pondered ordination, went methodically through the *Spiritual Exercises* of Ignatius, and entered into conversation with the Franciscans. When he made a Holy Week retreat in 1941 at Gethsemani Abbey, a Trappist monastery in central Kentucky, Merton knew he had at last come home. A few months later he returned to Gethsemani to stay.

The Seven Storey Mountain reveals a young man in love with the idea of being a monk, heroically and romantically turning his back on the world to embrace a life of cloistered solitude. For all the book's power and depth, it is not yet the work of a mature Christian soul, and Merton began moving beyond it almost the moment it appeared in bookstores. His later published writings include dozens more books and a stream of essays on spiritual, literary, and social themes, in both religious and secular journals. In these works Merton questions many of the assumptions that had made his autobiography such a sensation, pushes against the strictures of his order, and engages the world in startling new ways. As his fame continued to grow, a steady parade of admirers traveled to Gethsemani to talk with him — hardly the norm for a Trappist monk. His superior at Gethsemani, irritated and apprehensive, sometimes censored Merton's correspondence, a practice Merton called "absurd, crackpot, infantile" in a (presumably not censored) letter to a friend. He once said that "an author in a Trappist monastery is like a duck in a chicken coop. He would give anything in the world to be a chicken instead of a duck." Merton never second-guessed his monastic vocation, but he did try for a time to transfer to another monastery and eventually gained permission to live as a hermit in a cottage on the Gethsemani grounds, where he spent the last three years of his life.

Thomas Merton craved solitude, yet led retreats and delivered insightful, spontaneous addresses to novices (tapes of these talks survive), welcomed conversation with visitors, and corresponded with hundreds of people. Merton distinguished between solitude and merely being alone. He knew time spent alone could lead to self-absorption and a dangerous preoccupation with measuring one's spiritual progress. Though places of quiet encourage solitude, they are not essential to it, Merton said, and noisy environs do not necessarily destroy it. It isn't noise in the room or out the window that threatens solitude, but noise inside the soul, "that inner dialogue with self that is a jumble of frivolous thoughts, worrisome cares, and negative feelings," our goals, virtues, rivalries, and ambitions. A soul cluttered with these things has no room for God, Merton felt. Solitude is something quite different, involving detachment from worldly concerns. It leads to compassion because it teaches humility, acceptance of our rightful place in relation to other people. When we have abandoned our pretensions and illusions and have nothing left to prove, peace becomes possible, both within us and in the world at large.

Merton often distinguishes between the "false self" and the "true self." The false self is the person that we fancy ourselves to be and that we show to the world. It "wants to exist outside the reach of God's will and God's love — outside of reality and outside of life," he wrote in *New Seeds of Contemplation.* Driven to succeed, the false self compares itself to the false selves presented by others. Isolated and alone, it is a stranger to community (though it may seek crowded places). Far from being detached from the ways of the world, it is addicted to them. Its distinguishing marks are anxiety, fear, and competition. We mistake this mask for our true selves, living an illusion, a shadow, while our true selves remain out of sight.

The true self is the person God calls us to become, expressed in each person's unique character and personality, but always in union with God and with one another. This is what the biblical idea of the "image of God" means. Though we were created in God's image, that image has been covered over with the false self. How do we regain our true self? We don't and we can't. Only God can do it. This is one of the themes of *The Seven Storey Mountain* — that God was working in Merton's soul, drawing him home, even when he was unaware of it and his thoughts were far from God. His emphasis is always on the power of God within the soul, not on one's own energy or accomplishments. This is grace, "the sanctifying energy of God acting dynamically in our life." Though we are to seek God, it is less a matter of our seeking than of our "being found, loved, and possessed by God, in such a way that his action in us makes us completely generous and helps us to transcend our limitations."

Merton affirmed the importance of right belief and right behavior, but transformation from the false self to the true self requires more than that, he said. Right beliefs and behaviors can, in fact, be obstacles to transformation if we believe spiritual growth depends on what we think or do. Learning to live into the true self is hard because it requires us to abandon our trust in what the false self has relied on, including our skills, virtues, achievements — everything that is familiar. Transformation requires that we embrace what cannot be known. We must learn "to live by a power and a light that seem not to be there." The experience can be one of heaviness and defeat at first, but there is no other way. This new life is the goal of prayer and contemplation, and when the true self begins to bloom, a subtle but pervasive peace seeps into the soul. We are no longer captive to falsehood and illusion and are at last free to become the persons our Creator intends, liberated from confusion and imaginary needs and desires, united with and in God.

Important as solitude was for Merton, he came to see that the transformation into the true self cannot take place in isolation from others. The new life is meant to be shared. An almost mystical awareness of this, recounted in his *Conjectures of a Guilty Bystander,* came to Merton one day in 1958 in Louisville, in the center of the city's downtown shopping district. "I was suddenly overwhelmed with the realization that I loved all those people, that they were mine and I theirs, that we could not be alien to one another even though we were total strangers. It was like waking from a dream of separateness, of spurious self-isolation in a special world, the world of renunciation and supposed holiness. The whole illusion of a separate holy existence is a dream."

Merton's life and his writing now took a new turn, away from the understanding of monasticism practiced at Gethsemani and articulated in *The Seven Storey Mountain*. He now mocked the pious youth who had written that book as a "stereotype of the world-denying contemplative — the man who spurned New York, spat on Chicago, and tromped on Louisville." Engagement with the world replaced flight from the world in his vision of the faithful life (and Merton felt no need to apologize for changing his mind). "We all need one another, we all complete one another. God's will is found in this mutual interdependence," he wrote in *Life and Holiness*. The Christian way is that of spontaneous charity to our brothers, and "every man is, to the Christian, in some sense a brother." Articles on the spiritual implications of poverty, racism, and war now streamed from his typewriter. He took up correspondence with writers who were not only not Catholic, but not religious at all. The new Thomas Merton displeased his superiors and other American Roman Catholics, who urged him to stay put in the monastery and stick to writing books on prayer. But if anyone thought that in engaging the world Merton had abandoned his interest in the life of the spirit, they misunderstood him — he was merely extending its boundaries.

The circumstances surrounding Merton's death have intrigued and perplexed observers since the news was announced. He died in Bangkok. What was a cloistered monk from Kentucky, even one interested in social questions, doing in Thailand? Merton had long been interested in Eastern religions, an interest put on hold during his early years at Gethsemani, but one that flowered again in the 1960s. He saw that all the world's great monastic traditions taught, in one way or another, that the true self is realized through solitude. Always eager to learn and sure that others had much to teach him, Merton wanted to share experiences and ways of praying with like-minded seekers. He never thought of leaving his order or the church because he recognized that Eastern monastics stopped at discovering the true self, while for Merton and for Western monasticism generally, that was but a step along the way to knowing and loving God. Merton never veered from that goal. He had been scheduled to deliver a paper to a gathering of monastics from all the world's great religions. A few hours before he was to speak, on December 10, 1968, Merton was accidentally electrocuted when he touched an improperly grounded electric fan while stepping out of his bath. He was fifty-three years old.

IN HIS OWN WORDS

The human soul

When a ray of light strikes a crystal, it gives a new quality to the crystal. And when God's infinitely disinterested love plays upon a human soul, the same kind of thing takes place. And that is the life called sanctifying grace. The soul of man, left to its own natural level, is a potentially lucid crystal left in darkness. It is perfect in its own nature, but it lacks something that it can only receive from outside and above itself. But when the light shines in it, it becomes in a manner transformed into light and seems to lose its nature in the splendor of a higher nature, the nature of the light that is in it.

The Seven Storey Mountain

The will

The life of the soul is not knowledge, it is love, since love is the act of the supreme faculty, the will, by which man is formally united to the final end of all his strivings — by which man becomes one with God.

The Seven Storey Mountain

The world's logic

The logic of worldly success rests on a fallacy: the strange error that our perfection depends on the thoughts and opinions and applause of other men! A weird life it is, indeed, to be living always in somebody else's imagination, as if that were the only place in which one could at last become real!

The Seven Storey Mountain

Happiness

A happiness that is sought for ourselves alone can never be found: for a happiness that is diminished by being shared is not big enough to make us happy. There is a false and momentary happiness in self-satisfaction, but it always leads to sorrow because it narrows and deadens our spirit. True happiness is found in unselfish love, a love which increases in proportion as it is shared.

No Man Is an Island

Hope

He who hopes in God trusts God, whom he never sees, to bring him to the possession of things that are beyond imagination.

No Man Is an Island

Prayer

Prayer is inspired by God in the depth of our own nothingness. . . . The man whose prayer is so pure that he never asks God for anything does not know who God is, and does not know who he is himself: for he does not know his own need of God.

No Man Is an Island

Christ

A satanic theology . . . hides Christ from us altogether, and makes him so impossibly beautiful that he must remain infinitely remote from our wretchedness.

Conjectures of a Guilty Bystander

The beauty of the church

The beauty of the church shines also in those who are helped and who have nothing to give except the fact that they can be helped: which is a great gift to the church! It makes them most important in the church.

Conjectures of a Guilty Bystander

Saints

The eyes of the saint make all beauty holy and the hands of the saint consecrate everything they touch to the glory of God, and the saint is never offended by anything and judges no man's sin because he does not know sin. He knows the mercy of God. He knows that his own mission on earth is to bring that mercy to all men.

New Seeds of Contemplation

The devil's strategy

The devil makes many disciples by preaching against sin. He convinces them of the great evil of sin, induces a crisis of guilt by which "God is satisfied," and after that he lets them spend the rest of their lives meditating on the intense sinfulness and evident reprobation of other men. . . . In the devil's theology, the important thing is to be absolutely right and to prove that everybody else is absolutely wrong.

New Seeds of Contemplation

Humility

It is not humility to insist on being someone that you are not. It is as much as saying that you know better than God who you are and who you ought to be. How do you expect to arrive at the end of your own journey if you take the road to another man's city?

New Seeds of Contemplation

Believing

You can only believe what you do not know.

New Seeds of Contemplation

Faith

Faith is an act in which the intellect is content to know God by *loving* him and accepting his statements about himself on his own terms.

New Seeds of Contemplation

Your enemies

Do not be too quick to assume that your enemy is an enemy of God just because he is *your* enemy. Perhaps he is your enemy precisely because he can find nothing in you that gives glory to God.

New Seeds of Contemplation

Obedience and freedom

Obedience is not the abdication of freedom but its prudent use under certain well-defined conditions. . . . The mere ability to choose between good and evil is the lowest limit of freedom, and the only thing that is free about it is the fact that we can still choose good. . . . Only the man who has rejected all evil so completely that he is unable to desire it at all is truly free.

New Seeds of Contemplation

God's presence

The infinite God has no boundaries and our minds cannot set limits to him or to his love. His presence is then "grasped" in the general awareness of loving faith, it is "realized" without being scientifically and precisely known, as we know a specimen under a microscope. His presence cannot be verified as we would verify a laboratory experiment. Yet it can be spiritually realized as long as we do not insist on verifying it. As soon as we try to verify the spiritual presence as an object of exact knowledge, God eludes us.

Contemplative Prayer

Seeking God

We ruin our life of prayer if we are constantly examining our prayer and seeking the fruit of prayer in a peace that is nothing more than a psychological process. The only thing to seek in contemplative prayer is God; and we seek him successfully when we realize that we cannot find him unless he shows himself to us, and yet at the same time that he would not have inspired us to seek him unless we had already found him.

Thoughts in Solitude

Silence is salvation

My life is a listening. His is a speaking. My salvation is to hear and respond. For this, my life must be silent. Hence, my silence is my salvation.

Thoughts in Solitude

Prayer of trust

My Lord God, I have no idea where I am going. I do not see the road ahead of me. I cannot know for certain where it will end. Nor do I really know myself, and the fact that I think I am following your will does not mean that I am actually doing so. But I believe that the desire to please you does in fact please you. And I hope I have that desire in all that I am doing. I hope that I will never do anything apart from that desire. And I know that if I do this you will lead me by the right road, though I may know nothing about it. Therefore I will trust you always though I may seem to be lost and in the shadow of death. I will not fear, for you are ever with me, and you will never leave me to face my perils alone.

Thoughts in Solitude

Listening for God

Inner silence depends on a continual seeking, a continual crying in the night, a repeated bending over the abyss. If we cling to a silence we think we have found forever, we stop seeking God and the silence goes dead within us.

Thoughts in Solitude

Success

Be anything you like, be madmen, drunks, and bastards of every shape and form, but at all costs avoid one thing: success.

"Learning to Live"

Faith and doubt

Faith means doubt. Faith is not the suppression of doubt. It is the over-coming of doubt, and you overcome doubt by going through it. The man of faith who has never experienced doubt is not a man of faith. Consequently, a monk is one who has to struggle in the depths of his being with the presence of doubt, to break through beyond doubt into a servitude which is very, very deep because it is not his own personal servitude, it is the servitude of God himself, in us.

The Asian Journal

Learning from Asia

I am convinced that what one might call typically "Asian" conditions of nonhurrying and of patient waiting must prevail over the Western passion for immediate results. For this reason I think it is above all important for Westerners like myself to learn what little they can from Asia, *in* Asia. I think we must seek not merely to make superficial reports *about* the Asian traditions, but to live and share those traditions, as far as we can, by living them in their traditional milieu. I need not add that I think we have now reached a stage of (long-overdue) religious maturity at which it may be possible for someone to remain perfectly faithful to a Christian and Western monastic commitment, and yet to learn in depth from, say, a Buddhist or Hindu discipline and experience.

The Asian Journal

FOR REFLECTION AND DISCUSSION

What in today's world encourages us to live into the "false self"?
What in your life encourages solitude and what discourages it?
How did Merton's understanding of faithful living change as he matured?
Why does Merton think Satan wants us to think of Jesus as beautiful?
Write a prayer about the road ahead of you in the style of Merton's
    "prayer of trust."
Merton said to avoid success at all costs. If not as "successful," how
    would he describe the spiritual life he aspired to?
If "faith is not the suppression of doubt," what is it?

Chapter 30

MADELEINE L'ENGLE

1918-2007

Narrative Spirituality

"TELL ME A STORY." It isn't just children who make that request. Adults read novels, visit the theater, watch television, and listen to gossip to hear stories. As a preacher, I have noticed that people rarely remember the "point" of my sermons, but they remember the stories I tell.

The Bible is packed with stories, and Jesus was a renowned storyteller. These stories have been supplemented through the centuries with tales from the lives of the saints. Many such stories are accounts of historical events; others are made up. During the past century, academic scholars tried to isolate and identify the "truth" in these stories. "Truth" was seen as what actually happened (as distinguished from the story later told and handed down), or as the kernel of meaning to be extracted from the story. The story itself could then be discarded as no longer necessary. Conservatives and liberals have both, in their own ways, participated in this effort. Both sought a factual statement that could stand apart from the story. The result has been disappointing. Not only do the statements of "truth" often conflict, but they lack the power of the original stories.

More recent thinkers have begun to look at stories differently. Unlike propositional statements, they say, stories invite people to look for their own meanings or explanations. A story will in fact be many different stories, as each person filters it through the images, values, relationships, hopes, and fears of her life — that is, through her own story.

What then is a "true" story? When a tale is told or an event occurs, people experience it differently. This fact suggests that "truth" may be malleable, different from one person to another and from one time to another. Take, for example, the exodus story in the Bible. What actually happened when the Israelites crossed the Red Sea? One person might say, "A strong wind arose and blew the water away." Another might say, "Moses was smart and knew when to tell the people to get moving." Another might say, "The Egyptians stupidly followed the Israelites and assumed the wind direction would not change." And another might say, "The Lord delivered us with a mighty hand and an outstretched arm." And they could all be right. It is precisely this multifaceted character of stories that makes them suggestive, beloved, and memorable. To eliminate the story would be to obscure or diminish the truth it carries.

Among the foremost advocates of this understanding of truth — and a splendid storyteller — was Madeleine L'Engle. "I write stories because that's how I look for truth," she said in an interview. "We live in a world where it's very difficult for people to understand that a story can be truthful and not factual. . . . We're told to outgrow stories, that they're only for kids. That's one of the most terrible things that has happened to us as a people — we've been impaled upon literalism."

L'Engle occasionally wrote about stories and truth — *Story as Truth* is the subtitle of one of her books — but more often she simply told stories and invited readers to discover what they meant. It was her eighth book, *A Wrinkle in Time,* that brought L'Engle to the attention of the literary world when it won the Newbery Award for children's literature in 1963. *A Wrinkle in Time* is a fantasy in which a brother and sister travel through time and space in search of their lost father, a scientist studying time travel. They visit a planet called Camazotz, where they are drawn into a cosmic conflict between good and evil. L'Engle's winsome side emerges in her depiction of supernatural characters who, in interacting with the children, show themselves to be well-intentioned but as bumbling and perplexed as human beings. Two later books carry the story forward to its conclusion.

L'Engle's stories are marvelously diverse. She wrote over sixty books in several genres. Sometimes a character from one kind of story surprisingly appears in a story of a quite different sort. She regarded the characters in her books as "family" and said she didn't want to bid them good-bye at the end of a book, which is why they often pop up in subsequent books. Although best known for her works for children, L'Engle didn't consider herself merely or mainly a children's author. "If I have something that is too difficult for adults to swallow, then I will write it in a book for children," she said. She told a variety of stories for adults as well.

Several of L'Engle's adult books are autobiographical. A series of four volumes called the Crosswicks Journals relates her experiences as a wife, mother, and caregiver at the country home in western Connecticut where she and her husband, actor High Franklin, raised their children. They ran the country store in Goshen, Connecticut, a small dairy village, and quickly became part of the community. It was there, at the local Congregational church, that L'Engle had her first good experience of church life. The Crosswicks Journals artfully blend reminiscences of family life and people and events in the community, reflections on biblical tales, meditations on the ways of God, and comments on issues of the day. These stories often include homespun wisdom and gentle humor.

L'Engle's adult fiction offers complex, believable characters who struggle with faith and doubt, ego and humility, good and evil. Most are mature, creative people who have fulfilling careers, maintain healthy marriages, and raise their children attentively and responsibly. While none of this comes to them easily, L'Engle showed, both in her fiction and in her auto-biography, how it is possible to live faithfully even in difficult straits. Family life is central to L'Engle's stories. Her women are strong, confident, and engaged in the world, but never at the expense of her male characters. Though she was sympathetic to the goals of Christian feminism, it never figured prominently in her writing. Among L'Engle's works of adult fiction are a series of novels about the Austin family, beginning with *Meet the Austins* in 1960, and *A Severed Wasp*, published in 1982 and centering on the Cathedral of St. John the Divine in New York, where L'Engle served as librarian and maintained an apartment following the death of her husband in 1986.

Subtle biblical images and references are woven throughout L'Engle's works. She also published several explicitly biblical novels, probing and elaborating on the lives of biblical characters in the style of the Hebrew *midrash.*

In addition, L'Engle wrote several works of poetry and essays on art and writing. It is in poetry, she once said, that the Incarnation is best expressed and understood. She said that inspiration comes to a writer during the writing, not before. "My writing knows more than I know. What a writer must do is listen to her book. It might take you where you don't expect to go. That's what happens when you write stories. You listen and you say 'Aha!' and you write it down. A lot of it is not planned, not conscious; it happens while you're doing it."

Madeleine L'Engle was an only child, the daughter of well-to-do parents who loved her but were sometimes distant. Her father was a drama critic, her mother a pianist. Their lives were well established by the time their daughter was born, and they did not greatly alter their routine on her account. Most of Madeleine's childhood was spent in New York City, with long intervals at the home of her maternal grandparents in Jacksonville, Florida, where she acquired an understanding and appreciation of the American South. When Madeleine was twelve, the family moved to Europe, where she attended a Swiss boarding school. She was perceived as a nonconformist and often found her best friends in books. During her youth, Madeleine devoted much of her energy to writing stories, poetry, and diary entries, exhibiting a creative bent that was not always appreciated at school.

L'Engle credited her Episcopal upbringing for giving her an early awareness of language and imagery, but her early experiences at church were not always happy ones, and as a young adult, she was an agnostic. It was not church but science that brought her back to God. As she began to discover relativity theory, quantum mechanics, and the new physics, L'Engle found herself humbled and awestruck. Einstein was for her "Saint Albert, my favorite theologian." She was asking questions about the nature and meaning of the universe when she came across Einstein's comment that anyone not lost in rapture at the power of the mind behind the universe is "as good as a burned out candle." L'Engle began reading extensively until she grasped the major ideas of the new physics, finding herself increasingly in awe of the Creator of the universe. As a result, L'Engle never saw science and religion as conflicting. Both scientists and religious believers, she felt, become locked into conventional ideas and begin to think that truth revolves around them. Then when a new fact comes to light which suggests that truth is more vast or beautiful or subtle than their theories would allow, they resist it. "Scientists are as bad as Christians in hanging on to what they think they know," she said. The science behind her fantasy novels is sophisticated and informed, but never definitive or final. Her works encourage the asking of questions and are distrustful of quick answers.

Madeleine L'Engle has her detractors, especially in conservative Christian circles, where she has been accused of promoting universalism, denigrating organized Christianity, and promoting the occult. The Christianity in her writing is never blatant. Like real people, her characters struggle with spiritual and moral questions and are often perplexed and uncertain. This is as true in her biblically based works as in her novels. L'Engle didn't think of herself as a "religious writer," since the terms "religion" and "Christianity" are "encrusted with horrible meanings." For L'Engle, a writer who is a Christian doesn't urge people to believe certain things, but seeks to radiate hope, bring healing, and affirm the goodness of the universe. The main difference between a Christian and a secular artist, she said, is the purpose of the artist's work, whether it is story, music, or painting. A Christian artist seeks to advance the kingdom of God, to make people aware of their identity as children of God and "to turn our feet toward home." L'Engle called herself not a "Christian writer" but a "writer who is struggling to be a Christian."

IN HER OWN WORDS

Exciting search

The search for knowledge and truth can be the most exciting thing there is as long as it takes you toward God instead of away from him.

Meet the Austins

A holy death

"I think I would like to die a holy death, Stella. Does that give me away as being hopelessly old-fashioned? I suppose I am. But perhaps our death is the one strange, holy, and unique thing about us, the one thing we can *do*, as *ourselves*. Maybe in dying I will at least become me." She held one of the footposts of the bed to support herself. "I've always been a coward — " She gave a small gasp of pain. "I'll get into bed now."

The Other Side of the Sun

Humility

The moment humility becomes self conscious, it becomes hubris. One cannot be humble and aware of oneself at the same time. . . . Humility is throwing oneself away in complete concentration on something or someone else.

A Circle of Quiet

The human mind

We do have to use our minds as far as they will take us, yet acknowledging that they cannot take us all the way.

A Circle of Quiet

331

Structure and fun

The amoeba has a minimum of structure, but I doubt if it has much fun.

A Circle of Quiet

Compassion

Compassion is nothing one feels with the intellect alone. Compassion is particular; it is never general.

A Circle of Quiet

The mysterious

If we accept the mysterious as the "fairest thing in life," we must also accept the fact that there are rules to it. A rule is not necessarily rigid and unbending; it can even have a question mark at the end of it. I wish that we worried more about asking the right questions instead of being so hung up on finding answers. . . . One of the reasons my generation has mucked up the world to such an extent is our loss of the sense of the mysterious.

A Circle of Quiet

Guilt

It is only by accepting real guilt that I am able to feel free of guilt. . . . If all my mistakes are excused, if there's an alibi, a rationalization for every blunder, then I am not free at all. I have become subhuman.

The Summer of the Great-Grandmother

The Creed

. . . you can't understand the Creed like your Baedecker guide to Athens. It's in the language of poetry. It's trying to talk about things that can't be pinned down by words, and it has to try to break words apart and thrust beyond them.

The Summer of the Great-Grandmother

Myth

Myth is the closest approximation to truth available to the finite human being. And the truth of myth is not limited by time or place. A myth tells of that which was true, is true, and will be true. If we will allow it, myth will integrate intellect and intuition, night and day; our warring opposites are reconciled, male and female, spirit and flesh, desire and will, pain and joy, life and death.

The Irrational Season

This is the irrational season
when love blooms bright and wild.
Had Mary been filled with reason
there'd have been no room for the child.

The Irrational Season

How shall we sing our love's song now
In this strange land where all are born to die?
Each tree and leaf and star show how
The universe is part of this one cry,
That every life is noted and is cherished,
And nothing loved is ever lost or perished.

A Ring of Endless Light

Angels

I believe in angels; guardian angels; the angel who came to Gideon and told a shy, not very brave young man that he was a man of valor who was going to free his people; the angels who came to Jesus in the agony of the Garden. And, what is less comforting, avenging angels, destroying angels, angels who come bringing terror when any part of God's creation becomes too rebellious, too full of pride to remember that they are God's creatures. And, most fearful of all, fallen angels, angels who have left God and followed Lucifer, and daily offer us their seductive and reasonable temptations.

Walking on Water

Faith

My faith in a loving Creator of the galaxies, so loving that the very hairs of my head are counted, is stronger in my work than in my life, and often it is the work that pulls me back from the precipice of faithlessness. It is not necessarily an unmixed blessing to be a well-educated person in a secular society. [Someone once] wrote, "God must be very great to have created a world which carries so many arguments against his existence."

Walking on Water

Evangelism

We do not draw people to Christ by loudly discrediting what they believe, by telling them how wrong they are and how right we are, but by showing them a light that is so lovely that they want with all their hearts to know the source of it.

Walking on Water

Inspiration

To work on a book is for me very much the same thing as to pray. Both involve discipline. If the artist works only when he feels like it, he's not apt to build up much of a body of work. Inspiration far more often comes during the work than before it, because the largest part of the job of the artist is to listen to the work, and to go where it tells him to go. Ultimately, when you are writing, you stop thinking and write what you hear.

Walking on Water

In the end

I am convinced that not only is our planet ultimately to be freed from bondage to Satan, but with it the whole universe — all the singing, dancing suns and stars and galaxies — will one day join unhindered in the great joyous festival. The glorious triumph of Easter will encompass the whole of God's handiwork. The praise for the primal goodness of God's creation in the beginning will be rounded out with the final worship, as John has expressed it in the Revelation: "Worthy art thou our Lord God. . . . To him who sits upon the throne and to the Lamb be blessing and honor and glory and might for ever and ever. Amen!"

And It Was Good

Answered prayer

Like a human parent, God will help us when we ask for help, but in a way that will make us more mature, more real, not in a way that will diminish us. And God does not wave a magic wand. . . .

Two-Part Invention

Moments close to God

It is when things go wrong, when the good things do not happen, when our prayers seem to have been lost, that God is most present. We do not need the sheltering wings when things go smoothly. We are closest to God in the darkness, stumbling along blindly.

Two-Part Invention

Pattern?

There are many times when the idea that there is indeed a pattern seems absurd wishful thinking. Random events abound. There is much in life that seems meaningless. And then, when I can see no evidence of meaning, some glimpse is given which reveals the strange weaving of purposefulness and beauty.

Two-Part Invention

Word made flesh

I have long felt that the sacrifice of the mystery of the Word made flesh was a far greater sacrifice than the crucifixion. That was bad, yes. Terrible, yes. But it was three hours on the cross. Three hours. . . . there are worse deaths. And these deaths make no sense at all unless the mystery of the Word made flesh is present in them too; death makes no sense at all if the God who is in it with us is not in the dying body of the young man down the hall; the people killed, burned, in the most recent air crash, in my husband, in me, our children.

Two-Part Invention

Willing to change

As our knowledge changes, our images, our icons, must change, too, or they become idols. Our understanding of the universe today is very different from Joseph's understanding, but we, too, must be willing to allow our understanding to change and grow as we learn more about God's glorious work. We still tend to cling to our own ideas, or what we have been taught, or told, and to feel threatened if anything new is revealed.

Sold into Egypt

Judgmentalism

Too many answers lead to judgmentalism and to human beings (rather than God) deciding who can and who cannot go to heaven.

The Rock That Is Higher

How to spot a true Christian

Virtue is not the sign of a Christian. Joy is.

The Rock That Is Higher

Stories and *the* Story

We've heard the story of Jesus so often that our ears have become blunted. Story reawakens us to truth, the truth that will set us free. Jesus, the Story, taught by telling stories, quite a few of which on the surface would appear to be pretty secular, but all of which lead us, if we will listen, to a deeper truth than we have been willing to hear before.

The Rock That Is Higher

Prayer and condemnation

Words of prayer are the opposite of words of condemnation, and yet I must pray for forgiveness for my own condemnation of those who condemn. Even in my praying for the condemners, I am still, in a way, condemning. It is not easy. At least prayer is a beginning, as long as it is not coercive, as in "Lord, make these hard-hearted people repent! Convert them to *my* kind of Christianity!" More and more I am simply holding out myself, and those I love, and those I do not love, to a Maker whose love is beyond my comprehension but who is the core of my faith.

Penguins and Golden Calves

FOR REFLECTION AND DISCUSSION

Think of a story in your experience that expresses truth as you understand it. Tell it to someone and ask what that person makes of your story.
What makes something "true"?
Do you agree that "Myth is the closest approximation to truth available to the finite human being"? If not, what is? If so, then what is the use of creeds and catechisms?
Does God disclose himself through science? How do you respond when science and religion conflict or seem to conflict?
Why would one pose a question that she knows cannot be answered?

Chapter 31

JOHN S. MBITI

B. 1931

African Christian Spirituality

IN 1900 THE population of Africa was just under 100 million, of whom 9 percent were Christian, mostly European settlers or members of the historic churches of Egypt and Ethiopia. A century later the continent's population is over 800 million, of whom half are Christian, most of them native Africans. The rapid growth and vitality of African Christianity today (and in Asia and Latin America) suggest that the statistical center of gravity of Christianity may be shifting to the global South, and to Africa in particular.

Our best guide to African Christian spirituality is John S. Mbiti. Born in the Kitui district of Kenya, Mbiti herded sheep and goats as a boy. Mbiti's parents were Christian, and his early family life centered on the church. An intellectually curious youth, he excelled at the secondary school run by Kenya's Protestant churches and entered the University College of Makerere in Kampala, Uganda, in 1950, an external college of London University. There he studied English, sociology, and geography and earned his first degree. Although Makerere offered no courses in theology, Mbiti was active among the Christian students. He received a Fulbright scholarship in 1954 to study theology at Barrington College in Rhode Island (now Gordon College in Massachusetts). He then earned a doctorate in New Testament from Cambridge University.

Mbiti was ordained in the Church of England and briefly served a parish there before returning to Makerere in 1964. In the ten years since he had left, the University College had added a department of religious studies and philosophy, and Mbiti was asked to teach courses on theology, the New Testament, and African religion. Knowing little of traditional African religion and finding little in print, he plunged into original research. His book *African Religions and Philosophy* was published in 1969 (second edition, 1990). It was followed in 1970 by *Concepts of God in Africa,* in which Mbiti surveys and systematizes traditional understandings of God among 270 African peoples. A stream of additional texts and articles followed, many of which quickly became — and remain — standard texts in the field. From 1974 until 1980, Mbiti was director and professor at the World Council of Churches Ecumenical Institute in Bossey, Switzerland. Afterward he taught at the University of Bern in Switzerland and served as pastor at Burgdorf, near Bern. Now retired, he lives in Burgdorf with his Swiss wife, Verena, whom he had met in Cambridge and married in 1965. They have four children.

What accounts for the sudden flourishing of Christian faith in Africa? An obvious impetus, Mbiti says, was the great missionary influx from Europe and America that began in the nineteenth century and continues to this day. The missionaries brought with them more than Christianity — they also introduced Western economics, education, politics, and social patterns, sometimes disrupting local cultures and traditional values. Missionaries also usually worked with colonial regimes whose motives were mixed at best. But Mbiti gives the missionaries their due, praising their courage and self-sacrifice and acknowledging that they laid the foundation for the African church today.

However, Christianity began growing rapidly in Africa only when Africans assumed leadership of the missionary-founded churches and indigenous new denominations began flourishing alongside them. This was due to the evangelistic work of African Christians.

Even on so vast a continent, Mbiti sees themes recurring from place to place that enable him to make general observations about African religion as a whole. Perhaps his most intriguing — and controversial — suggestion is that traditional religion prepared the way for Christianity, providing the religious and spiritual environment in which Christianity would be readily received. Mbiti writes, "Traditional African religion . . . has prepared the religious and spiritual ground for many of its adherents to listen carefully to the teachings of the Bible, to reflect seriously upon them, to find a high degree of credibility in them, to discover meaningful parallels between their world and the world of the Bible, and in many cases to convert to the Christian faith without feeling a sense of spiritual loss but to the contrary thereby gaining a new outreach in their religious experience."

Mbiti speaks of the congruence, correspondence, and continuity of traditional religions and Christianity. Not only are both monotheistic, he says, but they share the same understanding of God as creating, guiding, and sustaining. Mbiti calls African religion *preparatio evangelica* (preparation for the gospel) and sees God's hand at work there just as in the early history of the Hebrew people. Western missionaries did not bring God to Africa — were that possible! — but rather, God brought the missionaries to Africa, to peoples who already knew God, Mbiti says. What was new and revolutionary was the person of Jesus Christ. In coming to Christ, then, Africans do not turn their backs on their heritage but build upon it, often unconsciously. They do not embrace the faith empty-handed, but bring words, concepts, and symbols from their religious heritage that resonate with biblical stories and images. Translations of the Bible use traditional vocabulary, and preaching builds on traditional worldviews.

Not everyone agrees with Mbiti's approach. Some Western missionaries and some Africans call for a sharp break with traditional religions. Others want to affirm traditional religions in their own right, not merely as stepping-stones to Christianity. But Mbiti's affirmation of the Christian gospel as the fulfillment of traditional African religion has been hugely influential throughout the continent. When I visited the Anglican diocese of Abakaliki in Nigeria in 2002, the bishop, Benson Onyeibor, explained how his church evangelizes: "You don't tell the people everything they've believed and done in the past is wrong and that they must turn their backs on it. You introduce them to something better and then let them decide. The traditional religion involved praying to ancestors to intercede with God to protect the people. You had to buy off the ancestors with offerings, a kind of bribe, and if you offered the wrong thing or made no offering, the ancestors might not represent your case convincingly to God, which could be bad for you. We explain that Christian faith provides a new and better Mediator, one who loves you and gives himself for you rather than demands gifts from you. And Christianity allows you to continue to reverence your ancestors and to obey the local chiefs." John Mbiti could have spoken those words, assuming the chiefs govern justly and without corruption.

Among the other features of traditional cultures and religiosity that Mbiti sees as having paved the way for Africans to receive the gospel are the following:

- *The Bible.* The Bible is a key factor in Africa's booming churches, Mbiti says. By 2005 it had been published in full or in part in 683 African languages, accounting for 28.4 percent of the world's 2,403 translations. When the Bible becomes available in the local tongue, the church springs to life. One reason, according to Mbiti, is that the biblical world is close to the African world. People encounter things in the Bible that are close to or identical to their traditional cultures; they see themselves in biblical experiences and traditions. Christians in Africa are also reliving the experience of the early church described in the Acts of the Apostles. (And most take their Scripture literally, which can produce friction at global church gatherings.)
- *Comprehensiveness of Belief.* Religion pervades African life and always has. "Africans are notoriously religious," Mbiti says. There is no distinction between the sacred and the secular. This resonates with the

Christian understanding that God sent the Son into the *world*, not just to human beings. Mbiti says that Christ came "to reclaim the entire person . . . the sum total of his activities and aspirations . . . the whole community . . . the whole humanity, the whole creation. . . . He came to make man so totally and absolutely religious that no department of man should be left untouched by his lordship."

• *Community.* Traditional African life, like life in biblical times, is communal. Individuals find their sense of identity and self as part of the community; one does not stand alone. Mbiti formulates this value in the following words: "I am because we are, and since we are, therefore I am." This means that when conversions occur, they eventually embrace entire families and communities and not merely individuals. Vincent Donovan, a Roman Catholic Marianist priest who worked among the Maasai people of East Africa in the 1960s, writes of his experiences in his book *Christianity Rediscovered.* After Donovan had lived in a village and told the Christian story, he called for those who had studied and prepared themselves for baptism to step forward, but told those who had missed too many classes they would have to wait. Tribal elders, however, asked why Donovan was trying to break them up. All would be baptized or none would be baptized, they said, even the lazy, the inattentive, the unworthy. No one could be separated from the group. That day, Donovan says, he learned a valuable lesson — and baptized the entire village.

• *Healing.* The church in Africa has reclaimed the ministry of healing and tapped into a centuries-old African healing tradition. Divine healing and other miracles are important to many African Christians. Conversions often follow a miraculous healing, especially in the indigenous churches where healing is a particularly visible ministry. Miracles are expected. Often dismissed as "witch doctors" or "medicine men" in the West, traditional doctors offer effective treatments. They have been the bulwarks of health care for millennia. I once interviewed a Western-educated Christian physician in Zimbabwe who explained that he uses Western medicine for viral infections and surgeries, but traditional African cures for diseases with a spiritual, emotional, moral, or personal dimension. Western medicine focuses on the individual human body, whereas traditional medicine treats the whole person, sometimes the entire family or village. Mbiti says that in traditional life before Christianity, people experienced God as powerful, present, and moving in the community — and as Christians they experience the same God. The two experiences are consistent.

John Mbiti is humble and quiet by nature, willing to talk about either his ideas or those of others but uncomfortable when talking about himself. When I corresponded with him in connection with this essay, he suggested I write about one of several other African thinkers. Of a fellow African theologian who had attacked his views and then died, Mbiti said that the man "had no malicious intention" and that his death was "a major loss for African theology." But perhaps Mbiti's greatest contribution, in an era of increasing religious polarization, is his affirmation of his own Christian faith while simultaneously recognizing that God has also manifested himself elsewhere and in other ways.

IN HIS OWN WORDS

African religion and Christian faith

The chief new element brought to African religiosity is the Lord Jesus Christ and his gospel. Whatever else they were and did, Western missionaries were carriers of news about Jesus Christ. African religion had already done the groundwork of making people receptive to the gospel of Jesus Christ. They already knew God through this traditional religion. But they did not yet know Jesus Christ.

Bible and Theology in African Christianity

Prayer

Prayer and praying are not foreign to African peoples. Prayer is a well-established and deeply-rooted tradition which has evolved over centuries and generations. Prayer was not introduced by Christian missionaries or by the church. . . . It strikes a familiar tune. It affirms that which is already there. . . . People do not spend time theorizing about prayer, or analyzing its academic meaning, or its form and structure. Praying is living spiritu-

343

ally just as walking or sleeping is living physically. Just as you live, so you pray, as an integral part of being a human being.

Bible and Theology in African Christianity

Mission

Christian discipleship commits one to mission. Our Lord had a mission. We cannot understand him, or come to him, or follow him, without integrating his mission into our concept of him. To be in Christ is also to be in mission with him and in him. Jesus did not call disciples into idleness, nor did he leave them without a purpose or duty to fulfil.

Bible and Theology in African Christianity

Conversion

Mission is more than evangelism, and evangelism is more than conversion. We need to sensitize African theology to explore the meaning and the process of conversion in the African setting. Evangelism should preach individual and community conversion in the broad sense of the term, as well as preaching the Kingdom of God in all its ramifications. Foreign missions in Africa have often left out the Kingdom of God. But the gospel is all about the Kingdom of God (Mark 1:14f). The work and teachings of our Lord Jesus are directed towards the realization of the Kingdom of God; and conversion is only a minor side effect. . . . The African understanding of mission must correct this imbalance. We have seen or heard too much conversion motif, and too little Kingdom of God motif.

Bible and Theology in African Christianity

Power

Both the power and [the] authority of carrying out mission belong to and derive from God. We have said that the church's mission is a participation in the mission of God. We must therefore look to God to equip the church for mission — equip it with the power of the Holy Spirit. Unfortunately we have tended to interpret power in terms of money, personnel, tradition, knowledge, and institutionalism from the churches that have been sending thousands of missionaries to Africa. The church in Africa has very little or none of these kinds of power. Its mission has to be based on other forms of power. It is here that we have to discover the role of the Holy Spirit in mission. . . . The mission of the early church derived its power, its direction, its authority, from the Holy Spirit — and not from mission boards, or missionary offerings, or missionary societies.

Bible and Theology in African Christianity

Christian resources

Resources carry power with them. Since Christians number one-third of the world's population, one might expect that one-third of world resources in general would be in the hands of Christians. In reality, however, Christians have far more than one-third, in view of the higher resources in the West, which is statistically overwhelmingly Christian. Several questions pose themselves in view of the present situation of Christians' resources. . . . Does it make any difference for Christians with the extreme minimum of resources possible for survival that they share the same word "Christian" with those who are at the other extreme with the maximum of resources? Are these really brothers and sisters in Christ? Or is the Body of Christ so disfigured by problems of Christian resources that the two extremes cannot really join hands of love, to have fellowship and spiritual oneness? Do Christian resources today help to destroy rather than help to discover communion with one another in the framework of communion with God?

Bible and Theology in African Christianity

Setting the African church free

The church in Africa knows best only how to be a "missionized" church, that is, initiated, directed, controlled and even enslaved by external structures, theological education, traditions and spirituality. Its umbilical cord has not yet been severed. The baby is out of the womb of its mother, but it still receives its nourishment through the umbilical cord. Until this cord is broken, there will not be a healthy relationship between mother and child; the child will not find its real identity as a human person on its own merits. It will also be unnatural for the mother to act as though her pregnancy were a perpetual gift from God. . . . Birth brings both parties to a new relationship through the bonds of mutual love, caring responsibility, familyhood and links with parents, relatives, friends, community and society at large. If any member of this relationship is treated like a perpetual infant, the whole relationship becomes sick and a burden to all concerned.

Bible and Theology in African Christianity

A Birthday Wish

> Erupt your grace in me, O Lord
> This day when I am five and twenty years.

And bear me to a lonely wasteland
A barren neglected point
Where north and south and west and east
Converge,
To that circling point
where the sun never sets nor rises
That single icy spot,
And let me there alone remain.

There at the top of the world
Lend me prolonged arms
That I may stretch my hands
To east and west and south
And embrace you, mother earth,
And whisper words of love
To you, humanity!
And let my east and west be one
That both my south may be
As on that northern point I stand

Where all the lines converge
And all the clocks together move
In a timeless concoction. . . .

   This, and only this give me,
   Give me this neglected heap of mankind
   And let me share my love with it.

Oh, for wings that were elastic
That with all this earth to embrace,
This round round ball
And hold it warm within my heart,
Forgetting east and west and south,
But standing only on my barren point
Where nothing flees beyond my reach
But always within the circle of my arms
Where all the routes converge
And the Sun circles round and round.

   This, let me have, O Lord,
   A bounteous heart and free
   With sufficient room
   T' enclose the world's frozen souls
   And whisper words of cheer to each:
   "I love you and you and you!"

From Poems of Nature and Faith

Universalism

There is not a single soul, however debased or even unrepentant, which can successfully "flee" from the Spirit of God (Ps. 139.1-18). God's patient waiting for the soul's repentance must in the end be surely more potent than the soul's reluctance to repent and turn to him . . . (II Peter 3:9). The harmony of the heavenly worship would be impaired if, out of the one hundred in the sheepfold, there is one soul which continues to languish in *sheol* or "the lake of fire."

New Testament Eschatology

Punishment not eternal

One finds it almost impossible to imagine that . . . punishment will last for all eternity in the same way that redemption is for eternity. For only the presence of God has this quality of eternity.

New Testament Eschatology

Identity with Christ

The only identity that counts and has full meaning is the identity with Christ and not with any given culture. Cultural identities are temporary, serving to yield us as Christians to the fullness of our identity with Christ.

"African Indigenous Culture in Relation to
Evangelism and Church Development"

The danger to ecumenism

The real danger to the ecumenical movement in Africa is not the ignorance of what it is all about, nor the opposition waged by a few sects. The dilemma lies in attaining a church unity which then becomes a theological stagnation for those who subscribe or belong to it.

African Religions and Philosophy

Christianity and the gospel

We can add nothing to the gospel for this is an eternal gift of God; but Christianity is always a beggar seeking food and drink, cover and shelter from the cultures it encounters in its never-ending journeys and wanderings.

African Religions and Philosophy

Jesus Christ

The strength of Christianity is in Jesus Christ. He is the stumbling block of all ideologies and religious systems; and even if some of his teaching may overlap with what they teach and proclaim, his own person is greater than can be contained in a religion or ideology. He is "the man for others" and yet beyond them. It is he, therefore, and only he, who deserves to be the goal and standard for individuals and mankind, and whether they attain that ultimate goal religiously or ideologically is perhaps irrelevant. Attainment of that full stature and identity demands that reference be made to an external, absolute and timeless denominator. And this is precisely what Christianity should offer beyond, and in spite of, its own anachronisms and divisions in Africa. I consider traditional religions, Islam, and the other religious systems to be preparatory and even essential ground in the search for the Ultimate. But only Christianity has the terrible responsibility of pointing the way to that ultimate Identity, Foundation, and Source of being.

African Religions and Philosophy

FOR REFLECTION AND DISCUSSION

Can more than one religious tradition be right? What does it mean to be "right"?

How can the Western church incorporate the reality of the global church into its life?

Mbiti says that "to be in Christ is also to be in mission with him and in him." What constitutes that mission? What does it look like?

What are the answers to the questions Mbiti poses in the quotation entitled "Christian resources" above?

Have you ever felt "missionized," as Mbiti uses the word? What did it feel like, and what was your response?

What do you think Mbiti means when he says that "Christianity is always a beggar seeking food and drink"?

Chapter 32

ROSEMARY RADFORD RUETHER

B. 1936

Feminist Spirituality

S OME MAY BE SURPRISED to find a chapter on Rosemary Radford Ruether in a book on Christian spirituality because they do not see her work as spiritual. Ruether doesn't write prayers or devotional pieces, and most of her prose is academic, analyzing history and evaluating ideas while revealing little of her inner life. Others might say Ruether isn't even Christian. She rejects large chunks of the Bible and historic Christian teaching in favor of ideas from other sources, and she says she finds most of her soul mates in small, autonomous "base communities" outside the institutional church. Raised a Roman Catholic, she was once asked why she remains in a church with whose leadership she is perpetually at odds. She is said to have replied (facetiously?), "Because the church has copiers."

Yet Ruether writes from within the church and to the church. Her loyalty to the church comes largely from her mother, she says. Ruether's father died when she was twelve. Her mother then relocated from Washington, D.C., to southern California. There she introduced her daughter to a "free-wheeling and humanistic" Catholicism, and the young Rosemary learned that when priests issued "narrow-minded statements," these "could be safely ignored." As an undergraduate at Scripps College in Claremont, California, she came to love classical Greek and Roman culture, and during her senior year she married political scientist Herman Ruether. They formed an egalitarian marriage, with both pursuing their academic interests. They later raised three children and wrote several books and articles together. Ruether earned her doctorate at the Claremont School of Theology, specializing in classics and the early church fathers. For most of her adult life, Ruether taught at Garrett-Evangelical Theological Seminary in Evanston, Illinois, a United Methodist institution — where she was beyond the reach of church authorities who might occasionally issue "narrow-minded statements." She has lectured at universities on five continents and teaches today, in semi-retirement, at the Pacific School of Religion in Berkeley, California.

Ruether sees herself as part of that large stream of dissenters that includes the Hebrew prophets, Jesus, and the Protestant reformers, challenging the institution to repent and recover long-suppressed elements of its identity. Western Christian culture, Ruether believes, has become an oppressive "patriarchy" that denies the full humanity of women and men alike. "By patriarchy we mean not only the subordination of females to males, but the whole structure of Father-ruled society: aristocracy over serfs, masters over slaves, king over subjects, racial overlords over colonized people," she writes.

What is needed, Ruether says, is a conversion not merely of individual souls but of the Christian church itself and of Western culture in general. Unlike some feminists, Ruether believes that the church is capable of renewal and can in fact become "the avant-garde of liberated humanity."

The church is hardly the avant-garde today, however. It must reclaim the vision and values of Jesus, Ruether says. Hers is a this-worldly Jesus. She has little use for creedal affirmations about the second person of the Trinity becoming human, still less for the ethereal Jesus of popular piety, but resonates with the human being she meets in the Gospels. This Jesus is a countercultural iconoclast who rebukes the social and religious leaders of his day — and of ours — by speaking and acting on behalf of the powerless and despised. He calls for a social revolution based on the principle that the last shall be first and the first last. The historic church, beginning as early as the pastoral epistles of the New Testament, has perverted Jesus' message, Ruether says, to the point where Christian teaching about the person of Jesus has often been used as a weapon of oppression.

This perversion of the gospel is seen in, among other places, the church's traditional teaching that because Jesus was male, women cannot be priests. Though the church denies it, the real assumption underlying this teaching, Ruether says, is that God is a male. She writes, "The Vatican Declaration against the Ordination of Women in 1976 . . . declares that there must be a 'physical resemblance' between the priest and Christ. Since this strange new version of the imitation of Christ does not exclude a Negro, a Chinese, or a Dutchman from representing a first-century Jew, or a wealthy prelate from representing a carpenter's son, or sinners from representing the Savior, we must assume this imitation of Christ has now been reduced to one essential element, namely, male sex." This is heresy, she says, for the Incarnation is about Jesus' humanity, not his masculinity. Throughout the centuries, persons and groups on the fringe of church life, often branded as heretics, have resisted the ruling patriarchy and preserved Jesus' vision of a fully liberated humanity. These have included the Gnostics and Montanists; mystics such as Joachim of Fiore, Julian of Norwich, and Jacob Boehme; the Quakers; the New England transcendentalists; the Rappites and Shakers; Mary Baker Eddy; and others.

All thinking about God begins with human experience, Ruether says. This is true even of so-called objective sources of theology, such as the Bible and tradition, which are actually reflections on human experience, written down and preserved over time. "One cannot start, as I had been taught to do, by asking if you 'agree with the doctrine.' Rather, one must first work back to the story, then to the dance, and finally begin to glimpse the experience that lies behind these expressions." The difference between feminist spirituality and traditional views is not that feminist spirituality is based on human experience, but that it includes an element of human experience overlooked in the past — *women's* experience. Ruether (unlike more radical feminists) does not reject or demean men or their experience, but merely seeks to give women's experience its due. Women typically experience life as less fractious and combative, more unifying and conciliatory than men do. The church and Western culture generally have ignored, suppressed, and silenced women's voices, Ruether says. This results in an "unbalanced" understanding of God and a way of speaking of God that destroy God's people. Ruether would correct this imbalance by referring to divinity as "God/ess," a term she admits is inadequate and unsuitable for worship, but that opens the way for new thinking by combining the masculine and feminine forms of the word while preserving the affirmation that the divinity is One.

The equality of women is for Ruether "one of the touchstones for understanding our faithfulness to the vision," and the promotion of the full humanity of women is "the critical principle of feminist theology." Sections of the Bible and of tradition that do not affirm the equality of women she rejects as unfaithful, and whatever promotes the full humanity of women is holy, regardless of where it comes from.

Nor does Ruether stop at seeking equality for women. In her best-known work, *Sexism and God-Talk*, she writes, "In rejecting androcentrism (males as norms of humanity), women must also criticize all other forms of chauvinism: making white Westerners the norm of humanity, making Christians the norm of humanity, making privileged classes the norm of humanity. Women must also criticize humanocentrism, that is, making humans the norm and crown of creation in a way that diminishes the other beings in the community of creation." Ruether is a kindred spirit to other recent Roman Catholic authors seeking to rethink Christian spirituality, such as Gustavo Gutiérrez, father of "liberation spirituality," which faults traditional Catholic spirituality for being too interior and ignoring justice and poverty, and Matthew Fox, father of "creation spirituality," based on the goodness and unity of creation rather than on sin and redemption. Known as a spokeswoman for Christian feminism, Ruether could easily represent these other spiritual movements as well. She has also written and worked extensively to combat anti-Semitism and to affirm the rights of the Palestinian people.

Relationships are central to Ruether's understanding of the Christian gospel. To live faithfully is to treat every other person, even the entire planet, as a "Thou" rather than as a thing to be used or manipulated for one's own ends. Revelation occurs when a person sees the social and economic contradictions that have defined human existence and moves toward a new life of freedom. This includes seeing how one has cooperated in maintaining these contradictions.

Underlying all these concerns is Ruether's conviction that all created things are kin to one another. Her approach to spirituality, like that of most feminists, is holistic, affirming viewpoints apparently opposed to each other. For example, she incorporates into her thinking insights drawn from the ancient Canaanite fertility and nature cults, with their worship of gods and goddesses, as well as those of the ancient Israelites. Ruether does not hesitate to embrace the ideas of Christian heresies — "dissenting voices," she calls them — as correctives to the dominant patriarchal tradition. To see things as either-or, good or bad, light or dark, true or false, is to devalue half of God's creation, and the half usually devalued is the physical, material, fleshly — and feminine, Ruether says.

Not surprisingly, Ruether (and other feminists) have many detractors. Some say she misconstrues traditional language about God, which was never intended to make the crude claim that God is male. They further point out that it was Jesus himself who bid his disciples to address God as Father, not oppressive patriarchs of a later time. Others say that Ruether misreads history and the Bible, distorting them to further her agenda. Her views have been shaped by modern culture, not Christian faith, critics say, and in picking and choosing which Scripture passages she will accept, she allows modern culture to judge the Bible rather than the other way round — is it Christian faith or modern culture that needs reassessing?

One can agree with some of these criticisms and still acknowledge that Ruether's call for a reconstruction of Christian teaching and a return to spiritual roots resembles similar calls by prophets of earlier eras who were once vilified but are now revered. And Ruether's critics sound disturbingly like those of earlier ages who sought to perpetuate a status quo rejected by later generations as falling short of the gospel. Even those who do not follow Ruether the whole way can learn from her and recognize in her work an authentic call to repentance and reform.

IN HER OWN WORDS

The starting point

The starting point for feminist theology, perhaps for all theology, is cognitive dissonance. What is, is not what ought to be. Not only that, but what we have been told is, is not always what is, and what we have been told ought to be, is not always what out to be.

Introduction to the second edition of *Sexism and God-Talk*

A new God?

Is the Cherubim throne empty? Perhaps it is this very idea of God as a great king, ruling over nations as his servants, that has been done away with by Jesus' death on the cross. With Jesus' death, God, the heavenly Ruler, has left the heavens and has been poured out upon the earth with his blood. A new God is being born in our hearts to teach us to level the heavens and exalt the earth and create a new world without masters and slaves, rulers and subjects. No, not even men come first with women behind in meek servility. This is what Jesus meant when he taught us to pray for God's Kingdom to come, for God's will to be done *on earth* as it is in heaven; to forgive each other, and not be led into temptation, but delivered from evil.

Sexism and God-Talk

Idolatry and blasphemy

Patriarchy itself must fall under the biblical denunciations of idolatry and blasphemy, the idolizing of the male as representative of divinity. It is idolatrous to make males more "like God" than females. It is blasphemous to use the image and name of the Holy to justify patriarchal domination and law. Feminist readings of the Bible can discern a norm within biblical faith by which the biblical texts themselves can be criticized. To the extent to which biblical texts reflect this normative principle, they are regarded as authoritative. On this basis many aspects of the Bible are to be frankly set aside and rejected.

Sexism and God-Talk

Rethink the whole tradition

An ecological-feminist theology of nature must rethink the whole Western theological tradition of the hierarchical chain of being and chain of command. This theology must question the hierarchy of human over nonhuman nature as a relationship of ontological and moral value. It must challenge the right of the human to treat the nonhuman as private property and material wealth to be exploited. It must unmask the structures of social domination, male over female, owner over worker, that mediate this domination of nonhuman nature. Finally, it must question the model of hierarchy that starts with non-material spirit (God) as the source of the chain of being and continues down to nonspiritual "matter" as the bottom of the chain of being and the most inferior, valueless, and dominated point in the chain of command.

Sexism and God-Talk

The use of human intelligence

We need to learn how to use intelligence to mend the distortions we have created and how to convert intelligence into an instrument that can cultivate the harmonies and balances of the ecological community and bring these to a refinement. We can turn the desert wilderness or the jungle into the garden. But we need to do that not simply by bulldozing what is and ignoring all other needs but our own, but by understanding the integrity of the existing ecological community and learning to build our niche in that community in harmony with the rest. We do this out of a genuine recognition of our interdependence.

Sexism and God-Talk

Jesus and religious experience

Prophecy is not canonized in past texts; the Spirit of God speaks today. Those of low or marginal status (Jesus and his disciples) speak not simply as interpreters of past traditions but as the direct word of God (with authority, not as the scribes and Pharisees speak). Jesus frees religious experience from the fossilization of past traditions (which doesn't mean he rejects those traditions) and makes it accessible in the present. And Jesus does not think of himself as the "last word of God," but points beyond himself to "One who will come."

Sexism and God-Talk

Feminists and the church

The more one becomes a feminist the more difficult it becomes to go to church.

Sexism and God-Talk

The true church

Whether we gather in living rooms, warehouses, or church buildings, the marks of the authentic church are the same. The church is where the good news of liberation from sexism is preached, where the Spirit is present to empower us to renounce patriarchy, where a community committed to the new life of mutuality is gathered together and nurtured, and where the community is spreading this vision and struggle to others.

Sexism and God-Talk

Our primary responsibility

It is the shaping of the beloved community on earth, for our time and generation to bequeath to our children, that is our primary responsibility as human beings. . . . It is not our calling to be concerned about the eternal meaning of our lives, and religion should not make this the focus of its message. Our responsibility is to use our temporal life span to create a just

357

and good community for our generation and for our children. It is in the hands of Holy Wisdom to forge out of our finite struggle truth and being for everlasting life. Our agnosticism about what this means is then the expression of our faith, our trust that Holy Wisdom will give transcendent meaning to our work, which is bounded by space and time.

Sexism and God-Talk

Charting one's journey

One has only limited objectivity about one's own biography. But, even more, one is always, at best, in midjourney. To be more and more fully alive, aware and committed, this is surely the meaning of a journey in faith. But this must mean that we are always reassessing and reappropriating the past — our own past experiences and reflections — in the light of new challenges. A side journey in our spiritual progress, one temporarily shelved, might suddenly become urgent again. In the light of new cultural demands, one might have to look again at some apparently closed questions from one's past to see what is usable.

Disputed Questions

Exclusivism

Although I have come to prefer a biblical world-view to that of classical humanism, I have never identified this with religious exclusivism. Basically I reject exclusivism, whether it be Christian over against Judaism or biblical religion as a whole over against nonbiblical religion. I have gone beyond, but have never forgotten, the theophany of the gods as an authentic manifestation of the divine. . . . I have never assumed that it [biblical faith] dropped out of heaven undefiled by historical gestation. Rather, I understand it as a product of a human quest for meaning that moved through many different stages and contexts. It is certainly not all of a piece, and it is incomprehensible to me why anyone would expect it to be. It is shaped by, dependent on, and yet responding to, the religious world around it.

Disputed Questions

To be truly catholic

Only God is one and universal. Humanity is finally one because the one God created us all. But the historical mediators of the experience of God remain plural. There is no final perspective on salvation available through the identity of only one people, although each people's revelatory point of reference expresses the universal in different contexts. Just as each human language points more or less adequately to universal truths, and yet is itself the product of very particular peoples and their histories, so religions are equally bearers of universal truth, and yet are particular in form. To impose one religion on everyone flattens and impoverishes the wealth of human interaction with God, much as imposing one language on everyone steals other people's culture and memories. If there is a messianic end-point of history that gathers up all these heritages into one, it can only happen through incorporating them all, not through suppressing them all in favor of the experience of one historical group. In order to be truly catholic, Christians must revise the imperialistic way they have defined their universality.

Disputed Questions

Goddess and God?

Ecofeminist theology and spirituality has tended to assume that the "Goddess" we need for ecological well-being is the reverse of the God we have had in the Semitic monotheistic traditions; immanent rather than transcendent, female rather than male identified, relational and interactive rather than dominating, pluriform and multicultured rather than uniform and mono-centered. But perhaps we need a more imaginative solution to these traditional oppositions than simply their reversal, something more like Nicholas of Cusa's paradoxical "coincidence of opposites," in which the "absolute maximum" and the "absolute minimum" are the same.

Gaia and God

Ecological spirituality

An ecological spirituality needs to be built on three premises: the transience of selves, the living interdependency of all things, and the value of the personal in communion. Many spiritual traditions have emphasized the need to "let go of the ego," but in ways that diminished the value of the person, undercutting particularly those, like women, who scarcely have been allowed individuated personhood at all. We need to "let go of the ego" in a different sense. We are called to affirm the integrity of our personal center of being, in mutuality with the personal centers of all other beings across species and, at the same time, accept the transience of these personal selves.

Gaia and God

FOR REFLECTION AND DISCUSSION

For Ruether, what is "the starting point for theology"? What do you think it should be?

Feminists are not the only Christians who see "a norm within biblical faith by which the biblical texts themselves can be criticized." Do you see such a norm? If so, list a few biblical passages that should be rejected on account of this "norm." If not, then how do you deal with biblical passages that endorse such things as slavery, polygamy, and genocide?

On what grounds does Ruether say we should put behind us the idea of a "hierarchical chain of being and chain of command" with God at the top? How do you feel about this suggestion?

How well does Ruether's understanding of the "marks of the authentic church" fit with the traditional understanding that the marks of the authentic church are that it is one, holy, catholic, and apostolic?

Respond to these remarks of Ruether:
- Jesus frees religious experience from the fossilization of past traditions.
- To be more and more fully alive, aware and committed, this is surely the meaning of a journey in faith.
- It is not our calling to be concerned about the eternal meaning of our lives.
- The historical mediators of the experience of God remain plural. . . . Religions are equally bearers of universal truth.

Acknowledgments

THE AUTHOR AND PUBLISHER gratefully acknowledge permission to quote material from the following publications:

Amy Carmichael. Prose and poetry excerpts. Copyright by CLC Publications. Reprinted by permission of CLC Publications, P.O. Box 1449, Fort Washington, PA 19034.

Donald Gee. *After Pentecost.* Copyright © 1945 by Donald Gee. Reprinted by permission of Gospel Publishing House.

Donald Gee. *Concerning Spiritual Gifts.* Copyright © 1972 by Donald Gee. Reprinted by permission of Gospel Publishing House.

Donald Gee. *Pentecost.* Copyright © 1932 by Donald Gee. Reprinted by permission of Gospel Publishing House.

Madeleine L'Engle. *And It Was Good.* Copyright © 1983 by Crosswicks, Ltd. Reprinted with permission of McIntosh & Otis, Inc.

Madeleine L'Engle. *A Circle of Quiet.* Copyright © 1972 by Madeleine L'Engle Franklin. Reprinted by permission of Farrar, Straus & Giroux, LLC. British copyright © 1972 by Crosswicks, Ltd. Reprinted with permission of McIntosh & Otis, Inc.

Madeleine L'Engle. *The Irrational Season.* Copyright © 1977 by Crosswicks, Ltd. Reprinted with permission of McIntosh & Otis, Inc.

Madeleine L'Engle. *Meet the Austins.* Copyright © 1960 by Crosswicks, Ltd. Reprinted with permission of McIntosh & Otis, Inc.

Madeleine L'Engle. *The Other Side of the Sun.* Copyright © 1971 by Mad-

Index